China Baby Love

COAT INC
238 NASH RD
GYMPIE 4570

JANE HUTCHEON

China Baby Love

ABC
Books

Most of the Chinese names in this book have been changed to protect identities. Most of the location names have also been changed except for Jiaozuo, the city at the centre of this book.

 The ABC 'Wave' device is a trademark of the Australian Broadcasting Corporation and is used under licence by HarperCollins*Publishers* Australia.

First published in 2017
by HarperCollins*Publishers* Australia Pty Limited
ABN 36 009 913 517
harpercollins.com.au

HarperCollins*Publishers*
Level 13, 201 Elizabeth Street, Sydney, NSW 2000, Australia
Unit D1, 63 Apollo Drive, Rosedale, Auckland 0632, New Zealand
A 53, Sector 57, Noida, UP, India
1 London Bridge Street, London, SE1 9GF, United Kingdom
2 Bloor Street East, 20th floor, Toronto, Ontario M4W 1A8, Canada
195 Broadway, New York, NY 10007, USA

National Library of Australia Cataloguing-in-Publication data:

Hutcheon, Jane, author.
Title: China baby love / Jane Hutcheon.
   978 0 7333 3433 7 (paperback)
   978 1 4607 0507 0 (ebook)
   Subjects: McCarthy-Shum, Linda.
   Women benefactors – Australia – Biography.
   Fund raisers (Persons) – Australia – Biography.
   Children – Institutional care – China.
   Orphans – China.

Cover design by Hazel Lam, HarperCollins Design Studio
Cover image: Hazel Lam
Typeset in Bembo Std by HarperCollins Design Studio
Printed and bound in Australia by Griffin Press
The papers used by HarperCollins in the manufacture of this book are a natural, recyclable product made from wood grown in sustainable plantation forests. The fibre source and manufacturing processes meet recognised international environmental standards, and carry certification.

For Michael and Isla

Contents

On a hazy summer day in 1930s Shanghai, a nine-year-old girl named Beatrice and her father Kit, arrived at The Bund to farewell visitors from Hong Kong. Aunt Rose and Uncle Alfred were heading home on a steamship, docked at the famous Shanghai waterfront. An outing to the pier was always exciting for a young girl. But suddenly, while she was still below deck admiring the cabin, she felt a shudder and realised the vessel was departing. It was too late to disembark. She didn't understand what was happening. Would her father, who was still waiting in the Studebaker on the pier, be worried or angry she wondered, as she raced out of the cabin to the deck and searched for him on the pier. She saw the black Studebaker first. Then she saw her father's silhouette against the smooth cream-coloured passenger seat of the car. His face was buried in his hands. He refused to look up.

Unknown to Beatrice, her father and his sister, her Aunt Rose, had hatched a plan. Without the child's consent, Beatrice was being taken from her home in the leafy French Concession of Shanghai. She had not been given the option to say goodbye to anyone and now she was being uprooted from her school, her friends, her two brothers and sister, her cousins, and being sent to the British colony of Hong Kong to live with her Aunt Rose, Uncle Alfred and cousin Alec. Everything in the plan had proceeded smoothly so far and now here she was on the ship with Rose and Alfred, heading for her new home and a new, unfamiliar life in Hong Kong thirty-six hours away.

As a child in Shanghai, Beatrice was unwell much of the time. A few months before she was sent to Hong Kong, she contracted diphtheria and was rushed to hospital where surgeons performed an emergency tracheotomy. When she was four, her beloved mother, Elsie, caught meningitis and died. She has one faint memory of Elsie sitting at a sewing machine. The absence of a mother, combined with the idea that Hong Kong might be better for her health, led to the arrangement with Kit's sister and brother-in-law.

Fortunately, though Aunt Rose was a disciplinarian and neither warm nor loving, Beatrice was doted on by her cousin and uncle and there were other relatives who showed her patience and kindness. She quickly found friends, a wonderful school and made a new and successful life for herself. This was very fortunate, because when Beatrice was fourteen, her father, Kit, still living in Shanghai with the rest of his family where he worked for a firm of chemists as a book-keeper, died suddenly. He had not seen his daughter since leaving her on the ship bound for Hong Kong. When Kit died, that made Beatrice, the youngest of four children, an orphan.

Beatrice is my mother. More than eight decades after she left Shanghai on the slow-boat to Hong Kong, she is still alive and well into her nineties. She often says that, although the early part of her life had its challenges, the latter part more than made up for the hardship. I'm thankful that she had relatives to care for her. Even though their care wasn't perfect, she wasn't given up to an orphanage. Losing her mother at such a young age would have been a terrible trauma, although in those days, any child who suffered a tragedy was expected to just get on with life. Setbacks unfolded, particularly around the time of the Second World War. But you didn't complain or feel like a victim. You were told to put one foot in front of the other. That's the way it was.

As a result of my mother's experience, child abandonment is something that has always tugged at my emotional core. From an early age, I was drawn to stories of orphans from Cinderella, and Peter Pan, to the world of Oliver Twist. I graduated to the comic strip Little Orphan Annie and later on when I had a daughter of my own, she introduced me to additional orphan characters like Sophie from the BFG and of course the boy wizard, Harry Potter.

My mother left Shanghai long ago – and happened to meet my father, who, like her, was born in Shanghai – so it would be fair to say that Shanghai, or China, has never really left me. China hasn't always been a love affair, but it's most certainly an ongoing fascination. So when I came across the work of an Australian woman named Linda Shum who decided to dedicate her life to an orphanage in what she likes to call 'the real China' (because it's not one of the big, flashy cities we usually hear about in the news), it was hard for me to walk past.

There are hundreds of foreign non-governmental organisations (NGOs), like Linda Shum's, working to improve the lives of China's orphans. Even NGOs that have legally registered partnerships with local orphanages (like Linda's organisation COAT has) feel they operate in a shadowy world where they can never be sure of what the future holds, where one wrong step or criticism can result in the loss of everything they have built up so far. Others face significant funding pressures as China becomes an increasingly expensive place to live in and to do business in. And of course, the biggest fear is that the children's lives that they have worked to improve, will somehow slip backwards.

On the other hand, there are international experts, including Professors Xiaoyuan Shang and Karen Fisher at the University of New South Wales, whose research is contributing to Chinese government policy and creating reform within China's child welfare system.

China is a country which produces an incredible array of statistics. It has a population of 1.38 billion, more than 300 million children, and more than one million orphaned or abandoned children. About 110,000 of these orphans are state wards, the majority of them (80 per cent) living in institutions and orphanages. An estimated 60 million children live separately from their parents who have left home to find work elsewhere in China. Parents leave their children behind because of strict residency controls which can affect education and healthcare.

China maintains that the one-child policy that was in place for thirty-five years from 1980 only applied to 36 per cent of its population and that 53 per cent were allowed to have a second child if the first was a girl. In the coming pages, you will hear about the negative side-effects of the one-child policy.

Linda Shum opened her world to me, introducing me to her network in China and beyond. The stories in this book belong to Linda and her ever-widening net. Linda is happy to ponder the deeper questions such as why a Chinese couple today is willing to abandon an infant with a physical disability such as a missing left hand. But she is more concerned about how to give abandoned children the best start in life, to give them an education and, if necessary, to guide them to adulthood. I admire her work. However, I am often speechless concerning why child abandonment remains widespread and why so little is done by the Chinese government to reduce abandonment and address disability discrimination.

The stories you're about to read don't all have happy endings, but there are many triumphs along the way.

Linda Shum likes to tell her volunteers a story from the Chinese classics:

Yu Gong was a man who was laughed at by his whole village because he said he could move the local mountains to a better spot. He took a shovel and began to dig up the mountains bit by bit. Yu Gong got older, but still he shovelled and shovelled and again, the villagers laughed at him. They said he would die before the mountains were moved... but Yu Gong insisted that his children, their children and great-grandchildren would persist in order to move those mountains.

That's what Linda Shum is doing. She is moving mountains; one shovel at a time.

CHAPTER 1

A Rendezvous

I searched for my name, or something resembling it, on the sea of whiteboards at Zhengzhou Airport. No such luck. Haven't heard of Zhengzhou? It's the capital of Henan Province, the third-most populous province in China with almost 100 million people. Unlike China's best known cities – Beijing, Shanghai, Guangzhou and Chongqing – Zhengzhou is a city of the future. It's one of thirteen super-sized cities that is currently under construction.

The last time I arrived in Zhengzhou in 1998, the city was a demolition zone and the new, gleaming airport with its rippling ceiling like the wings of a giant bird, had only just opened. Travelling with my ABC colleagues, we had come to report on a man who had become one of China's super-rich through the American organisation, Amway. Everyone around us seemed in such a hurry. 'To get rich is glorious', they were told. But even within that sparkling new airport, the 'other' China was plain for us to see. A family of farmers in blue Mao suits were on a self-guided tour. They held hands as they shuffled through the halls in awe of the modernity, looking completely out of place.

Thirteen years after I left, I'm back. It's October 2013. The advertisements in the airport show the Chinese as sophisticated, sexy, middle-class, jet-setting, smart, connected. The reality around me is different. There are certainly Chanel handbags and Dolce & Gabbana sunglasses. But my fellow passengers are impolite. I've been pushed, tripped over, people have jumped in front of me in the queue. And now, out in the arrivals hall, as I check my watch, I'm in danger of being rolled over by trolleys.

As my host was nowhere in sight, I decided to check outside the hall, edging out of the sliding doors where men in leather jackets; taxi-drivers, prepare to pounce.

'Taxi?' a man asked out of the corner of his mouth.

I shook my head.

'*Mei wenti*' (No problem), he replied, already eyeing up his next catch.

Mei wenti was a phrase I used to hear 1.3 billion times a day in China. It's the equivalent of the Australian 'no worries' which usually means there's something to worry about.

The smog caught my nostrils like the plume from a genie bottle.

Why am I back in China?

I had gone to Beijing as ABC Television's China correspondent in November 1995 and remained until 2001. It was my first international posting before I travelled further afield to the Middle East and Europe. I remember my friends telling me NOT to say to the interview panel that the China job was *meant* to be mine. So I told them I'd been studying Mandarin for two years. Both my parents were born in Shanghai when it was known as the 'Paris of the East'. My Mum was half Chinese. I grew up in Hong Kong and spoke Cantonese. And the clincher was that as a child, I owned a pink toy rodent named Mousey Tung, although I wasn't sure who Mao Zedong was at the time. All I knew was that he was always in the news.

And then, just as I was leaving the interview, I told them the China job was *meant* to be mine. And two days later, it was.

There was a vibration in my pocket.

'WHERE ARE U?' read the text. It was from Linda Shum. The person who was supposed to be meeting me.

I left the smog, returned to the arrivals hall and wheeled my luggage across the smooth, marble floor. A large Caucasian woman dressed in black approached from the far end of the concourse. Though it was cold enough for me to wear a down puffy jacket, she wore a long summer skirt and top with a light scarf draped around her shoulders. She wore Jesus sandals instead of enclosed shoes. Her hair was very short, dyed brown but greying at the roots. And, to put it bluntly, she was obese. As she came closer, she waved, and although it was the first time I had met Linda Shum in person, I could tell something was wrong.

Next to her was a small Chinese boy in a wheelchair. He looked around five-years-old, but he worked the wheelchair like a junior Kurt Fearnley. As the two approached, Linda hesitated. I was about to step forward to hug her, but something made me hold back.

'I bet we stink,' she said. Well, that was a strange greeting.

She leaned forward to give me a hug while trying not to press against me.

At that point I inhaled the unmistakable odour of vomit. The stench made me gag. I realised now, why Linda didn't want to get too close. All her clothes were wet because, she said, they'd been trying to clean themselves up in the bathroom.

'I gave him the iPad on the bus,' she said pointing to the boy in the wheelchair. 'What a dumb thing to do. He threw up all over both of us.'

The boy looked up, a polite smile on an otherwise wan face.

'I always like to bring one of the kids with me,' she said. 'It's good for them to get out.'

It dawned on me that he was one of the orphans. *Weren't they all supposed to be girls,* I wondered?

'We must stink,' Linda repeated. 'I'm so sorry.'

I gathered my wits. Then I breathed through my mouth.

'I can't smell a thing,' I lied.

'I suppose we'd better put something back in his stomach before we head back to Jiaozuo,' said Linda.

Our destination, Jiaozuo (pronounced *jow* as in *wow* and *zor* as in *bore*), was less than 100 kilometres away. It's what China calls a 'prefecture-level' city, one of 300 smaller cities in the country. Linda calls Jiaozuo 'the real China' because, apart from a few McDonald's outlets in the centre, there are no other Western shops or restaurants. Even butter was impossible to find.

'We're going to take the public bus back to Jiaozuo. Are you up for a coffee or something first?'

Linda spotted a cafe down the hallway.

Coffee! I didn't need reminding about how foggy I felt. Coffee sounded very good although I forgot decent coffee outside a major city was as rare as a Ming vase. I gathered my bags and the three of us did a u-turn for the cafe. As we talked and ambled, I was acutely aware we were the centre of attention. People often stare in China. But this wasn't staring, this was gawking. All eyes were directed, not at the large or even the small Australian woman, but at the boy in the wheelchair. Living in Beijing in the mid-90s, the only disabled people I ever saw on the street were beggars. Whenever an important foreign dignitary came to town, the beggars were shooed off the pavements for a week. They always returned after a while. It was a kind of game.

9

Linda and the boy were oblivious or more accurately, accustomed, to people's stares. A boy pushing himself in a wheelchair clearly wasn't something Chinese people encountered every day. Nobody bothered to hide their surprise or discomfort.

Coming face-to-face with Linda was not what I had expected. She had an awful lot to say. She talked for all of us, about the eventful ride to the airport on the public bus; about all the orphans, her Chinese 'grandkids', as she called them, in the city of Jiaozuo; her three adult children back home in Australia and her nine grandchildren in Gympie and Tasmania. She talked about her dead husband and soul-mate Greg. And she talked about her ageing father, Charles, whom she cared for. Charles got sent to 'the kennel' as she called his aged-care home, whenever she travelled to China, two, three or four times every year.

I nodded, too tired to take it in. Even Linda seemed to lose the thread of her stories a number of times. I wasn't sure if she was lonely and grateful for company or just extremely chatty. My attention shifted to the boy who didn't wait for anyone to get him seated. He lifted himself like a professional gymnast out of the wheelchair into the restaurant chair, effortlessly swinging his legs under the table.

'This is Wen Xuan. He's almost ten, but he's small for his age,' said Linda looking at the boy with pride. 'He was born with a hole in his spine. It's called spina bifida.'

I'd heard of spina bifida but had no idea what it was.

'Was that the reason he was abandoned?' I asked.

'That's right,' Linda said matter-of-factly. I could tell she had been a teacher. 'The police brought him to the orphanage when he was only a few weeks old.'

'He could still move his legs then. At one stage when he was very tiny, he got very sick with chickenpox. The orphanage medical staff stuck needles into his skull to feed him Chinese medicine. I always hated it when they did that.'

She paused, anxious not to elicit pity. 'Eventually, he came through.'

Wen Xuan reached for a menu and opened it, revealing laminated pages of photos for foreigners who couldn't read Chinese. His fingers moved quickly, almost gracefully, as if he was flicking through the pages of a musical score. His eyes darted back and forth as he concentrated on the important choice he needed to make. Then he rested on an image of an exotic-looking club sandwich decorated with an orchid and a delicate paper umbrella. It looked like something out of a resort magazine. A long index finger slowly uncoiled towards the photo and ever-so-lightly tapped it. It wasn't every day he got to order a $10 sandwich from the airport cafe. This was a boy who'd spent his entire life in a welfare institution.

Linda and I opted for cappuccinos. They were $10 each. $30 for two coffees and a sandwich. Sydney prices.

She started to tell me more about Wen Xuan's life story, explaining that Chinese doctors had operated on him when he was a baby. They had purposely cut the tendons in his legs to stop them retracting. As a consequence, he lost the use of his legs. I shook my head, feeling sickened.

Linda also shook her head and tsked at the short-sightedness of the procedure. She wasn't convinced it was necessary at all, but it was a common thing to do in China at the time, she said.

'In Australia we stopped doing that kind of thing in the 1950s,' she said quietly. 'He has no feeling from the waist down.'

Her candour took me by surprise.

Taking a sip of coffee and putting the upsetting thought aside, she glanced at Wen Xuan again like a proud grandmother. 'He has really overcome so many obstacles in his life so far.'

Her mood quickly brightened at this thought.

'When he was four, he got about by crawling on the floor. The carer in the foster home accidentally locked herself out, leaving babies, toddlers and Wen inside the apartment.'

'Stuck outside with the children on the inside, she became frantic. She asked Wen Xuan to try to open the door, but wondered to herself how on earth he would do that.'

The boy had searched around and noticed a pile of plastic stools against the wall. He proceeded to drag them using one hand, while crawling across the floor with the other. Within a few minutes he had built the stools into a staircase. Like a monkey, he swung himself onto the first step and climbed up the stools until he could reach the handle. Then, using both hands, he managed to unlock the door and let the carer back in.

A young woman dressed like a 1950s American diner waitress, emerged from the kitchen with the coffees and sandwich. She carried the tray nervously, then stood behind us, just so that she could stare at Wen Xuan. Once again, he was oblivious to the attention. His focus was on the club sandwich in front of him. To my mind, it didn't quite live up to the photo in the menu. There was no orchid or paper umbrella. It was held together by a wooden toothpick. That didn't bother Wen in the slightest. His spindly fingers gathered up the sandwich, which he virtually inhaled within seconds, leaving just the toothpick on the plate. After licking his fingers, he reached for Linda's iPad, long fingers tapping the screen while we finished our conversation.

I first heard of Linda Shum during Australian Prime Minister Julia Gillard's visit to China in April 2013. A ground-breaking deal was going to be signed; a strategic economic dialogue between Australia and China which was supposed to give our government access to the uppermost echelons of China's ruling Communist Party, a privilege given to only a handful of countries including Russia, Japan and Britain.

At the time, I hosted a nightly program on the ABC news channel. The producers were searching for a fresh angle to tell the story of Australia's engagement with China. I was keen to find a human element to this political story but time was running out. Then, out of the blue, a message appeared from a social media site I rarely used. It was from a woman in Queensland named Linda Shum. I guessed she was Chinese.

'I need your help,' she wrote.

It felt like one of those hoaxes when someone stuck in a foreign country asks for money which they promise to re-pay.

But Linda Shum wasn't asking for money although she seemed anxious. She was the CEO and founder of a charitable organisation that ran foster homes for orphans in a small Chinese city. She said a fire had recently swept through a foster home in central China. Seven children – all of them with special needs – had died. As a result of the fire, Linda Shum feared foster homes all over China were about to face a backlash. Her organisation wasn't far from the scene of the accident. She was worried it would be closed down.

I Googled the incident. Reports said the fire broke out in an unofficial foster home managed by a Chinese good Samaritan. She had sheltered abandoned and disabled children over many years.

I knew China to be a place where rules and regulations could sometimes be quite fluid, particularly beyond the city limits of Beijing. The fire had raised many questions and caused widespread debate about the government's obligation to protect abandoned babies and children. The woman who had cared for the orphans had done so out of the goodness of her heart. Her service was personal, not official.

After the fire, the central government stepped in quickly. It ordered authorities to strengthen the regulation of foster care delivered by NGOs and individuals. Linda Shum feared she might have to return all the children in her foster homes to the orphanages they originally came from. It was a soul-destroying prospect after fifteen years working to remove children from damaging institutions and giving them an experience of regular family life. I continued reading her message.

'I really want t...'

That was the end.

My fingers drummed impatiently beside the keyboard.

Was it a hoax? She didn't ask for money, so what did she want?

I clicked on the return email address and wrote in the subject line:

'*Can you email me please Linda?*'

A few hours later, a reply appeared.

'Hi Jane, what would you like me to email you about? Faithfully, Linda.'

'*I got a message from this address about a fire in a Chinese foster home?*'

And then came a torrent of words. This woman was clearly driven by passion and commitment, but lost me in the detail of China's welfare system. It was too much information for a first conversation and I didn't follow half of what she was talking about.

I'd never heard of her organisation, COAT, but I was intrigued. I hoped I could find the thread of a story somewhere amid her verbose outpouring. Still, she had effectively snared her first big fish in the media and I had found the human interest interview that would nicely explain the people-to-people relationship between Australia and China.

Two nights later when Prime Minister Julia Gillard wrapped up her visit to the Asian powerhouse, home to one fifth of humanity, Linda Shum appeared at the ABC's Southbank studio in Brisbane where I interviewed her for *The World*. I was in Sydney, in the so-called 'fishbowl' studio because bystanders could look in at you from the foyer. When Linda's picture popped up, I saw that despite her surname, she was Australian, not Chinese. She looked older than I expected, with a solid face and body to match. In front of the camera, she was much more formal than she'd been over the phone. I wasn't sure if the interview did her justice, but then you can never be sure.

Journalism for me involves researching and immersing yourself in someone else's life for as much time as a deadline allows. From your basket of research, you craft questions, the interview happens, and then, when it's over, you say goodbye and move on to the next subject or story.

But once in a while, you don't want to move on. On this occasion, the story behind the woman with a tendency to give too much information, continued to gnaw at me. In fact, after the program went to air, I had even more questions than I had before although none of them had anything to do with the Australia–China relationship.

How did a retired teacher from regional Queensland (who didn't study Chinese) end up building an organisation, raising money and caring for the needs of Chinese orphans half a world away? Who were these children? How many of them were there and what was the Chinese city Jiaozuo – which I'd never heard of – actually like? She mentioned God a lot. She was clearly religious. Was she a missionary?

When I worked in China in the 1990s, I confess I didn't think the one-child policy was much of a news story. It had been around since 1980 and it didn't take great powers of observation to notice that everywhere you went in Beijing, the pavements, the squares, the parks, the lakes, the department stores, even the courtyards of the Forbidden City were crammed full of people. I just accepted the premise that the one-child policy was necessary because there were too many people in China. I thought the nation had done the planet a favour. Since meeting Linda, I've changed my mind.

Not far from the airport cafe, an advertisement flashed an image of a man in a surgeon's gown, holding a giant syringe to the flawless face of a pretty Chinese woman. It was curious to see a plastic surgery ad at an airport. During my time in China as a correspondent, the focus of the nation was on lifting hundreds of millions of people out of poverty. Was there still poverty in China if middle class Chinese could afford plastic surgery? I wondered whether other aspects of Chinese life had changed since I had lived there. The list of questions were starting to mount. If China could afford to build a telescope to search for extraterrestrial life, why couldn't it afford to care for its own orphans? What effect did the one-child policy have on China? What did the future hold for orphans like Wen Xuan, the boy in the wheelchair who I met at the airport, and who turned heads everywhere? And why was a retired Australian school-teacher permitted by a patriotic government proud of its own achievements to assist Wen and orphans like him?

'Shall we catch the bus?' Linda asked bringing me back to the moment, reminding me that we had another leg of the journey to go before reaching our destination.

'Do you ever wonder why Wen Xuan was abandoned?' I asked. 'Was it because, if his parents could only have one child, according to the policy, they wanted it to be a perfect child?'

Linda thought for a moment.

'I think he was abandoned because of ignorance and superstition,' she said. 'I don't believe it is ever the mother's choice to let her child go. It's the grandparents who only get one chance at a grandchild and they think it should be male and he should be perfect.'

She paused again.

'There's a black mole on Wen's back which is hairy and ugly. You see, some families consider a deformity to be a curse. Villagers are quite superstitious about this kind of stuff. Historically, there's been very little outside help for disabled children. When Wen Xuan was born his parents knew he wouldn't be any good for working in the fields. He would be a burden to the family.'

I looked across at Wen who was peering at us with big orphan eyes. He reminded me of Mark Lester, the actor who played Oliver Twist in the 1960s film. Wen Xuan was my Chinese Oliver Twist. Even in his post-nauseous state, there was something about his eyes. They were alert and a little vulnerable. It was hard to imagine a couple putting him down, turning their backs on him and leaving him forever.

The hawk-eyed waitress watched me put two notes on a tray. She took it back to the counter and checked each note against a lamp to ensure I hadn't passed her any counterfeit money. She was probably right not to trust a journalist. Who knows, she could end up in a book.

I sensed a long journey was beginning and not just the one to Jiaozuo city.

CHAPTER 2

Unwanted

From all accounts, the New England town of Inverell after the end of the Second World War was an idyllic place to grow up. Renewal was the buzzword. Optimism replaced austerity and the Australian economy began to ramp up production. Australians themselves ramped up production and a baby boom was in full swing. Linda McCarthy Shum's early life, recalls a safe, simple time. I could sense this when I visited Inverell in 2014 as the black swans gathered in the bends of the Macintyre River, sheltered by the fronds of billowing willows.

There is no shortage of churches or pubs in Inverell, where Linda spent her first twelve years. Her father, Charles McCarthy, used to tell a story about his sister's birth at the Inverell Hospital. There were several pubs between the hospital and the registry office where Charles' father, Stan, was despatched after the birth. Stan had been instructed to register the child as Gabrielle Anne. But after several celebratory beers, by the time Stan reached the registry office, he had forgotten his daughter's full name. On the birth certificate, she was simply 'Gay'.

Linda remembers mostly happy, carefree times as a small child. Grandmothers, cousins, aunties and uncles all lived close to the family home at 8 Howard Street, a fine hilltop location on a street lined with trees filled with the chatter of birds and cicadas. Howard Street rises from a suspension footbridge which crosses the Macintyre River and connects to a path leading to the town centre. Standing at the front gate of the old house, you had, and still have, a perfect view of the town. Every now and then, church bells interrupt the birdsong.

Linda roamed Inverell by bike with her cousins. Her uncle Harold taught her to swim, first by doing breast-stroke on the grassy verge before graduation to the murky river. Most working families grew their own vegetables and roasted hogget, a cheap cut of meat, for Sunday lunch. For entertainment, they gathered around the wireless to take in the daily trials of Dr Gordon in the much-loved ABC radio drama *Blue Hills*.

Linda's parents, Charles McCarthy and Molly O'Brien, met at a social dance. Charles, who was twenty-four, had returned to Inverell from Sydney after his war service in Borneo and Indonesia. Molly's family ran a garage. She was just eighteen.

'She was a very attractive, outgoing woman who liked people to notice her,' Linda's long-time friend Beth McNeil recalled. 'She was Catholic, but not a good Catholic. She didn't go to church. None of the O'Brien's did.'

The McCarthy's, on the other hand, were Anglican, and while Charles' father, had he been alive, would have balked at his son marrying a Catholic, Charles' mother reluctantly agreed. While there were exceptions, in those days there were still sectarian divisions. Catholics and Protestants didn't blend well.

Molly, whose father was dying when she first met Charles, was a vulnerable young woman. She and Charles were immediately attracted to each other and romance led to a proposal. Molly had grown up in a culture that taught her it was questionable whether Protestants could get to heaven, that any marriage outside the church was not worth the licence it was printed on and any children from that marriage would be considered illegitimate. She insisted on a Catholic wedding. Reluctantly, Charles' mother conceded. The priest made Charles and Molly promise to bring up their children as Catholics, yet despite jumping through all the hoops, in the end they couldn't be married in the church itself because of a small matter which was a very big deal in those times. Molly was pregnant. As a compromise, the ceremony was held in the presbytery where the priest lived.

Perhaps because she had a fraught relationship with her own mother, Molly desperately wanted to give birth to a boy. She prayed for a son but when Charles brought her to the Inverell Hospital to give birth on 21 October 1948, it was a little girl he lifted gently into his arms. They named her Ethne Linda McCarthy, but the intention was always to call her by her middle name, Linda.

As well as Molly's disappointment at giving birth to a girl instead of a boy, Linda's arrival marked the beginning of Molly's life-long struggle with depression. Mental illness wasn't well-understood or much talked about in those days. After Linda's birth, Molly was miserable. She yearned for the unconditional love of her father, who died before the wedding, crying rivers of tears, sometimes in sync with the baby. It was a miserable start for a new family.

Molly's mother was known to Linda as Gan. Gan never attempted to disguise her disapproval of Molly conceiving a child before the wedding. 'It wasn't something Gan could forgive or forget,' Linda said. Whenever mother and daughter argued, which was frequently, Gan brought up the 'offence' to drag Molly down. As a small child, Linda often remembered Gan calling Molly 'a little slut'. It sent Molly into fits of sobbing.

On top of a glass display cabinet at Linda's home in Gympie near Queensland's Sunshine Coast, she keeps a large photograph of Molly in her late teens. Soft dark curls roll away from a porcelain face. Her lips are colourised in harsh burgundy. Molly's piercing eyes, like tiny almonds, seem vacant or lost. She was certainly very pretty, but as I mulled over the portrait, trying to absorb what Linda had told me, I sensed that this attractive young woman wasn't happy.

'I was a huge disappointment to my mother. She was always glamorous. I was always frumpy. We had lots of differences right from the start,' Linda said pointing to another photo of her mother, looking trim in a fitted suit. She is holding Linda's hand. Linda is wearing a white dress with a white bow in her hair. Contrary to what she said, she didn't look like a frumpy child. Whenever she speaks about difficult emotional subjects, Linda becomes matter-of-fact. She was adamant that Molly didn't want her. To prove it, she sent me an account written by her father, Charles, a few years before his death in 2015. Charles wrote simply, 'Molly hoped that her baby would be a boy. She was disappointed when it was a girl.'

One day when Linda was about four, Gan, pulled the suitcases from under the beds and started packing them with holiday clothes. As she dressed the child, she divulged something that would be imprinted on Linda like a tattoo.

'Your mother does not want you, so I'm taking you to Sydney with me.'

Linda insisted that she took the news in her stride. On her holiday in Sydney, she never gave her mother a second thought.

'I slept with Gan in a big bed and felt very safe. I always remember the cooing of pigeons which reminded me of a happy childhood. About Mum's rejection, I just thought, oh well, it doesn't matter. I belonged to Dad. I was secure in his love and the love of my grandmothers and Dad's sisters.'

Two years after Linda's birth, Molly and Charles had the baby boy Molly was so desperate for. They named him John (Molly called him Little John until her death). For a while after John's birth, Molly seemed happy. But when he reached the age of three, Molly became depressed. Rage followed melancholy followed rage which was squarely aimed at her immediate family. In the community, there was little sympathy for her condition.

'All Molly McCarthy needed was a good kick,' the family doctor told Charles.

Molly was sent to see a psychiatrist in Sydney and remained in treatment for a year. During her absence from Inverell, Linda was put on a plane to Brisbane (her first flight) where she stayed with her Aunt Trudie and Uncle John in Redcliffe. The couple were childless and doted on Linda, lavishing her with beautiful dresses, shoes and ribbons for her hair.

When Molly eventually returned home she was offered a job as a book-keeper by her brother Jack, fourteen years her senior. Jack ran a construction business, O'Brien Sands and Metal. Part of Molly's wage paid for a nanny to clean the house and look after John. The other portion was set aside as savings.

Before she started primary school, Linda began taking Little John with her around Inverell thinking she was doing Molly a favour by giving her some peace. One day, she took her brother down the hill to play by the riverbank. When her mother found the two of them by the water's edge, she stormed home to grab the dreaded 'woolly duster', a cane with a clump of wool on the end used for cleaning, which she used to beat the back of Linda's legs leaving her with thigh-to-ankle welts. After that incident, Linda tended to leave John well alone.

The big picture, however, was looking up. For a while there was harmony in the McCarthy household and Molly felt fulfilled and happy. The job was to last six years and gave her independence and a bit of distance from the children. Now that they were upwardly mobile, Molly and Charles were keen to buy a big consumer item that was taking Australia by storm in the post-war years; a family motor car.

One day, the family ventured down Howard Street, across the bridge over the Macintyre River and into town. They were headed for the Holden dealership, F Gaukroger and Sons, for a glimpse of 'Australia's Own Car'. Not long after the visit to the showroom, the 'parp' of a car horn sounded outside the front door at Howard Street. There was Charles triumphant in the driving seat of a brand new FJ Holden. It cost one thousand pounds and had been paid for by Molly's savings. The FJ had a gleaming grey body and a sleek, red leather interior; the height of fifties sophistication.

'It was one of the cheap models,' Linda quickly pointed out. 'It didn't have blinkers (as indicator lights were called then). 'The cheaper model meant the driver or passenger had to wind down the window and use a hand-signal before turning.'

The car brought a new sense of freedom to the family. Their world suddenly became much bigger as they visited towns and cities further afield. On one occasion, the family drove to an outdoor cinema at the town of Delungra, 30 kilometres away. It was screening *The Inn of the Sixth Happiness* starring Hollywood movie legend Ingrid Bergman.

The 1958 film was based on the book *Gladys Aylward: The Little Woman* about a poorly-educated Cockney desperate to become a missionary in China in the 1930s. China was in the grip of civil war, and in the midst of widespread upheaval, the Japanese invaded the north of the country. Arriving after an arduous journey on the Trans-Siberian Railway, Gladys was shocked by the extraordinary poverty and backwardness of the country. She was put to work with an old missionary, Jeannie

Lawson, but Mrs Lawson died after a fall. Gladys tried to take her place but was woefully unprepared. Eventually she made a name for herself as a saviour of abandoned children. Then as now, it's a story that resonated deeply with Linda.

'I know *The Inn of the Sixth Happiness* off by heart,' Linda said. 'Whenever I feel down, I put the DVD on and it gives me a bit of a lift.'

A few months before he died, Linda's husband, Greg, bought her six DVD copies of the film. 'I think you're going to wear them all out,' he said. He was right. All of the copies were used, scratched to oblivion and eventually discarded. 'Thank God for YouTube' Linda says, which has the film in its entirety.

I watched it at Linda's suggestion, pausing at the point Mrs Lawson, the old missionary, calms Gladys after she witnesses a public execution. Mrs Lawson says:

> There's much that is horrible in China, as in any country; babies left to die in ditches, the poor preying on the poor, many things. But they [the Chinese] will change. One thing at a time with the help of The Lord and that's what we are here for in this dirty room, to try to help...It's a hard life for a young woman, but it won't seem hard, I promise you. When you are my age and look back, it will only seem beautiful.

For her lifetime of service, the Chinese awarded Gladys Aylward the title 'Virtuous One'.

Curiously, like me, Linda always paused at the section following the execution. She found the old missionary's message transformational.

'I internalised those words,' she said, 'Even as a child, I wanted to emulate Gladys.'

The film gave me a sense of what motivated Linda to go to China from her very first viewing under the canvas of a starry night.

In 1960, the family upgraded the Holden FJ to the Holden FB model. Charles sold the house at 8 Howard Street and the family packed up and headed north to Toowoomba in south-east Queensland. Four years later, they were on the move again, this time to the town of Stanthorpe where Charles was appointed manager for Beaurepaires Tyres.

Though Molly was pleased to escape from her mother and brother in Inverell, she wasn't able to settle into life in Stanthorpe and a familiar cycle began. Linda by now was a teenager while Molly had become a heavy drinker and continued to suffer from depression. She and her daughter argued incessantly. During school holidays when Linda was fifteen, one of their arguments became so heated that Molly ordered Linda out of the house. Then Molly dumped the entire contents of Linda's bedroom onto the front lawn. Linda was barred from entering the house during the day so she was forced to camp in the Holden which was parked outside Charles' office. By this stage, Linda clearly understood that she had been rejected.

One of the first things Linda told me about herself was that she has lived a sheltered life.

'Don't be ridiculous,' I responded.

But as our friendship progressed, I began to agree with her. Linda had moved from bubble to bubble. Her early life was spent in a Catholic bubble. She went to Catholic schools and was only ever taught by nuns. She attended mass every Sunday, because it was considered a mortal sin not to, as well as on the first Saturday of the month and several early mornings during the week. She went to confession every Saturday in order to take Holy Communion on Sunday.

'I loved God,' she said, 'but it was fear that drove my actions when I was a child. I didn't want to go to hell. So I obeyed all the rules. I was very religious. I was in Year Eleven when I first felt a strong urge to get closer to Jesus by giving him not just my life, but my whole self. I never felt called to go off and convert the heathen. I felt called to become a teaching nun, to spend time with God and to care for his children.'

At the age of seven, Linda had a dream or a vision. She thinks it must have been while she slept and it was the first time she'd experienced anything like it. In the dream, she met Jesus who stood towering over her. Understandably frightened, she kept her head bowed. It was then that she noticed his feet. Jesus wasn't wearing shoes and his feet were dirty. She recalls seeing black hairs on his big toes. While Linda quivered in his presence, Jesus eventually spoke.

'Come be a sheep in my flock,' he said in a kindly voice. 'Feed my lambs.'

She interpreted this to mean that Jesus wanted her to devote her life to looking after small children. She has never questioned the significance or her part in the deal even though this happened over sixty years ago. It remains as vivid and emotional for her today as it was when she was seven.

Sometimes during our conversations, I found Linda's fire and brimstone Christian language difficult to relate to. She regards the Bible as the word of God and likes to quote it a lot, so perhaps it's not surprising that she says things like 'Come be a sheep in my flock'. Linda turns to the Bible for direction many times every day. She wears her faith on her sleeve. She speaks of her 'calling'. Everything she accomplishes she attributes to God. Miracles occur around her. 'Satan' gets a regular mention in our chats. It's not language I'm comfortable with, although I can still admire what she does and how she conducts herself.

In the early 2000s, a few years after she began visiting China, her brother John drove to Gympie to see their father Charles and found Linda in the shed, milking a cow. John was battling cancer of the jawbone. Leaning on a gate, bitterness fell from his mouth, contorted by his disease.

'My fat-arsed stuck-up sister lowers herself to milk a cow,' he said, sneering.

'He made me feel two inches tall,' Linda recalled. 'I had been telling him about the Chinese orphans and how I was trying to give them comfortable lives in a loving environment.'

John wasn't interested.

'There goes my sister,' he muttered as he turned to leave. 'Mother Bloody Teresa.'

After finishing high school, Linda left Stanthorpe for Brisbane in 1968 to become a teacher.

She loved her studies at Kedron Park Teachers' College and with her outgoing nature, she made friends easily. One day as she ate lunch with a group of companions on the grass in the sunshine, a bespectacled young man appeared around the corner. She had seen him around although he wasn't really her type. He was quiet and serious. A voice in her head, that she took to be God's, told her 'marry him.'

'You have got to be kidding!' she remonstrated. 'One day he's going to be bald and fat!'

But not long after that, she found herself sitting next to the quiet young man in a social studies class. His name was Greg Shum.

'I didn't tell him then that the synthetic shirt he was wearing needed to be washed every day. That came much later. He began to hang around with me and my circle of friends. He liked to watch me doing phys ed where our uniform was a pair of bloomers with a short tunic over the top. My legs weren't too bad in those days,' she said with a twinkle.

Greg, like Linda, was a devout Christian. But Greg's brand of Christianity was not liked by conventional Christians. He was a Pentecostal, part of the evangelical movement which emphasises the work of the Holy Spirit, which includes healing, speaking in tongues and prophesy.[1] Its modern incarnation began to spread in the United States in the early 20th century. In the 1960s, Pentecostalism was still widely ostracised as a fringe sect by mainstream Protestants and Catholics.

Linda continued her argument with God. Not only did Greg wear synthetic clothes, but to marry him would involve one of them having to convert.

'After what happened to my parents, I didn't want a mixed marriage,' Linda said. 'And if I became a Pentecostal I'd have to give up my family, my friends and my Catholic religion. What was God thinking?'

Despite Linda's misgivings, Greg persisted. He chauffeured Linda and her friends to barbecues in his FE Holden ensuring there was always a free seat next to him. By the end of their first year at teachers' college, their relationship had deepened. The following year, they drew up a list of the controversial elements of their faiths as they saw it. One of them was the existence of purgatory and limbo. Another was the infallibility of the Pope. They spent long hours in the library and consulted several Catholic priests to arrive at their own conclusions.

'We looked at the history of these things and found them to be man-made rather than scriptural. And we looked at the history of the Popes and found many of them to be nothing more than wicked men.'

The two had involved and heated conversations, 'which caused Greg to love the real me,' Linda said.

Today Pentecostals say their faith is one of the fastest growing Christian denominations in Australia and the world. Included under the Pentecostal umbrella known as the Australian Christian Churches, is the Hillsong Church founded in Sydney's western suburbs in 1983 by pastor Brian Houston. Hillsong's website asserts: 'The Australian Christian Churches [is] a movement of 1,100 churches and more than 250,000 believes across Australia' and is also connected to 'tens of thousands of other churches around the world'.

I asked Linda if I could accompany her to a Hillsong Conference in July 2014. An estimated 30,000 people packed the stadium at Sydney Olympic Park. They were mostly families and people under fifty. It was like a United Nations advertisement with people from varied backgrounds. They sang with their eyes closed and arms held high as mist swirled around the performers on a stage in the centre of the arena. The music was trance-like. My chest reverberated from a drumbeat that seemed in sync with my own heart. Linda, her daughter Debbie, and two of Debbie's teenage daughters were also on their feet. Linda had one arm held up as if she were bringing the traffic to a halt. I was the only one with my hands by my sides and I didn't know the words. Everything on stage was relayed through giant screens so you didn't miss a thing, wherever you sat. The whole effect was tantalising.

Veteran ABC broadcaster John Cleary sees Pentecostals as having a reputation among other churches as 'very good at community' but weak on critical reflection. 'The role of the charismatic preacher has been central,' he told me. Despite Hillsong's claims of more than a quarter of a million devotees in Australia, John Cleary believes there is some evidence of a high turnover rate among followers. He says that until recently, Pentecostalism has been seen as 'a religion of permanent adolescence'.[2]

Pentecostal Christians foster a personal, emotional connection with God. It gives them the opportunity to teach their faith as an individual journey.

There are also controversial elements of Pentecostalism, in the eyes of mainstream Christians, which I view from my agnostic perch with scepticism. They come with their own Pentecostal vernacular:

1. The laying on of hands (healing).
2. Speaking in tongues (when a person experiencing religious ecstasy utters sounds they believe are a language spoken through him or her by God).
3. Prophesying (God rather than a clairvoyant telling people what's going to happen).
4. Being slain in the spirit (being overcome by the Holy Spirit so that you are literally knocked over).

I don't take the Bible literally. As Uniting Church pastor and CEO of the Wayside Chapel, Graham Long told me, 'It's like the Bible dropped out of the sky one day and bingo, [fell] into somebody's hands. "God had given us a cookbook, just follow all the instructions!" Well, you know, that isn't what happened. That isn't how we got the Bible. It's [been] through a very messy history. I think it's really hard to take the Bible seriously and literally at the same time.'

When I mentioned to Linda that some elements of her faith – particularly speaking in tongues – troubled me, she said they had troubled her too, long ago. But then she decided to believe only what was written in the Bible. She remembers attending her first Pentecostal prayer meeting with Greg in Chermside, near the teachers' college, before they became engaged.

'The whole room seemed to be "drunk". They were rolling on the floor, crying out to God. I then understood why some people called them "Holy Rollers",' she said. 'There were people lying on the floor, rocking, crying tears, praying up a storm. I got such a shock, I knelt down and said a rosary for protection,' she recalled.

'It really frightened me. But I was impressed too. It was inspiring.'

With many of their misgivings put to rest, Greg and Linda married in an Assemblies of God Church in Brisbane in August 1970. Linda's decision to marry outside the Catholic bubble was the equivalent of joining the Dark Side.

'My wedding day for me was quite sad,' she said. 'I felt my father should have given me away, but another man did, because Dad was too scared to come.' Some close school-friends stayed away too, as did nuns and priests that she respected. All except for one beloved high school teacher. But as always, a decent cohort from her father's family including her grandmother and several aunts and uncles showed up.

Linda's mother Molly did not speak to her daughter after the wedding. By then, Charles and Molly had adopted two sons – Christopher and Michael – just before Linda's departure for teachers' college. However, the joy of having two baby boys quickly faded. Nothing seemed to rid Molly of her depression. In 1976, when Christopher and Michael were aged nine and eight, Charles had Molly committed for being mentally ill. He took care of the boys. After Molly's release, she refused to return to Charles and they separated. Charles rented a unit for her and she survived on a deserted wife's pension and Weetbix.

Molly didn't speak to Linda for twenty-one years, until shortly before her death. Despite the split with her mother, Linda continued to remain very close to Charles. She and Greg bought a small plot of land in Gympie inland from the Sunshine Coast, but before settling there, they relocated to small towns in regional Queensland for teaching assignments. Molly missed the births of her grandchildren; Jason (born 1973), Debbie (1974) and Damien (1976).

In 1980, the Shums moved to a tiny place called Yuleba, with a population of a few hundred, 420 kilometres west of Brisbane. Greg became principal of a school with just five teachers. Linda was a stay-at-home mum at the time, caring for the couple's three young children. Their youngest son, Damien, suffered a serious asthma attack one night. The nearest doctor was 60 kilometres away in Roma. After that incident, the Shums became involved in running a community-based ambulance service. A seventeen-year-old ambulance that had been kept in the council shed was dusted off and readied for service. Linda received first aid and CPR training and two nights a week plus every second weekend she worked as a volunteer ambulance bearer, helping to transport injured and sick patients to Roma Hospital.

One night, a motorist demolished his car on an infamous bend in the road. The black spot was known ironically as 'The

Feather Bed'. The young man had been catapulted onto the gravel on the edge of the road. He was seriously injured and his face was a bloodied mess. Greg was supposed to mind the children but he left them sleeping in the house alone in order to get help. He and Linda headed to the crash scene with a policeman from a neighbouring town. Greg's role was to help the police by gathering accident statistics. He began to take measurements at the scene of the crash. Linda spotted the policeman and started to give him orders on how to load the patient into the ambulance.

'Who IS that woman?' the officer asked Greg incredulously.

'That's no woman!' Greg replied. 'That's my wife!'

Once the patient had been settled for the ride, 'The Feather Bed' was soon in the distance behind them. But as the ambulance approached the outskirts of Roma, the young man stopped breathing.

Linda, sitting beside him, looked at his mangled face where the skin had been buffed away by the gravel. She couldn't find a heartbeat. He was so young and yet his life was going to be cut short on this lonely road without his family around him. The oxygen resuscitator was empty. Someone had forgotten to refill it. What was she supposed to do?

Linda did the only thing she could think of. She panicked. And then she prayed. Loud and hard. The driver asked her whether the boy was ok. She called back that he wasn't and that maybe the driver, who was travelling at 100 miles per hour, shouldn't go so fast. Then the young man took a rattling breath. Linda prayed more loudly. He continued to breath as they reached Roma Hospital. He was still alive. In the coming days, he drifted in and out of consciousness and called out several times 'Jesus! Jesus! Jesus!'. Staff and visitors thought he was cursing, however Linda maintains her prayers reached into his subconscious. Eventually, he made a complete recovery.

Linda learned so much from her experience as an ambulance bearer but she saved people who weren't accident victims too.

Linda's daughter Debbie remembers her tenth birthday party when Linda insisted on inviting a little girl from the neighbourhood.

'I didn't want her to come so I told her she wasn't welcome,' Debbie said. 'Mum was furious and flogged my butt with a belt. I couldn't jump on the trampoline because my bottom was so sore!'

What Debbie didn't know was that the girl had been sexually assaulted by the neighbourhood boys. She was ten.

'Mum knew though. She looked out for her and took her under her wing. I was a selfish little girl who couldn't see past the end of my nose,' Debbie said. 'It was a well-learned life lesson.'

Following her separation from Charles, Molly McCarthy was in and out of mental institutions and hostels for the homeless. Over the years both Greg and Linda wrote and sent photos of the children to Molly attempting to stay in touch. Once, Greg took the three children to meet their grandmother, but it turned out to be so stressful, it wasn't repeated.

A few years ago, Linda discovered Molly's diary. She read this: 'That bastard Greg Shum came to see me today. How could such a fat, ugly bastard have fathered such a pretty little girl?'

Linda put down the diary angrily. Though it hurt to read those words, she felt it important to remember the essential part of the relationship with her mother.

'Just before she died, when I left the room I overheard her tell a nurse, "That's my daughter, I am so proud of her!". Then one day, I was changing her incontinence pants and she seemed so tiny and vulnerable. At that moment, I looked into her eyes and said "I love you Mum". Tears rolled down her face. She was dying from emphysema. But after so many years of sadness she managed to say "I love you too". That meant everything to me.'

Reflecting on Linda's life before she found China, here was a woman shaped by three things: faith, resilience and compassion. Linda attempted to answer all my questions about her religious practice. She was never judgemental towards me. She did not try to convert me. She listened to my views and asked me lots of questions and still does. From my perspective, she peppers her conversation with far too many biblical references. But I never saw her speak in tongues. She wanted the orphans to learn about Jesus, but that's as far as it went. She really did say 'God' quite a lot. But who am I to judge?

CHAPTER 3

The Dying Rooms

In June 1995, a few months before I arrived in Beijing to begin my posting as the ABC TV China correspondent, an international scandal erupted. Britain's Channel Four television network aired a documentary called *The Dying Rooms*. Filmmakers posing as American orphanage workers used hidden cameras to film government-run orphanages around China. The footage showed conditions of appalling poverty and neglect. The central allegation in *The Dying Rooms* was that orphanages – which in the early to mid-1990s were extremely overcrowded – deliberately left babies to die through starvation and withholding medical treatment.[1]

In *The Dying Rooms*, producer Kate Blewett spoke of what she called 'evidence that babies really are dumped on the street like kittens in a sack.' In the final minutes of the investigation, the team uncovered a hidden room in a southern Chinese orphanage. There, a little girl they called 'No Name' had been left to die. 'No Name' was emaciated and without any human contact. Four days after the filming, she died 'of plain neglect,' Blewett said in the voice-over.

The Chinese government responded with a TV report called *The Dying Rooms: a Patchwork of Lies*. China denied that babies were systematically left to die. But the denial failed to extinguish widespread condemnation of China. Beijing was already smarting from the loss a few years earlier of its bid to host the 2000 Olympics. *The Dying Rooms* was viewed around the world and ended up winning a swag of international awards including an Emmy. It was singled out for praise by Oprah. Though the internet was in its infancy in those days, *The Dying Rooms* was what we would describe today as viral.

By the time I arrived in China at the end of 1995, the shockwaves from the documentary were still being felt. I remember finding China such a riddle as I ventured out in my green cashmere coat, so perfect in Sydney and next to useless in a face-tingling northern Chinese winter. I thought, somehow, that China would be more familiar than it was. My mother was Eurasian; both her parents were half Chinese. I had learned Mandarin and spoke Cantonese while growing up in Hong Kong where my father (whose parents were Scottish and English) was a newspaper editor. My mother too had been a journalist, giving up her career to have children. And so I became a reporter, firstly on radio and then with a TV station in Hong Kong. My first big assignment was to Beijing to cover the visit by the Queen in 1986. And yet, years later standing on Tiananmen Square as the new ABC China correspondent in my inadequate coat in early December, nothing conformed to what I thought I knew.

Modern high-rise buildings stood wedged between steely Communist architecture. Police at the intersections used funny hand gestures to control the traffic (it was a trend) as if they were robots. At night when the police disappeared, the traffic became chaotic. Nobody wanted to give way. On intersections, there were so many poor people selling mass-produced goods and street food, like baked sweet potatoes, out of baskets and carts. It was one big stir fry; exhilarating and baffling at the same time.

I devoured virtually all the books penned by China experts and correspondents. Many of them made outrageous predictions about the future. 'China has five years, perhaps ten before it falls' (written in 2001), 'China will be democratic by the turn of the century', 'If China sneezes, the world catches a cold', 'The endgame of Chinese Communist rule has now begun'. You had to wonder whether anyone really knew what was going on in the halls of power in this big, strange nation of more than a billion people.

In early 1996, a few months after my arrival, Human Rights Watch (HRW), a respected NGO, released a report building on the accusations made in *The Dying Rooms*. The agency asserted that thousands of children in state-run orphanages had perished as a result of 'deliberate starvation, medical malpractice and staff abuse.'[2]

The HRW report, *Death by Default*, was based on the testimony of a Chinese doctor Zhang Shuyun, who worked at the Shanghai Children's Welfare Institute. Records revealed between 1986 and 1992 more than 1,000 children died unnatural deaths in this one institute alone.[3] After attempts to expose the situation were quashed by officials, Dr Zhang (not her real name) grabbed the evidence and fled China.

Human Rights Watch alleged 'most orphaned or abandoned children in China die within one year of their admittance to state-run orphanages' and accused the government of a 'policy of fatal neglect'. The Shanghai Children's Welfare Institute according to HRW had 'practised a deliberate policy of child murder in numerous cases', and cited a mortality rate from the late 1980s to early 1990s that 'was probably running as high as 90 per cent'.[4]

With the watchdog's co-operation, Channel Four aired a second documentary called *Return to the Dying Rooms* which elaborated on some of the claims in the report.

'To stop these children screaming of hunger and thirst, they (orphanage staff) either tie them to the bed so they can't move, or they give them huge amounts of sleeping pills or inject them with sedatives. This way they are unconscious and can be slowly left to die,' Dr Zhang said in *Return to the Dying Rooms*. The second documentary was every bit as damning as the first.

Every newsroom in the industrialised world clamoured for a response from the Chinese government. Just two months into my posting, as a newly anointed correspondent, I assumed, as it was a UK documentary, there was little I could do from Beijing. There would likely be a dry statement from a spokesperson at the weekly Chinese Foreign Ministry briefing. However, there was no way I could get anywhere near the Shanghai orphanage in question. Apart from that, most of the key players were either in Hong Kong or further afield. I didn't think there was much more I could add so I didn't offer a story to any of the programs I reported for.

Bad call Jane.

The next morning I got a message that a producer from *The 7.30 Report* in Sydney was looking for me. I returned her call. She said the program was interested in a follow-up to the orphanage story. Actually, she said, the presenter was surprised I hadn't offered anything.

'Kerry is really keen on this story,' she said referring to the program's high-profile presenter, Kerry O'Brien. Apparently he'd taken a personal interest in it. Before I could speak, the handset was jerked out of the producer's control. The formidable KO'B was on the line.

I don't remember precisely what he said, because I was in shock. He was calm. I think he said something along the lines of, 'If anything big like the orphanage story happens again, just get on the phone to me and we'll give you all the help you need.'

From Kerry, it was a mild rebuke. When he wasn't happy, his reaction could be legendary. But a few years earlier when I worked with him on the program *Lateline,* his dissection of my research briefs always taught me something. Just weeks into my new posting however, my run-in with Kerry had left my confidence shattered. So naturally, I have never forgotten *The Dying Rooms.*

CHAPTER 4

Population Control
From Mao to Now

To understand how China arrived at the one-child policy in 1980, you have to wind the clock back to the 1950s. China was backward and poor when Mao Zedong and the Communists swept to power. The two biggest issues Mao faced were, how was China going to feed itself and how was it going to modernise?

The Communist government embarked on China's first national census assuming as most international experts did, that the population was between 430 and 480 million. But the head-count came in at 582,603,417. Each decade from 1949, when the Communists took power, added 135 million more Chinese to the tally, the vast majority rural and poor according to Harvard anthropologist Professor Susan Greenhalgh.[1] In the early 1950s, Chinese women on average had more than six children each.

In a campaign known as The Great Leap Forward in the late 1950s, Mao planned to drive up agricultural production by using something China had plenty of: people. Soon, communes took over farming communities. 'Communism is paradise and the people's communes are the way to get there,' was one popular slogan. However, the transition to communal living caused much misery as private property was confiscated and land handed over to the state.

One of the most bizarre public campaigns of the time was exterminating the Four Pests: mosquitoes, flies, rats, and sparrows. It was partly about hygiene but mostly about getting rid of vermin which consumed China's hard-won grain output. The whole country was mobilised to kill or scare little birds away from the trees. People came out of their homes, beating pots and pans so the birds eventually dropped out of the sky in exhaustion. Even schools were rewarded for the volume of pests they eradicated. It didn't occur to officials that killing sparrows would result in an ecological imbalance that would cause the number of other pests, including locusts, to multiply.

Then, in an act of hubris, Mao Zedong announced that China would double its steel output, supplementing mass production by building crude backyard furnaces. Every conceivable form of metal (including kitchen utensils, tools and scrap iron) was smelted in huge melting pots in order to raise the production level to equal Great Britain's.

Chairman Mao declared, 'With 11 million tons of steel next year and 17 million tons the year after, the world will be shaken. If we can reach 40 million tons in five years, we may possibly catch up with Great Britain in seven years. Add another eight years and we will catch up with the US.'[2]

Mao saw it as a short-cut to face off with one of the great Western powers. But it was nonsensical. Most of the steel produced by the backyard furnaces was unusable. Not surprisingly, the plan failed dismally. Relations between China and its ally, the Soviet Union, were rapidly declining by this time so that the USSR eventually withdrew aid to China. What followed in 1958 was the start of three years of devastating floods and crop failures, producing disaster on an unimaginable scale. The natural and policy-driven calamity was known as China's Great Famine.

I discovered something that Linda and I both have in common. We are both admirers of Li Cunxin, artistic director of the Queensland Ballet. Most Australians came to known him through his best-selling autobiography *Mao's Last Dancer* and the film of the same name. Apart from his book, I was able to glean so much more about The Great Famine during an interview with him for my program *One Plus One*.

Li Cunxin was born in China's northeast in 1961. He was the sixth of seven sons born to peasants who lived in a commune which produced wheat in winter and corn, yams and sorghum the rest of the year. The government would take the biggest portion of the produce at a set price. The rest was divided among the peasant workers. In addition, Li's family had been allocated a plot of land for their own use which was one twentieth of an acre or about 200 metres square, fifteen minutes walk from their home. The entire family worked their tiny piece of land on Sundays, their day off.

His parents were loving, but poor. A major preoccupation of the entire family was their empty stomachs: where was the next meal going to come from?

'We saw people dying around us of disease, starvation, even a simple cold that might turn into something more serious,'[3] he told me. 'Every day, we struggled for basic food. And we dreamed of having a full stomach before we went to sleep.'

Li was born during the final year of China's Great Famine. Millions of people were reduced to eating anything from bark to bird-droppings. Tens of millions perished. Because the Communist Party still rules today, there has never been an official investigation or apology for this event or the plethora of other damaging policies during Chairman Mao's rule. The truth has been locked away. Thankfully, enterprising individuals have managed to uncover lost or hidden details of the atrocities.

Dutch historian, Frank Dikötter, used a brief window of openness and transparency during the lead-up to the Beijing Olympics to conduct research in China's provincial archives. Of course, the open window was soon shut, but it enabled Dikötter to uncover what had previously been off limits. He's written a riveting history called *Mao's Great Famine* about the era many Chinese refer to as The Three Bitter Years. He estimates at least 45 million deaths can be attributed to The Great Famine.

In another investigation, retired Chinese journalist Yang Jisheng also accessed archives never intended for public consumption and wrote a history called *Tombstone*. It hasn't been published in China. Yang believes there were 36 million deaths directly due to starvation including that of his own father. The Chinese government's official toll is 15 million fatalities. Whether you accept the numbers of the historian, the journalist or the government, it was a time of acute suffering which had a devastating impact on the Chinese people and is seared into the national memory.

Most Chinese aged fifty and over are still young enough to remember how difficult life used to be. It's why the Chinese people put so much store in wealth and education which are seen as keys to future advancement. When Li Cunxin was a boy, however, a completely different attitude prevailed. Society was focused on survival. And having sons was the answer.

'At the back of my parents' minds, they thought that by having many sons one of them might get lucky. The lucky one may have better genes or above average intelligence so he could be more than a farmer. Then if he became successful, one day he'd return to the village and come to the rescue of the rest of the family. When I was growing up, we were always told that if you do well, it's your responsibility to come back and help the rest of the family.'[4]

The Li family had initially been willing converts to Mao's socialism. 'Mao was a God,' said Li 'and we did whatever he asked of us.'

'My father would hide his few cents under his pillow or up in the loft. He'd save up for the entire year just so that we could buy enough ingredients to make dumplings at Chinese New Year, so that we could have one great meal.'

Li turned out to be the lucky ticket in his family.

After training as a ballet dancer for Madame Mao's dance troupe (she was the despised wife of Chairman Mao) during The Cultural Revolution, he defected to the US and eventually migrated to Australia. When he stopped dancing, he turned to his new passion: observing 'the machinery of capitalism' and becoming a stockbroker. But the main reason he went into share trading was to help his family.

'Sending money home was not going to set them up for life,' he said. 'I wanted to help my brothers start businesses so they could help their children and their grandchildren; give them a better education. So I've helped my brothers with different businesses at different times and they've done very well. I've played a small part in their success.'

In the early 1970s, a voluntary, but heavily-promoted birth-control program called *Wan Xi Shao,* meaning 'Later, Longer, Fewer', began rolling out nationwide. Its objective was to reduce population growth by encouraging women to marry and have children later, wait longer before having the next child and have fewer children overall. It was astonishingly successful although this downward trend in fertility occurred in many other countries as well. Between 1971 and 1978 China's birth-rate halved to 2.98 births per woman. So why didn't the Communist Party just continue with 'Later Longer Fewer', rather than taking the big-stick approach of the one-child policy in 1980?

The answer, is that a new mindset was taking hold in China after Mao's death and the power struggles that followed. Mao's successor, Deng Xiaoping, who was influenced by Western thinking, was firmly of the view that a bigger population was counterproductive to prosperity. He was swayed by the work of a Russian-trained missile scientist named Song Jian, who in turn was inspired by thinkers like American biologist Paul Ehrlich, (author of *The Population Bomb*) and the influential Club of Rome scientists who called for limits on population growth. Dr Song's theory was that if left to grow, China's population would reach 4.5 billion by the second half of the 21st century.[5]

A target of 1.2 billion people by 2000 was set (the 2000 census revealed that target had been exceeded by more than 65 million people) and Dr Song's cohorts concluded, 'during the next two decades each married couple should be encouraged to have only one child.'[6]

The one-child policy was officially born on 25 September 1980, the publication date of an open letter to the party faithful. When I was in China, most people called the policy *Jihua Shengyu* meaning 'birth planning'. But in the West and even officially in China, it was known colloquially as the one-child policy. All Chinese who lived in cities, as well as others in densely populated rural or suburban areas, were limited by law to one child per family with an exception for China's ethnic minorities.

In rural China, where 75–80 per cent of the population lived, the policy proved deeply unpopular, where, as Li Cunxin's story illustrates, the tradition was to have many children and preferably boys (this story is also told in Chapter 19). As a concession, in 1984 under an amendment called Document 7, local governments were allowed to tweak the policy to a one-son/two-child rule. If a couple's first child was a boy, they could have just the one. However if it was a girl, the couple was permitted to try for another child after a break of a few years.

However, the result of introducing flexibility (the Chinese government called it 'opening small holes' in the policy), was that it was applied with an iron fist. As commentator Amy Klatzin noted, 'the slightly more lenient policy was enforced much more vigorously in rural areas than the previous one-child policy had been. As a result orphanage populations sky-rocketed.'[7]

Those Chinese couples that were desperate for sons often abandoned their second-born daughters to the orphanages to try for a son. Other families abandoned children with disabilities to try for a son or a daughter – this is where *The Dying Rooms* came in. During the 1980s, thousands of children were left in the care of state orphanages.

On top of this, China passed its first adoption law in 1992. It discriminated against domestic adoptions by requiring adoptive parents to be over thirty-five and childless. But it opened the door to a large, well-regulated international adoption sector, a movement which has seen an estimated 140,000 Chinese orphans, most of them girls, finding homes overseas.[8] This has been the subject of much controversy both in China and beyond. Each international adoption earns the orphanage approximately US$3,000 per child. Was international adoption a humanitarian response to overflowing orphanages, or was it a regulated trade? Regardless of the conclusion, the international adoption floodgates were finally closed in 2007 when new rules came in favouring domestic over international couples. And even before this time, healthy daughters had become increasingly valued in Chinese society.

Chinese officials claim 400 million births were 'averted' over three decades as a result of the one-child policy although that figure is questioned by several international demographers. There is a swag of research on the phenomenon known as 'missing girls' meaning the female fetuses or infants who were 'disappeared' in order that their parents might try for a child of the opposite sex. It's fascinating, but tangential to this very brief history of the policy and how it relates to orphans.

The unintended consequences of what Professor Kay Johnson calls this 'collision between policy and culture'[9] is now obvious:

- China has a gender imbalance of 118 boys born for every 100 girls, against a global average of 103 to 107.[10] This means 30 million Chinese men will be 'bare branches', as China calls them; they will be unable to find wives, according to Mei Fong, the author of *One Child*, a powerful history of what she calls China's most radical experiment.[11]
- Trafficking in women and children is a huge problem for the country (again, mainly in rural areas) as desperate couples attempt to procure that which they don't have.

- China now has an acutely ageing society which means fewer workers to support the elderly. According to Mei Fong, 'Right now China has a dependency ratio of about five working adults to support one retiree. In about twenty years that's going to jump to about 1.6 working adults to support one retiree.'[12] This is probably the key reason why China finally relaxed the one-child policy in late 2015.
- At least a million children have been abandoned (experts say it's likely to be higher) creating a generation of orphans.

Xiaoyuan Shang, now Professor Shang, grew up during The Cultural Revolution when schools and institutions were closed across China. When the universities re-opened in 1977, she was among the first intake of students. In the 1990s, she relocated to the UK with her husband, an academic, and son. Her doctoral research focused on interest groups and social security reform in China. After hearing about *The Dying Rooms*, she joined her colleagues, switching on the TV in the common room. When the scathing documentary finished, she sat back in her chair, unable to speak.

'I was shocked,' she said. 'To be honest, I didn't really believe it,' she said of the previously unseen footage of child neglect.

She couldn't put the disturbing images out of her head. Surely this wasn't possible in her homeland, she thought, that children were being left to die? In a bid to discover the truth, she began to focus on China's child welfare system and government policy relating to orphanages. In effect, *The Dying Rooms* marked a new direction in her career. She was keen to find out whether government officials were complicit in the deaths of children, as *The Dying Rooms* and Human Rights Watch claimed. She travelled back to China where she was given high-level access to the Ministry of Labour and the Ministry of Civil Affairs.

'During my fieldwork, one labour official assured me that Chinese government officials had no motivation to kill children,' she said. Despite the assurance, she found there was plenty of work to do to improve the well-being of China's orphans.

Around the time of the 2000 Sydney Olympics, Xiaoyuan Shang, landed a position at the Social Policy Research Centre at the University of New South Wales where she's now an associate professor. She began to team up with Professor Karen Fisher, an expert in China and disability.

While researching China's orphanages for this book, the names Shang & Fisher kept coming up as fixtures in the body of academic research on China's welfare system. I looked them up and found that not only were they working for an Australian university, their base at UNSW wasn't far from my home. After entering a maze of offices, I finally found my way to Xiaoyuan Shang's office. There, amid a riot of books, papers, two desktop screens and a mountain bike, I came face-to-face with Professors Shang and Fisher who patiently answered my questions, beginning with the documentary which started it all. They said *The Dying Rooms* told a simplistic story of how the one-child policy created China's orphan problem but it wasn't the complete story.

Associate Professor Shang conducted the first national census of China's orphans in 2005. At the end of the 1980s, there were 5,000–6,000 children in state orphanages. By the end of 1997, just before Linda Shum's arrival, there were nearly 24,500 children. By 2011, the orphan numbers had more than quadrupled to around 110,000.[13]

In the early 1990s, Xiaoyuan Shang met the head of an orphanage in a south-eastern province who told her new babies were abandoned at the front gate every morning. One particular day, eleven babies were left there. Funding allocations to orphanages were made at the start of each year, so any new arrivals weren't accounted for. At busy times, the orphanage grouped three children in a bed. The orphanage director also told her the child mortality rate in that orphanage was 80 per cent, most of them girls. Something had to change.

CHAPTER 5

The Road to China

The Assemblies of God (now Australian Christian Churches) chose the Sunshine Coast for its 1997 Queensland women's conference. About a thousand women gathered at Caloundra's town hall for a weekend of Pentecostal sisterhood. Arriving delegates were assigned their accommodation and conference packs. Caloundra buzzed with expectation. No-one left these conferences uninspired, particularly with a theme that threw down a personal challenge to each woman: what purpose does God have for you?

Linda remembers the conference fondly. 'It was like a rock concert,' she recalled, 'Little old ladies were coming out of sessions literally drunk with the Holy Spirit, swaying from pillar to post.'

After one session, Linda returned to her room, barely able to walk in a straight line because of her exuberant state. Her mind was racing, so she had a warm shower to wind down and flopped between the bedsheets. The shower didn't help. She couldn't unwind and she knew she would never fall asleep in this mood.

She picked up her conference pack and started flicking through the newsletter. It fell open at an article about Chinese orphans. It said something along the lines of, Chinese babies and children were being held in dehumanising orphanages. She remembers the line 'Chinese children are dying from a lack of mother-touching'.

Her attention froze on the phrase 'mother-touching'. The touch of a human-being. Nurturing. Her adrenaline-charged brain dialled-up memories from her childhood in Inverell and the pain of being an unwanted daughter. She knew the feeling, however she'd also had plenty of love to make up for her mother's uninterest. The Chinese orphans didn't have anyone to love them. Now, here was this article claiming there were thousands and thousands of unwanted, unloved Chinese babies. This was tragic.

Linda's head began to spin. She couldn't shake the words or the thoughts from her mind. Restless in bed, she conjured up images of sweet little bundles lined up on the pavements of heartless China. There was no chance of sleep now. In frustration, she sat up.

'I started to argue with God,' she said. 'Here I was enjoying the Sunshine Coast and He was urging me to go to China. I was turning fifty the following year. I told him I was too old to make a difference.'

But the conversation didn't end there.

'He kept saying to me, "You can do this. Your mother is dead, your three children are grown up and your husband can care for your old Dad while you're away looking after the orphans."'

And on went the conversation.

By morning, Linda felt like an electric current had passed through her. She knew she had to throw her hat into the ring, to somehow contribute to the cause of China's orphans. She didn't know exactly what to do or how to do it, but she was determined to live up to the conference theme and discover God's purpose for her.

The following day, after the gathering ended, her mind was still filled with images of defenceless Chinese orphans. She drove back to her hill-top home in Gympie amid the swaying gumtrees and kookaburras. She barely had time to put down her bags and kiss husband Greg hello, when she realised they were about to head out again for evening worship at their local church. She didn't say a word about the orphans. She still wasn't sure exactly what it was she was going to do in China and she worried that Greg's initial response was going to be negative. His default response was usually dismissive.

At church, the pastor asked everyone who'd attended the women's conference to make themselves known. He invited them to come forward and give a single sentence about how God had touched them during the gathering. Linda stood up and joined a line of women. She watched as the others stepped forward to deliver their insights. And then her turn came.

'I'm going to China to save orphans,' she blurted out, without being sure exactly where the voice came from. She glanced around and noticed the looks of surprise on her friends' faces. Others in the congregation called out, 'Praise God!'

Greg wasn't one of them. His face had turned tomato red.

'I looked at him and thought, "What have I done?" It probably didn't help his blood pressure,' Linda said mischievously.

But though the moment felt secretly delicious, she could sense his fury. Greg managed to hold himself together until they got into the car.

'How could you be so selfish as to go off to China and leave me?' he bellowed before rattling off a string of reasons why she shouldn't go. She could get a disease, the plane could crash, she would so obviously get lost because of her poor sense of direction and, NOT ON HIS LIFE would he ever be going with her.

Over the next fortnight, Greg and his close friend Pastor John Pohlmann had several deep conversations.

'Let her go and get it out of her system,' the pastor reasoned. Greg trusted Pastor John and thought the advice made good sense. Surely she would pack her bags away for good after one trip? Pastor John then gave Linda a contact for a Christian NGO which arranged visits to Chinese orphanages. The Christian organisation declined to be named for this book although it has a website and a public Facebook page. It's still operating, conducting visits to orphanages, and sending in teams and Bibles in Chinese to spread the Christian word. This publicity-shy organisation describes orphanage trips as 'Mercy Missions'. Each participant pays his or her own costs and the organisation provides access to a particular orphanage where members of the team can spend time with the children.[1] Linda didn't know much more than that when she signed up. But whether Greg approved or not, Linda was going to China.

The next available 'Mercy Mission' to China departed eight months after the Caloundra conference during the Easter term break of April 1998. Linda said a cheery goodbye to her class of five-year-olds at Monkland State School and boarded a Singapore Airlines flight from Brisbane to Hong Kong, which would be the team's first port of call. Linda peered out at the disappearing coastline of Australia until it became a distant canvas of orange earth, vivid ocean and dreamy clouds. It was all falling into place. Her colleagues from school were bemused. Her three grown children seemed busy with their own lives and challenges. Her father, Charles, was worried about Linda's international adventure: being in a strange country, with strange people, speaking a strange language and eating strange food.

'I was never worried about the criticism,' she said. 'There were so many things I wasn't capable of. I just decided to get on with what I could do in my little corner.'

After decades as a teacher, wife and mother, Linda couldn't believe that here, finally, she was embarking on an adventure that was all her own making. She was about to arrive in the former British colony of Hong Kong where the incoming flight flew low over the haphazard housing estates of Kowloon City. Laundry hanging from bamboo poles outside the apartment windows looked close enough to touch. After clearing the neon advertisements, the landing gear emerged and the plane gracefully descended into Hong Kong's Kai Tak International Airport.

The 'Mercy Mission' (fifteen including five translators) was first taken to a Christian hostel outside the semi-rural district of Shatin where it spent three days acclimatising, praying, getting to know each other, sharing experiences of home and learning about the work of Christian missions in mainland China. Team members were told never to mention the name of the organisation. They were given very few details, only that they were going to an orphanage somewhere in central China. At the time, China was in the throes of a crackdown on religious and spiritual groups. The team was told it must tread cautiously so as not to draw attention. While the visit was primarily humanitarian, the ulterior motive was to bring Christianity to the Chinese people.

Linda kept a journal noting instructions on Chinese culture. 'We need to be like little children and have ears, but not the mouths,' she wrote.

It was during the preparations in Hong Kong that she first heard about the Chinese concept of 'face' which relates to reputation and dignity. Linda learned it was important for Chinese 'to look good in front of people. They would die rather than lose face and it impacts on all relationships.'

A Singaporean man led the conversation. He said the visitors should be aware never to crinkle up their faces when something wasn't acceptable.

'We were specifically told not to criticise Chinese toilets. If we detected bad smells we had to pretend we didn't in case someone 'lost face' over it. He also told us it was his own view that the Chinese people needed to be delivered from this burden, but until that time, we had to accept it and avoid causing any Chinese person to 'lose face'.'

The culture lessons were the first time Linda heard the term *guanxi* which is the art of relationship-building. *Guanxi* describes a connection between two people in which one person asks another for a favour. For example, two friends go to school together and one becomes a policeman and the other a bank clerk. The clerk discovers he needs to deal with a traffic fine. His policeman friend can help. The policeman may do this freely or accept a small 'gift' on the side, but either way, he saves red-tape – and potentially 'face' – for the bank clerk. In future, the policeman may reverse the process and prevail on the bank clerk to help him obtain a housing loan. This relationship also binds them both into their network. Reciprocal favours are a key factor in maintaining *guangxi*.

Finally there was the matter of the orphanage itself. The tourists were told that 'many dinners and cups of tea' were shared with Chinese officials to get the secretive Christian organisation to where it was that day, trusted enough to bring foreign teams to visit the orphanage. In the aftermath of *The Dying Rooms*, such visits were still sensitive. The Christian visitors were frequently reminded when phoning home, not to tell their friends or family where they were or what they were doing.

Excitement mounted. Apart from clothes – and it would still be cold in China where it was early spring – the travellers weren't sure what supplies to bring. Hong Kong was the place to stock up on everything. So, the women filled their suitcases with medicine and mountains of disposable nappies. Linda also brought knitted toys, colouring books and pencils donated by church-goers and other Gympie residents.

Linda telephoned home to Gympie. Greg was out so she left a message on the answering machine.

'I have never seen anything like this in my life,' she gushed, 'Like a National Geographic show, only times three better and this is real life! Thanks for letting me come.' She hadn't even reached the orphanage yet.

From Hong Kong, the group took a circuitous route to China because it was the cheapest available. After crossing the border from Hong Kong, the Christians boarded a bus to Guangzhou (formerly Canton) on the mainland.

'This is China!' Linda wrote in her journal during the bus journey. 'New apartment blocks are going up everywhere – cement monstrosities that quickly go black with mildew and soot.'

From Guangzhou, the team boarded a domestic flight for the three hour journey to Henan Province in central China. Henan is around two-thirds the size of the state of Victoria but its population is four times that of Australia's. Enveloped in dense smog, the plane landed just after midnight in Henan's capital city, Zhengzhou.

In her journal, Linda wrote: 'National Geographic in 3D with Smellavision!'

'That first visit broadened my mind extraordinarily,' said Linda. 'It opened my eyes to so many things that were different from my life in regional Queensland. I hadn't travelled very much before that.'

The group gathered their luggage from the carousels and emerged into the gloom of the socialist-style arrivals hall at the old Zhengzhou Airport. They were told a brand new airport was due to open in a few months' time. Feeling blurry yet buzzing at the thought they were finally close to their destination, Linda prayed for a hotel and a warm bed. The plan all seemed to be moving in the right direction as a large welcoming party of local government and orphanage officials converged on the foreigners, grabbing their suitcases and belongings as they swarmed across the car-park and boarded several battered 15-seater buses. The hosts easily outnumbered the team. That was how it was done in China. Maximum respect to your visitors. But someone hadn't done their sums properly and there weren't enough seats for everyone. Wedged into a window seat, her feet one on top of the other, her huge back-pack on her lap, Linda shifted, grateful to have a seat at all.

It was only a few degrees outside in the early hours of the morning when the buses, complete with flashing lights and sirens and tailed by a tribe of officials in big black cars, departed from the airport. Instead of heading into the centre of Zhengzhou, the convoy drove straight through the provincial capital and onto a poorly lit highway. Was there no end to this journey? A collective sigh rose from the foreigners. They soon discovered the brave new world of driving in China, an experience in thrillseeking. Drivers adeptly dodged the smorgasbord of traffic: over-stuffed trucks raining cubes of coal, sedans, rickety box-vans with heavy loads strapped to their roofs, farm carts and even a few bicycles. None of the vehicles had headlights on.

'Everyone drives on the wrong side of the road,' Linda noted in her journal, referring to how Chinese drive on the right-hand side. 'The bus-driver uses his horn as a kind of tracking device. This lets everyone know where he is on the road. The rule is, if your nose is ahead of the other car, you are the winner and the other guy has to let all of you in!'

She was fascinated by the antics on the road and couldn't take her eyes off the scenery unfolding in the shadows of the ghostly light. There were tents made of striped plastic erected along the banks of the Yellow River and she could see people watching television outside the tents. Someone told her the name of the province they were in, Henan, translates as 'south of the river'. Then the coach suddenly veered to the opposite side of the highway into oncoming traffic. To dodge potholes, she was told later. A local official explained that a section of the highway fell between the jurisdiction of two counties. The governments had been arguing for a decade about which one should pay to repair the road. They could never agree and so a certain section of the highway gradually turned into something resembling the surface of the moon.

The coaches continued bumping along the highway heading towards Jiaozuo, a small city of around half a million people, founded in the 1950s by the Communists. It had once been famous for coal production but like hundreds of small Chinese cities, it was really a town, consuming the surrounding farmland as it spread. The ninety kilometre journey from Zhengzhou took over five hours in 1998. In 2013, when I first visited, Jiaozuo had grown to 3.5 million people. Gone was the potholed highway, replaced by a divided six-lane tollway shortening the journey from five hours to two. By the end of 2015, the journey became even faster again after a high-speed railway line opened slicing travelling time down to just thirty minutes.

A washed-out dawn began to break as the two buses reached the outskirts of the city. Eventually the weary travellers were deposited at Jiaozuo's most luxurious hotel. The reception was dripping in gold and silk and Linda felt quite grubby in comparison. By now, most of the chatter had died down from exhaustion. The volunteers trudged silently to their rooms. Linda was looking forward to a warm shower and bed. In the shower, she reached for the mixer, but it didn't matter in which direction she turned it, the water was always freezing. Nevertheless she was clean and more than ready for bed. Sinking between stiff, white sheets on an extra-firm mattress didn't faze her and she fell into a blissful sleep.

Four hours later it was morning. She awoke to Richard Clayderman's piano (he is very popular in China) belting out *Auld Lang Syne*. Someone thought it would be a good idea to pipe music into the guest rooms. Then to the strains of *Dr Zhivago*, she managed to locate the hot water tap in the shower. Downstairs, a bountiful breakfast banquet awaited the travellers with salted duck eggs, rice congee and fluffy steamed buns, arranged around a giant carrot carved in the shape of a kangaroo. Every morning there was a new carrot sculpture which was always recycled at the lunch table.

Everyone on the team felt weary, but at least clean and comfortable. The Chinese officials also appeared for breakfast, helping themselves with gusto. They remained with the group for the duration of their stay. In fact, the officials didn't let the foreigners out of their sights. They even went shopping with them, saying it was their duty to keep them safe. The Chinese were completely unbending in their timetable right down to the twenty minutes allocated to brushing teeth.

'All I wanted to do was to hold a child,' wrote Linda in frustration on the first day, 'Just one'.

The hosts didn't understand this need. In the late 1990s, Western businesses were knocking each other over in a bid to get a foothold in China. The officials thought foreign Christians, who had sent teams to Jiaozuo since 1996, must be interested in something other than orphans.

'They tried to get us to visit a factory and then they wanted us to visit a pig farm so we could invest in it. It took a lot of convincing and several visits before they got the message that all we wanted to do was to help the children,' said Linda.

Finally, there were no more excuses. The buses turned into a long dusty road with fields on either side. At last, Linda was on her way to a Chinese orphanage.

CHAPTER 6

The Orphanage

The Jiaozuo orphanage was a series of dilapidated low-rise buildings next to the railway line near the commercial heart of the city. You entered via a *paifang*, a gateway or entrance, consisting of a brick structure with a decorative Chinese roof. That too was dilapidated and unwelcoming. The Chinese characters for 'welfare institute' were peeling off the walls of the gateway. It didn't improve once you were through the gates where there was a large yard with a roundabout in the shape of a tiered wedding cake filled with abandoned flower beds. Then you came to the buildings. They too were crumbling. With a high brick wall surrounding the compound, it didn't feel like a home for vulnerable children. It felt like a prison.

It was a bitterly cold day. A layer of grime lay everywhere, a reminder of the city's mining origins. In the dormitories surrounding the orphanage courtyard, the temperature didn't change when you went indoors. It was like walking into a freezer sprayed with coal dust. Each time foreign visitors arrived, they were told a new orphanage was being built in a new city suburb. That explained why the orphanage was in a state of decay and looked as if it hadn't been maintained or cleaned for years.

In Chinese, an orphanage is known as a 'welfare institute'. If it houses children, it is called a 'children's welfare institute'. In theory, a child remains in a children's welfare institute until he or she reaches eighteen. The facility in Jiaozuo had a children's orphanage, a home for destitute elderly and a section for people with psychiatric problems.

The elderly people were on the edge of the courtyard, housed two to a sparse, dirty room. All the walls were smeared with, something. During the day, the old people sat in the courtyard chatting, smoking, sipping from their tea-jars, playing cards and Chinese chess. Their smiles revealed terrible teeth, crooked and black because dentistry was a privilege of the rich. Their smiles wore the legacy of hunger, poor nutrition and inadequate health care. Not all the elderly were sociable. Some sat by themselves, faces towards the sun, no words exchanged.

Around the corner was a kitchen. In the centre was a huge coal fire and two large copper pots. Sometimes the kitchen staff used these to steam round buns or *mantou* in their hundreds. One cauldron was always kept for the soup, rice or noodles prepared for the orphans twice a day. The 200 plus occupants of the orphanage were fed from that kitchen.

In the children's section at the damp end of the compound, around twenty children spent their days, largely ignored by staff. The highlight of the day was the bell signalling lunch. 'This is where they paced, sat, played, slept, ate, suffered or died,' Linda said in a newsletter from the time.

Red buckets filled with soup were carried to the children's wing at the far end of the courtyard. Lunch was usually a thickened broth made of corn with beaten egg, noodles and some vegetable. There were no second helpings. The inmates ate twice a day and it was never enough. There was another courtyard beyond the first. This one was for intellectually-impaired men. Unwell and largely untreated, they had been boys once who had grown up in the orphanage. Or they were abandoned as adults once they became either too dangerous or too difficult to take care of at home. Now they were part of China's hidden army of unwanted people.[1]

When Linda and the other volunteers arrived at the front gate on their first visit, they were directed to a two-storey building past the children's section, upstairs to a reception room. It was the best looking room in the entire compound, with freshly painted institutional walls: green on the lower portion, white on the top. Plush armchairs covered in starched grey cloth ringed the room. In front of the armchairs were small tables holding red thermos flasks and glass tumblers. At the base of each tumbler was a ball of chrysanthemum tea leaves.

Linda's heart sank when she saw the reception room. It wasn't that she didn't welcome a hot cup of Chinese tea. All she had wanted to do since reading about Chinese orphans at the church conference eight months earlier was to *hold* some of the children; to nurse them and give them the 'mother-touching' she had read about. But as they were forced to walk past the children's quarters, the translators reminded the volunteers about Chinese protocol. Visitors were supposed to remain in the reception room until they were excused. So the team sunk into the plush sofas as the battalion of Chinese officials, from government departments as well as the orphanage leaders, stood up in a procession, to address the visitors. The speech session lasted well over an hour. Each cadre seemed to take an interminable length of time using flowery compliments and anecdotes about the weather to welcome the foreigners. Once the speeches were delivered, they had to be translated. Then it was the foreigners' turn to respond, followed by translations into Chinese. All the while attendants dressed like doctors in grubby white lab-coats, shuffled around the room, topping up the tea tumblers with boiling water. Linda soon discovered that the white coats were ubiquitous in China. They were the uniform for all orphanage workers, domestic helpers, factory workers, and doctors among others; anyone engaging in hands-on labour.

When the last Chinese speaker finished with a two-handed toast of his tumbler, two girls, blind twins were ushered into the room to entertain the guests with patriotic songs. The girls wore bright red tops and black trousers and their hair had been cut into matching severe short bobs. Linda remembers their names – Fu Na Na and Fu Juang Juang. How curious she thought, that they had the same name. The translator set her straight, telling her that the Chinese used their surnames first and that all orphans were given the surname Fu. *'Fu'* means fortune or good luck. These days, orphans are often named after the sign of the zodiac depending on the year of their arrival at the orphanage.

After the speeches and the performance by the twins, orphanage officials finally allowed Linda and the other volunteers to go down to the courtyard to meet the children. An old man called The General stood 'guard' at the bottom of the stairs. He wore a People's Liberation Army uniform which in those days, you could buy in any general shop. The sleeves were held up with safety pins. On his head was an officer's hat and a comically large pair of dark glasses. A string with dozens of keys hung around his neck. Linda greeted him with a cheery *'Ni Hao'* (How are you?) and he grinned back at her, revealing his missing teeth.

'He is kindly but probably a little senile,' she wrote in her journal, 'not unlike myself.'

Deeper into the courtyard, Linda registered the stench of a powerful disinfectant, phenyl, mingled with faeces and urine. You would never forget this once you've smelled it. It didn't matter which part of the courtyard she went to, it followed her, making her eyes water.

It didn't seem to bother any of the little people looking at her. She was staring into the faces of sixteen children looking like the urchins out of *Oliver!*. Their clothes were filthy. Their hands left black marks on Linda's clothing. Snot and food were smeared over their faces. Most of them had physical or intellectual disabilities.

The toddlers ran around in *kaidangku* or open-crotched pants (it's still very common in China) so they could go to the toilet when and where it suited them. It was cheaper than putting the children in nappies. Many Chinese believed this was the most efficient way to toilet-train a child although it was unhygienic to have excrement and urine lying around in such a confined space.

Another group of children sat in a row of 'potty chairs'. These were modified chair frames with small tray tables. The chairs had holes in the seats and a bucket or enamel bowl underneath to catch the mess although they were rarely in the right spot. Most of the children in the potty chairs were incontinent and had been strapped in for safety. At least that's what the staff told visitors. Linda noticed one big boy, who sat on top of a bucket every day she was there. He was eleven and had been born with the birth defect spina bifida so he was incontinent and couldn't use his legs. Linda rationalised that on the plus side, at least he didn't need to use the toilet block.

Taking in the scene of dejection around her, she poked her head into the adjoining rooms off the courtyard, sensing something was missing. 'Where are the babies?' she wondered.

Surprisingly, there were none in sight. Not a single one. Before she had time to ask, a boy with a strange face bounded up to her. He was very friendly. His eyes seemed to have melted over his cheekbones and he was deaf and mute. Despite his appearance, he was very energetic, always cheerful and willing to help. Fu Yang was seven and like the other kids, he knew to avoid the toilet block. He learned to stand at the doorway and with his 'great stream' as Linda called it, hit the back wall to the block, four metres away. 'The toilet' consisted of an open sewer a metre below the concrete pavers. The pavers were badly broken so that smaller children were always at risk of falling into the channel.

Out in the courtyard, there were washing lines and two disused bathtubs propped up against the brick wall. In the centre of the courtyard was a rusty roundabout which no longer went around. Sometimes on sunny days, the staff hung laundry on it. There were no washing machines in the orphanage until the foreign volunteers came. If clothes were washed at all, it was in a brick tub, using cold water, near the toilet. For hot water, you had to walk around the courtyards to a boiler house powered by a coal furnace.

The cement walls had holes big enough to fit fists through. Gaps were stuffed with rubbish. The walls had been whitewashed once, but were covered in black coal dust as well as children's scribbles with crayons given to them by the foreigners. Was the writing on the wall a sign of rebellion or a cry for help? Nobody knew for sure. You just knew not to touch anything you didn't have to. Linda had seen poverty like this in the Queensland towns where she and Greg had lived during the seventies and eighties. But back then the poverty was restricted to one or two families. This was one orphanage in one city in one province of modern China. She wondered what the other orphanages must be like.

'Someone said that the orphanage was built in 1979,' Linda said. 'I just couldn't believe that. It looked 400 years old.'

One of the intellectually impaired boys ran around without pants. He cavorted about like a puppy with a giant smile on his face, especially when the foreigners gave him a ball in the courtyard. His name was Bing Bing.

Linda noticed a girl with an older face sitting among the smaller children. Her name was Chun Hua. She looked around ten years old and was intellectually impaired. Linda decided to give her a bath. There was no bathroom so it had to be done in the courtyard in plastic tubs the volunteers had brought with them. Through the translator, the kids told Linda their last bath was just before winter and they didn't usually have another one until May when it began to warm up. There was one towel which all the children used one after the other. If they couldn't wipe their faces for whatever reason, The General, who had greeted Linda on the first day, came and did it. Not surprisingly, conjunctivitis, spots, snotty noses and coughs were rampant.

Linda prepared to bath Chun Hua out in the open. As she returned from the boiler room with the hot water, one of the officials rushed towards her imploring her not to take off Chun Hua's clothes. Despite her appearance, Chun Hua wasn't a child, the official said. She was a woman in a child's frame. Linda was astonished. So few of the children were seen by doctors. To this day, Linda isn't sure whether Chun Hua's condition has ever been diagnosed. She moved the tub behind a wall for privacy and began to take Chun Hua's clothes off. Linda discovered her skin stuck to her underclothes. She had menstruated several times into her underwear without any protection. After the bath, Linda put her into a brand new set of clothes. Delighted by the transformation, her face blossomed into an enormous smile. From then on, Chun Hua took charge of handing out all the new clothing in the orphanage. She had a special knack of finding the right piece of clothing in the right size for the right child.

Apart from impromptu baths, the volunteers weren't exactly sure what they were supposed to do now they were on the ground in China. They tried to round up the children who were mobile to play *Ring a Ring a Rosy*, but the children didn't speak English and had never interacted with grown-ups like that before. The Chinese didn't play that way and the children had no idea what they were supposed to do. Then there were the five blind kids. They sat in hard wooden chairs rocking themselves backwards and forwards for stimulation.

Despite confronting scenes in every corner of the orphanage, Linda's experience as an educator in rural Queensland had prepared her. 'In my teaching, I had seen dirty children, badly-treated children, all sorts of children had come through my classroom and none of them had shocked me. Snotty noses, dirty hands, bare feet because kids couldn't afford shoes. I had dealt with them all. When faced with a problem, my job always was simply to try to solve it.'

A shrill bell rang. It was 11 am. Lunchtime is traditionally early in China and it was the first meal of the day for the orphans back then. The children perked up at the sound of the bell, Linda recalled. However, the volunteers – who were there as guests of the Chinese government – were not allowed to stay. They were herded out of the orphanage onto coaches and taken to a banquet back at the hotel. The meal was completely over the top for a simple lunch. Platters of cooked vegetables, meat, fish, noodles and rice streamed out of the kitchen. After the meal ended, the officials excused themselves for their customary nap. The foreigners were also expected to rest in their rooms. At 2 pm they were promptly summoned and driven back to the orphanage where they were allowed to stay until 4 pm.

That was day one.

The following day, Linda awoke feeling more resolved. Once again, the volunteers were brought up to the reception room with the starched sofa covers for the obligatory speeches and compulsory tea. This time, as well as the tea, there came fresh fruit and roasted sunflower seeds (a popular snack). The officials cracked open the kernels and slurped their tea during a slightly shorter session of formalities. Eventually the foreigners were excused and allowed downstairs. Linda tried to save her fresh fruit so she could give it to the children, but the orphanage staff forbade it because, they said, 'fruit makes them sick.'

The foreigners came to know a little more about the orphanage and the children. One day, they were allowed to see inside the children's dormitory. The children slept in connecting rooms heated by rusty radiators and several antiquated briquette braziers to generate warmth during the freezing winters. Each room had a grimy window. Despite being only a few degrees Celsius outside, all the windows were open when the volunteers visited, to let in the 'fresh smog' as Linda described it. 'At least it was better than keeping the fumes from the coal braziers inside.'

The rooms smelled like 'century-old urine' according to Linda. Blue metal cots lined the walls like a baby-prison. There was also a single bed with a hard base and no mattress. It had two quilts, one to go on the wooden base and one to cover the children. Four older children slept in this bed. Everyone, it seemed, urinated freely in the beds and cots. The bedding wasn't changed afterwards. Despite the state of the room, Linda felt comforted knowing that the children could huddle together for warmth at night.

One afternoon, a newcomer showed up at the orphanage. A baby boy in a basket was brought in by the police. He had been abandoned, but beyond that, no-one knew the full story. Linda could see the bundle rising and falling, so she knew he was alive. Two orphanage workers, known as *ayis* in lab coats wrapped him in a wet cloth and placed him next to the open window in the dormitory. Linda found this perplexing given the chilly weather. She went over to the child and started to sing to him, afraid that picking him up would make the staff angry.

A doctor from Texas was among the volunteers. He wanted to examine the baby properly but for reasons he couldn't fathom, he wasn't allowed. When the staff eventually left the room, two of the foreigners stood guard. Linda, ever-so-gently unwrapped the damp bundle, removing the filthy quilt which was soaked in blood and urine. The baby was naked except for an old T-shirt wrapped around his bottom as a substitute nappy. The little body felt like it had just come out of a fridge. As Linda pulled back the T-shirt nappy, somebody noticed that the baby's umbilical cord was still attached and moist, suggesting he was just a few days old.

Linda stroked the boy's face. Unlike the softness of a healthy baby, this child's skin was taut and cold. The doctor turned him over and indicated a hole, covered by a thin membrane, on the lower part of the baby's spine. It was the tell-tale sign of spina bifida: a congenital defect where the spinal cord doesn't form properly. In Australia, the incidence of these defects has declined since the 1990s as a result of widespread public health campaigns and fortifying food with folic acid. In China however, corn, a winter staple for poor people and farmers, contains a fungus that prevents folic acid from being absorbed. Farmers were reluctant to give up their seed to obtain fungus-free corn. It wasn't until 2009 when China, which has the highest incidence of neural tube defects in the world, began providing free folic acid supplements to rural women seeking to get pregnant.

Here in the orphanage, it was a lottery of life and death. Linda felt it powerfully on that first visit. She found out later that the baby had been purposely placed by the window, so that hypothermia could hasten his death. Given the shortage of funds in China's orphanages, she was told this was a common response. Orphanage staff operated a triage when faced with so many lives that were deemed unviable.

The volunteers felt strongly that the baby should have the dignity of a name. They decided to call him Moses, because he had arrived in a basket.

The arrival of Moses marked the point where Linda became more than a casual observer. It was the moment that she felt she had something worthwhile to contribute.

'I looked around and I knew I could love these children as I had loved my own kids. I honestly felt that if Moses was going to die, it was better that he died in someone's arms.'

For the remainder of the trip, the team leader put Linda in charge of administering affection. With her previous first-aid training as a volunteer ambulance bearer she was confident she could warm Moses up and make him comfortable. She drew up a roster to ensure the baby wasn't left alone and he got as much physical contact as the volunteers could give before they left China. Within the next few days, other babies arrived at the orphanage. Their parents had left them in public places like the railway station or outside the police station. One of the boys, named Joe by the volunteers, weighed under two kilos and had feet that pointed towards each other. Without treatment, Joe was unlikely to be able to walk.

'That would have been so easily fixed in Australia,' said Linda. 'His legs could have been put in plaster for six weeks, because the bones were still forming. That would have solved his problem.'

Another little girl had an oversized head due to hydrocephalus (water on the brain). The volunteers named her Hope. Linda carefully bound the baby girl to a pillow so that her heavy head didn't snap her neck. Like Joe's feet, it was a medical condition routinely treated in the industrialised world.

The babies kept coming. There was a girl named Miriam (in the Bible, the sister of Moses). Her bile duct was blocked giving her jaundice. There was baby Aaron (Moses' brother) who had a cleft palate, which could easily be repaired if there were funds. Finally, there was a toddler the volunteers named Luke. He arrived in an extremely weak and drowsy state. His parents had given him a hair-cut, put him in clean clothes and left him at the orphanage gate.

By the end of Linda's visit, a total of six babies had arrived at the Jiaozuo orphanage within the space of a fortnight. She wished she could take them all home with her, but they belonged to China, not to her. As she realised her visit was coming to an end, she thought about everything she had learned; the protocols of banqueting with Chinese officials, how a Lazy Susan worked on a dining table, how to get your cup of tea filled, how speeches weren't just made at weddings, how to navigate Chinese squat toilets, the importance of *guanxi* and the necessity of 'face'. However, she still didn't understand why the children had been abandoned by their parents.

Every day Linda noticed new things. The orphans seemed undernourished. The ayis never washed the bottles the babies drank from and everywhere you looked there was dirt, rubbish and the most persistent flies. So many children with severe disabilities clearly required medical attention beyond what the orphanage could afford. Babies and children needed stimulation from other humans to enable them to develop, what Linda called 'mother-touching'. But the Chinese way was practical and not tactile. The ayis propped the bottles up against the quilts and let the babies drink by themselves.

Linda knew at the very least, she could provide affection to the abandoned children of Jiaozuo. She went home to Gympie with her head reeling, armed with a video that one of the female directors had filmed during the volunteers' stay at the orphanage. The officials were very wary of people taking video in the wake of *The Dying Rooms* documentary where the film-makers had posed as orphanage workers. Linda hoped to use the video and photos to raise awareness back in Australia.

And what of the six babies who'd been brought to the orphanage while she was there? She had kissed Moses goodbye, convinced she would not see him again. Deep down, she was sure two out of the six babies would not survive more than a few weeks. Within a fortnight of her return, she heard news that she wasn't prepared for. All six were dead.

'Something broke in me,' said Linda. 'The waste, the futility and the cruelty of it. Nobody thought these kids were of any value, so the orphanage officials didn't bother with them.'

Later that year, Linda would turn fifty. Mid-life. 'My own three kids, Debbie, Jason and Damien had already grown up. My arms were empty, open and waiting. I came home to Australia feeling that I could have given those Chinese children something. They could have died in my arms.'

CHAPTER 7

Saving Babies

After Jiaozuo, Linda returned to her classroom set amid undulating bushland at Monkland State School in Gympie, but it was the orphans forced to pass their days in potty chairs who dominated her thoughts. She started to think about ways to raise money and involve her community, which she was confident had expertise to offer. She accepted speaking invitations from community groups like Rotary, schools and church groups and in return she received donations.

Most of those closest to her admired her enthusiasm. John Pohlmann, the pastor at her local church sang her praises.

Linda's daughter Debbie, who's in her early forties and like her Mum a teacher, said she struggled with the idea of Linda being away at first. 'It took her away from her grandchildren and from her children when two of us were in failing marriages and had little kids. We wanted them to be doted on as we all lived in the same town.'

'However we knew Mum was a passionate and giving woman and always had enough love to go around for all. We learnt this as children as she cared for half the neighbourhood kids while their parents played golf with my Dad. We soon discovered that Mum was able to easily juggle all of our needs and dote on us to our heart's content. While she was in China, we kept in touch via Skype, email and Facebook. Mum was always closely connected to us whether she was overseas or here.'

The Shum's eldest son, Jason, is forty-four. He has two sons and now lives in the main house on Linda's property while Linda has the granny flat. Jason is a forestry supervisor. Born two months' premature, he stopped breathing nine times and was not expected to live.

The Shum's youngest son, Damien, was in his twenties and living at home when Linda first went to China. He now lives in Hobart with his wife, Claire, and their four children where he supervises a federal government call centre. Both Debbie and Damien are Pentecostal Christians like their mum.

'Mum had the passion and it was her dream. I mean it wasn't a surprise. As kids, we used to have to watch her favourite film, *The Inn of the Sixth Happiness,* about this missionary called Gladys Aylward, over and over and over again!' he laughed.

Greg's side of the family, particularly his sisters, Elva and Joy, strongly supported Linda from the beginning. Greg, on the other hand, did not like his wife travelling to a foreign country and leaving him alone. In the space of two years she had already been to China three times. When he realised Linda's commitment was deepening instead of waning, he decided he had to put a stop to it.

From childhood, Greg had found relief in order and predictability. Growing up in a quiet country town he had his own bedroom and he kept it immaculate. His sister, Elva, remembered him giving strict instructions to the family not to meddle with his toys.

'We didn't dare touch anything in his room. Not his toys or trucks. He was very tidy. Then he married Linda who was a bit different,' she said with a wink.

As an adult, Greg suffered from several serious health issues as well as a mental illness that took decades to diagnose. After a stressful period in the late 1980s when he worked long hours for weeks at a time, he suffered a nervous breakdown, falling heavily and rupturing two discs in his back in the process. Linda cared for him at home as he lay listlessly, unable to recognise his own wife for three days. Doctors later operated on his spine but his left leg was partially paralysed. As a result of the injury, he suffered chronic pain and needed a stick and a brace to walk at times. Eventually, he took early retirement at the age of thirty-nine.

Sometimes, when Linda returned home from school, she found her husband sitting on the steps of the house with his head in his hands, sobbing uncontrollably. He thought he was just sad. The doctor prescribed antidepressants for Greg which he took for a period but always stopped once he started feeling better. But the mood swings, mania and depression lurked a few steps behind him like an imaginary friend. Linda counted nine episodes of depression since they were married, but she didn't recognise the first few for what they were until she had her own experience of clinical depression following her mother's death.

A brain scan in 2001 revealed nothing out of the ordinary. Soon after, Greg was referred to a psychiatrist. After hours of interviews with both him and Linda, Greg was diagnosed with bipolar disorder. By that time he was almost fifty-five. From then on he took regular medication which controlled his mood swings. That Greg's condition finally had a name came as a huge relief to everyone around him.

'He hid his depression very well,' son Damien said. 'He'd have lists of things to do in a particular order. They had to be done his way. And if we went off and did it a different way, he'd say "Why didn't you do it like this?" It always had to be Dad's way. He always had to be right, even when he knew he was wrong. As we were growing up, I always had the thought that you have to let Dad think he's right.'

One day, as Linda and Greg were taking a dip in their pool, shaded by a few straggly gumtrees, their conversation took a nasty turn. Greg declared Linda to be a bad wife, a bad mother, a bad grandmother, a bad teacher and as if they weren't enough reasons to give up China, then here was one more, he said. She simply wasn't holding up her 'end of the stick' at church or at home.

Linda felt like she had been slapped in the face. For years, she had worked herself to exhaustion bringing up their children almost single-handedly because Greg was busy with his teaching career, and had a short fuse when he was in the down phases of his mental illness.

He gave Linda six months to choose. 'You can have me or you can have China,' he said in his resonant voice, 'but you can't have both.'

Linda didn't believe in divorce. She believed in the vow she had exchanged at their wedding in 1970, that she and Greg had agreed; 'until death do us part'. Despite all of their dramas including her mother cutting off ties, changing denominations, two miscarriages, three children, his health problems and their career challenges, she took the vow seriously. On the other hand, she didn't see how she could give up on her 'Chinese children' as she called them. Caring for them was what she had been called to do since she'd had the vision of Jesus who told her to 'feed my lambs'.

A few months later, Greg went away to a church leadership conference near Brisbane.

On his return, he put his bags down in the hallway and slipped in beside Linda who was sitting at the breakfast counter. Linda could tell instantly that something was different. 'Boy! Have I got news for you!' he exclaimed.

Wild scenarios ran through Linda's head: he was terminally ill, he'd found a mistress, he was homosexual or perhaps – please no, she thought – he had fathered an illegitimate child. It turned out to be none of the above.

'God,' Greg said, 'has punched me.'

'What did you say?' I interjected.

'Yes,' Linda said, 'God hit him. Literally.'

Not sure what I was hearing. I asked her to continue.

'During worship, something out of the blue hit Greg in the stomach. He was winded for a moment. He straightened up. Then, it happened again.'

She described her husband as a 'large' man (130 kilograms) and the punches had knocked him to the floor. When he peered around in amazement, his friend Pastor John Pohlmann was standing next to him, completely oblivious.

'Greg said John's hands were raised in worship. It couldn't have been him doing the punching,' insisted Linda.

Lying dazed on the auditorium floor, Greg crawled under a pew, curled up and stayed there for the rest of the session. 'While under the seat, God had words with him,' Linda recalled. In fact, God told him in no uncertain terms, 'Go to China and serve your wife.'

'Greg found the experience deeply humbling,' Linda said. When he finished the story, he declared that despite his reservations, he would accompany her on her next trip to

China in September 2000 serving both Linda and the orphans as God had instructed him to.

I wasn't sure what to make of Greg's supernatural boxing match.

As a teenager, I regularly went to an Anglican church until I finally had the confidence at sixteen to tell my parents I wasn't sure whether I had any faith at all. I've continued to search in various ways and in the different places I have lived, but I still can't feel comfortable with the idea of worship or calling myself a Christian. However, I've discovered amazing people who do incredible things in the name of God and Jesus, and Linda is one of them. I don't think Greg had a bout with God. But I think he believed he did. And so did Linda.

I wrestle with Linda's brand of faith and some of the strange things she has shared with me. Shortly after I interviewed her for ABC News in 2013, Channel 7's *Sunday Night* program produced a segment about Linda's work. They called her 'Grandma Angel'. Beautifully reported by Alex Cullen, it was a ratings winner. After the show, COAT received a flood of donations (around $60,000 as a direct response) and a stream of people wanting to visit the Jiaozuo orphans. The program was viewed by as many as two million viewers in Australia and New Zealand.

Curiously, Channel 7 neglected to mention Linda's Pentecostal Christianity. That part was just missing. In fact, while she was being interviewed for the show, the producer instructed her 'not to say God so much'. Did God make her less inspiring or did the evangelical stuff complicate the 'whites in shining armour' story?

A possible explanation of Greg's experience is that he hallucinated due to his medication or, he just hallucinated.

I used to think hallucinating was a type of delusion but neurologist Oliver Sacks changed that view. Dr Sacks wrote: 'Hallucinations tend to be startling ... they happen to you, autonomously – they appear and disappear when they please, not when you please ... they are involuntary, uncontrollable.'[1]

I believe there's truth when he says: 'It is not always easy to discern where the boundary lies between hallucination, mis-perception, and illusion.'[2]

A survey in the US in 2008 found almost 61 per cent of respondents believed in angels.[3] The Baylor Religion Survey found one-third of respondents experienced a direct encounter with them. Professor Rodney Stark, one of the authors of the report, noted 'mystical experiences are widespread ... this is the taboo subject in American religion. No-one studies it, but there is a lot of it out there.'[4]

Among those I love and admire, several individuals have reported spiritual or supernatural experiences. Something inexplicable happened. It was real for them, in that moment.

I can't know for certain what Greg Shum experienced that day but I know it's consistent with what Pentecostal Christians believe about cultivating a close personal relationship with God. Linda thinks that most readers will think it's a fairy story.

What I can say is this: something made Greg change his mind about Linda's work in China. He and Linda attributed it to divine intervention.

The Shums set out on their first trip together in September 2000 as a Mercy Team under the banner of the secretive Christian NGO. They travelled with Lyn, a third volunteer from Gympie, lugging five enormous suitcases between them stuffed with nappies, terry-towelling jumpsuits, bouncinettes,

sheepskin rugs, toys, children's clothes, baby formula, medicine
and vitamin supplements. All had been donated by people from
the church and the Gympie community.

From the Sunshine Coast, the Shums drove to Brisbane,
boarded a plan for Shanghai and then a domestic flight to
Zhengzhou. The last leg was the slow bus to Jiaozuo where
they met their translator, Belinda, a volunteer from Singapore.
Their mission was to consolidate the partnership with the
Chinese and continue to find ways to improve the lives of the
250 orphans in the Jiaozuo orphanage. First, Linda and Lyn set
to work cleaning everything up, changing nappies and washing
the hands and faces of all the children and babies. Greg found
he quickly connected with the young boys at the orphanage
who loitered in the yard. Soon, ideas started coming to him.
Maybe, he thought, he could be a role model for them and
teach them some basic maths and English.

As she gained confidence in her dealings with the staff, Linda
began giving instructions on improving hygiene and reducing
infection and illness among the children. As she watched the
ayis work, she reminded them frequently about washing hands
and general cleanliness. The orphanage seemed reluctant to
carry out her instructions. They probably thought she had
no right to tell them what to do. After all, she was going to
disappear in a few weeks' time. She discovered any advice
meted out was promptly forgotten. So she repeated it over and
over. Within a few weeks of her departure, as she suspected,
the old habits returned.

In those early years, she visited China only once or twice a
year (Greg came once a year) because she was still teaching full-
time. To try to embed these new Western practices, she decided

to find a set of friendly eyes and ears at the orphanage. She looked around for someone whom she considered dependable although there wasn't a huge pool to choose from. Eventually, she discovered an adult orphan named Tao Mei. Tao Mei was eighteen and should have left the orphanage by now, but she had no other home. She was brought to the orphanage at age eight with her younger sister and brother. They were found alone after their mother was taken to a mental institution and their father died soon afterwards. Apart from suffering this loss and living without supervision for a time, the three children were in good physical shape.

The orphanage paid Tao Mei a nominal wage of 10 yuan ($2)[5] every month to help with simple chores like feeding babies and doing laundry which she did by hand. Linda decided to employ her, giving her an extra 300 yuan ($60) a month, half of which was paid by Linda's church, the rest by the Shums themselves. It was a respectable salary in the late 1990s and earning the extra money delighted Tao Mei. She was responsible for the care of sixteen orphans, some as old as twenty. Linda taught her the importance of nutrition and hygiene. She taught her to carefully wash milk bottles, which until then, the orphanage workers regarded as a strange foreign habit. Before the foreigners arrived, orphanage staff had never washed used milk bottles. They had simply refilled them after each use with cheap sweetened milk.

There was also conflict over the lack of skin-to-skin contact with the babies. The workers didn't like getting messy or wet from holding the infants and thought cradling a child was an indulgence which they didn't have time for. The usual feeding method at the orphanage (which still exists) was to prop the bottles against a pillow for the babies to manage themselves. Linda knew from her research that the science of infant development concluded uncategorically that touch and emotional engagement were vital for tiny brains and there was a critical window. Stimulation was everything and it was being denied to the orphans.

Linda found the Chinese staff, including Tao Mei, had very fixed ideas on the care of babies and children. Though she and the other volunteers instructed Tao Mei to hold the babies while they fed them, it took many training sessions, constant reminders and much vigilance before Tao Mei accepted the wisdom of washing bottles and teats with hot soapy water. Getting her to wash poo off the soiled bed linen was another battle. She preferred to flick off the dry residue.

The ayis were state employees. They were rarely trained, poorly-educated and most of them had worked in allocated jobs most of their lives in accordance with socialist ideals. It was hardly surprising many of them had little connection with the children.

I remember visiting a motor-cycle factory near the Yangtze River as China restructured its lumbering state-owned enterprises. There were hundreds of men hanging around the assembly lines. My Chinese colleague laughed when I asked what they were doing.

'This is what all Chinese factories look like,' she said.

In the 1990s, some of the enterprises were eventually closed while others were privatised or went into partnerships with foreign companies. The result was that more than 20 million jobs were cut from the state sector between 1994 and 2005.[6] If the only employment going was with children who weren't valued by society, it was infinitely better than no job at all.

Linda found it wasn't just motivation that was a problem, it was the mind-set. 'I wanted the children to have fresh fruit every day,' said Linda. 'Tao Mei insisted that fruit made them sick. At first she wouldn't give the little ones baby formula for the same reason. I really hoped she'd eventually come through, although in reality, we just didn't have an alternative to her.'

Employing Tao Mei caused friction among the staff. Because she herself was considered a lowly orphan, the other staff looked down on her and wouldn't accept her as an equal. One day Linda asked her to do an inventory of the storeroom where all the donated clothes and medicine were kept. The orphanage staff refused to give her the key. Other battles were ongoing. When Linda wasn't around, orphanage staff ridiculed Tao Mei for persisting with all the laborious tasks the foreigners insisted on. She told Linda, 'We Chinese think our ideas are better.' There were also cultural differences. Chinese staff didn't tend to play and interact with children like the foreigners did.

With money donated by Rotary, Linda bought a twin-tub washing machine for the children's courtyard. It stayed there while she visited but as soon as she left, it was commandeered by the staff for another section of the orphanage. During the summer, orphanage staff tied the small children into potty chairs and left them outside in the yard. It was convenient for the staff and prevented the children from coming to harm in the decaying orphanage. With all the excrement and exposed bottoms, the courtyard was a fertile breeding ground for flies. Insects stuck to the children's faces and to the corners of their crusting eyes. Eventually, the orphanage doctor agreed that introducing nappies was a good idea to reduce the flies. It took him longer to be convinced that new white nappies, rather than old rags, were a more hygienic option.

In the winter of 1999, Linda found a six-month-old girl sitting amid a group of children propped up in potty chairs. She was almost touching a burning radiator. In pulling her chair away from the heat, Linda noticed the child couldn't sit up yet. She was weak and as floppy as a puppet. Linda crouched down so that she could look into the child's face. The little girl's eyes flicked from side to side. There was just emptiness there: she was blind.

The infant didn't have a name, but after Linda and another volunteer, Jenny, began taking an interest in her, the orphanage named her Lin (Linda) Jie (Jenny). Linda liked this name. She disapproved of the way well-meaning foreigners gave Chinese children Western names like Declan, Ryan and Madison. She found it offensive when the children were Chinese by birth so she vowed not to do this herself.

Lin Jie was tiny for her age. Apart from congenital blindness, she was lethargic and didn't seem interested in food. Within a few minutes of Linda playing with her, and tickling her, she perked up immensely. However, Linda noticed that the orphanage staff made no effort to encourage her to eat. In that very direct Chinese way, an ayi told her that the child wasn't 'worth' anything because she was blind. She was, the worker told Linda, a 'throwaway child'.

A throwaway child? Did she really hear that correctly?

Linda was learning about the harsh reality of many of the children in front of her. The definition of orphan in China is different to how we understand it in the West. While most definitions mention the death of one or both parents, China's definition includes children who are abandoned. Foundlings. The wispy-haired, blind infant Lin Jie most likely had parents who were still alive somewhere in China. So did most of the other children. Abandoning a child, though illegal, was seen as an acceptable option in extreme circumstances. How could a family afford to keep a disabled child if they were barely able to feed themselves?

Linda thought of a plan. She proposed to the directors that if she personally paid for Lin Jie's food and care, would the staff allow her to live? They said they would. So Linda and Greg became Lin Jie's sponsors. From Gympie, they posted tins of Sustagen and huge packets of formula and rice cereal. When they were in Jiaozuo in person, they gave the equivalent of $40 a month directly to the head of the orphanage, Director Lan, for Lin Jie's care.

From that time, Linda focused on the idea of sponsorship, realising that a reasonably small but regular contribution could mean the difference between life and death for an orphan. The idea proved popular among Linda's friends and fellow church-goers. Within a few months, twelve children had sponsors, each paying $40 per month for their upkeep. Greg helped by creating photo montages of the Australian families who took out sponsorships, superimposing the face of their orphan onto the photo. Linda laminated the images and stuck them onto the wall next to the beds of the sponsored children. The ayis, she discovered, always stopped to admire the photos. They were impressed that a foreigner would pay money to support a 'throwaway' child in China. It made the orphans seem more worthy in their eyes. The flipside was that staff continued to ignore the children who didn't have sponsors.

Linda made a note of all the children with serious physical conditions. One little boy named Shan Shan had turned feet and a quivering lower lip as he was constantly on the verge of tears. In those first few months, he essentially lived in his bed while staff ignored him. Linda convinced one of the volunteers, a woman named Marolyn to sponsor Shan Shan and a photo montage of the little boy with his Australian family went up next to his bed. As a result of his Australian 'Mama' and the extra attention from the ayis, he regularly broke into smiles.

One day, Linda caught sight of a baby girl lying in a basket in the courtyard. The baby's forehead and left cheek were badly scarred. She had been out with her mother who had placed the child in a ditch to protect her from the cold while her mother worked in the fields. While her back was turned, rats began to gnaw at the baby's face. Although the mother returned and eventually chased away the rats, the baby's face was covered in blood and disfigured. This was the reason, according to the orphanage workers, her parents abandoned her to the care of the state.

'After being attacked, she wasn't perfect,' said Linda. 'Quite often it's not the fault of the parents but the paternal grandmother. She only gets one chance at having a grandchild and of course it has to be perfect and preferably a male.'

'It's not for us to judge,' she said repeatedly at the time, 'but to do what we can to make their lives better.'

Though we can never be sure, there were several reasons why a child might have been abandoned. While Jiaozuo was a city of half a million people in the late 1990s, it had evolved from a town and was still semi-rural. Rural Chinese had virtually no welfare support at the time. In 2003, only one per cent of China's 800 million rural people had health insurance coverage. Many farmers wouldn't have had the first idea how they could afford to fix the damage done to an otherwise healthy baby girl. Her parents may have assumed it was unaffordable, or they may have taken her to a hospital and been given an exorbitant estimate of what it would take to repair her face. It's also possible that if the girl's parents were poorly educated, they perhaps saw the opportunity to try for another child in the hope it would be a boy.

Back in Australia in the calm of an early winter's morning in 2002, the phone rang at the Shum's home in Gympie. Still half asleep, Linda stumbled into the office and took the handset. She was surprised to hear the voice of Frank, one of the directors from the NGO which managed the teams of volunteers visiting Jiaozuo. Frank had no idea what time it was in Queensland. He had called to break some bad news. The NGO was pulling out of Jiaozuo city and officially terminating its support for the orphanage. The group didn't want to stay in Henan Province, Frank said bluntly. It was turning into an uphill battle. Officials there, he said, were too corrupt, too wicked and too cruel.

Linda felt numbed by his words. She had invested four years in the Jiaozuo orphanage and they were so much more than an investment to her. Those years had rescued and revived her spiritually. Despite the filth, poverty and pollution, she believed improvements were gradually being made to the children's lives. Small steps every day. Wasn't that what it was all about? She felt like someone had died.

Greg, by this stage, had woken up and came to sit beside his wife. He put his arms around her.

The reasons cited by the director for pulling out, were exactly *why* the group should remain in Jiaozuo. Instead, the NGO planned to move to a different part of China where, Linda suspected, they could influence a greater number of Chinese people through spreading the Christian message. This was its unspoken goal. It wasn't Linda's.

'If you feel so strongly about it,' said Frank 'why don't you start your own charity?'

Blimey, Linda thought. *Me?*

'I was a grade one teacher. What would I know about starting a charity to help Chinese orphans?' she said.

As she put the phone back on the receiver, turmoil overtook her mind and the faces of the children she had come to know over the past four years peered at her pleadingly. She had always followed her heart and deeply believed that she was doing the right thing by travelling to China. She couldn't bear the idea she might be letting down these vulnerable children. Now she was feeling frightened and adrift. Would *she* become the latest adult to abandon the children?

Linda knew her activist credentials were not particularly impressive up to this point. Despite early attempts at fundraising and a few functions at church and at school, Linda had no management experience. Her own children and her husband loved her dearly but otherwise she was just 'Mrs Shumbum' to her class of five-year-olds. She had no business contacts. And she was really quite disorganised.

'There were so many things I wasn't capable of, but this was also liberating. It meant I didn't have to worry about criticism. I just had to get on with what was possible,' she said.

Could she take over the work of the publicity-shy Christian NGO? Could she lead an organisation providing support for the Jiaozuo orphans? Would the Chinese allow her to? Would they co-operate with her? Some of the terrible things orphanage officials said came back to haunt her; that orphans were worthless unless a foreigner sponsored them and that they were 'throwaway' children. But she was already starting to turn around the negative self-talk as a growing sense of determination rose inside her. No child, whether abandoned or not, she vowed, would be labelled as worthless if she had anything to do with the matter.

CHAPTER 8

Eating an Elephant

In China's whirlwind transformation from rural underdog to superpower, the orphanage did not miss out. After the cleaver came down on Communism, China began opening up to the world in 1978, and despite a significant challenge to the regime with the pro-democracy crackdown at Tiananmen Square in 1989, the Chinese Communist Party has retained its captaincy for almost seventy years. 'The reform and opening-up' as the post-Mao phase was called, was like converting a shack into a Buckingham Palace while the existing family stayed put during the building works. Today, the palace isn't perfect or finished. It doesn't work in many places, but the goal is still a palace and the renovation continues.

At the start of the millennium, a new city welfare compound, including an orphanage, grew out of the wheatfields in Jiaozuo city's *Jie Fang* (Liberation) district. Every so often, Chinese officials invited the foreign volunteers to inspect the site. Linda went along and found the entire process fascinating. The buildings were erected brick by brick by hand. There were very few machines. The workforce were not professional builders but itinerant farmers, known as China's 'floating population'. They were cheap to hire, sometimes paid less than $100 per month. In some places, they were so plentiful, they formed armies on street corners, at railway stations and on ferry piers, advertising their skills on handwritten signs or sitting on curbs waiting for work. Their uniform was a blue Mao jacket and a bamboo hard-hat.

Over the past few decades, increasing numbers of Chinese have rented out their farmland to find work in ever-growing cities. Even an unskilled labourer in a city like Jiaozuo earned in one month the equivalent of his annual farm income.

These days, apart from 260 million migrant workers, there is another statistic; that of the 'left-behind generation'. An estimated 60 million children live alone or are cared for by relatives while their parents work in other parts of China. The reason their parents leave them behind is because of the *hukou* system: strict household registration laws – providing access to education, health insurance and welfare, but which only apply to individuals in their place of residence. Benefits are not transportable to another province. So if adults travel, and their children follow, they become unregistered and known as *hei haizi* – black children.

Once the farmland had been cleared to make way for the welfare compound, workers erected a rickety brick kiln. Bricks were fired and stacked in their hundreds, ready for use in the coming days. Though the men worked quickly, every night people from the surrounding villages broke into the government site and stole bricks by the cartload. They'd return to their homes and arrange the loot in tidy rows outside their bungalows. The villagers knew that if they were to build another storey onto their shacks, in the likelihood their villages were the next to be demolished, two-storey dwellings would entitle them to bigger apartments as compensation.

In a changing society where rules were constantly shifting, many Chinese people adopted a 'get rich quick' mentality. From party officials down to men and women on the street, everyone was weary of decades of poverty and austerity. 'Black cat, white cat,' paramount leader Deng Xiaoping had said, 'as long as it catches mice, it's a good cat.' The message to ordinary people was that if prominent officials could do a bit of skimming to feather their own nests, surely a few bricks paid for by the public purse weren't going to harm anyone?

When the Shums arrived in Jiaozuo for their annual visit in October 2002, they found the new welfare compound hidden away at the end of a long, narrow road – a stark contrast to the villages surrounding it. But the new location was a vast improvement on the bleak, ramshackled place they had come to know. Apart from a children's wing with a vibrant playground as the centrepiece, the new compound included an old people's home, a small hospital, an administrative building and a hostel for visitors so they didn't have to commute from a hotel every day.

As the boss of a new organisation to support Jiaozuo's orphans, Linda had naming rights. She wanted an acronym that was easy to remember. She admired the shape of a traditional Chinese silk jacket or coat, with its high collar and knotted buttons. Coats are warm and comforting, went the reasoning, and so her charity became COAT: the Chinese Orphans Assistance Team. She formed a committee from church friends, relatives, people she met through teaching and others in the community. Their role was to advise her on everything from medical treatment and physiotherapy to education. In 2017, the COAT committee consists of eleven, based in Gympie, Bundaberg, the United Kingdom and China. They meet via Skype every month for a 'Lazy Susan' round-table, as Linda calls it, where everyone gets a turn to talk.

The Shums viewed COAT as a pipeline between the orphanage and the outside world. The first snapshot of children in Chinese orphanages by UNSW's Xiaoyuan Shang in 2001 (via a sample survey of eight child welfare institutions) confirmed their numbers were no longer dominated by healthy girls. By 2001, 81 per cent of children had disabilities. Just over half (55 per cent) of the residents were female, however disability had replaced gender as the main cause of child abandonment.[1]

The orphanage was funded by the Chinese government and provided food and shelter for the children. If COAT could raise money and gain the trust of the directors and government officials, it might be able to provide solutions to some of the orphanage's shortcomings. Some things were easy to accomplish. COAT purchased water heaters for the bathrooms so the children could have warm showers. This encouraged the children to want to have showers in the first place. However, other issues were not as easily resolved.

The first floor (what we'd call the ground floor) was where the dormitories and outdoor yard for older children with intellectual disabilities were located. They were the most neglected children in the facility and it was a dispiriting place to be. Sometimes, as a matter of convenience, the children were locked in their room or tied to the railings of their beds, to prevent them getting into trouble, or as the ayis insisted, 'to protect them'. To be fair, the orphanage workers were under a great deal of pressure. They worked long hours in a lowly career which gave them no sense of pride. The children on the first floor were difficult customers, because, not surprisingly due to their conditions, they rarely co-operated and required constant attention. The ayis had to feed, clean, wash and care for the children as well as doing all the housekeeping.

'I had some agendas,' Linda said, 'the officials had some agendas and sometimes the two didn't match. I had to listen, negotiate and stick to my guns if I thought it important, as well as be prepared to bend my ideas if their requests seemed reasonable.' She heard of a Chinese saying that fitted the situation perfectly: when the wind blows, the reed must bend or it will break.

But the inequitable treatment of the children by orphanage workers was something that Linda couldn't easily accept. Most of the attention was focused on the healthy children because the orphanage could earn US$3,000 per child if adopted to a foreign couple. In her book (the Bible) however, Christians were told to care for 'the least of these', meaning, those in need. But poorly paid, uneducated ayis focused on the pragmatic elements of their job. Most of them didn't know or understand about conditions like autism and cerebral palsy and viewed 'different' behaviour as disobedience. Being warm and caring wasn't part of the job plan. Linda, on the other hand, wanted a longer-term emphasis on a child's emotional as well as physical well-being.

'I have a selfish reason to be involved in this,' Linda said of her work during one of her early trips. 'I love it. It makes me feel my life counts.'

Apart from being close to the orphans, the best gift of all was having Greg working beside her. She marvelled that a man who didn't like to leave home, endured a long-distance flight once a year. Any crowd or new situation usually caused Greg extreme anxiety yet he was prepared to risk his life in a country of more than a billion people. He didn't like Chinese food and travelled with a fork in his shirt pocket. Linda packed instant mash potato and Surprise Peas so he wouldn't go hungry and they found a red sausage in the shops that became Greg's staple food while in Jiaozuo.

The Shums spent hours every day bouncing babies on their laps until all of them had a turn jumping and clapping and laughing. Greg, who had been aloof with his own children when they were small, now enjoyed himself more than ever. Linda asked him whether he could ever have imagined spending afternoons playing peekaboo with babies.

'Never in my wildest dreams!' he'd replied, realising that he hadn't only survived the journey to a strange new country, he was happier than he had been in a long while.

'From that time, he became my greatest fan, my greatest advocate and the next five years were the pinnacle of our lives together,' said Linda.

Greg and Linda Shum surrounded by some of the children at the first COAT school and play area in 2004.

When their son, Damien, saw photos of his father lying on the hostel floor playing hide and seek with the orphans, he laughed in astonishment. 'This was out of the norm for Dad,' he said. 'He had always been very practical before, but with the orphans, he softened and became a lot more loving. Even to his own children.'

Damien smiled recalling his father's involvement in COAT. Greg had been a meticulous organiser and book-keeper. Everything had to be done above board.

'Mum's attitude would be, "We need a thousand toothbrushes." Dad was different. He'd say, "Could the money be better spent doing something else?" But he always made sure there was money for the high priorities.'

Three-day old twins were found on the steps at the gate of the welfare institute. They were mirror twins, both with cleft lips and cleft palates. They couldn't suckle because of the split in their lips and their mouths and their desperate cries filled the hallway.

As staff unwrapped the blankets swaddling them, they found a note on brown paper that had been slipped between the infants: 'Dear caring people, We are poor and incapable of providing for our twins. Please keep them. They were born on 12 September 2003.'

The orphanage ayis tried various methods to feed the girls, including spoon-feeding them milk. Nothing worked. If the babies didn't get sustenance soon, they would suffer from malnutrition, which was a common outcome for cleft babies at the time. That would affect their development or it could kill them. Later that day, Linda stepped off the bus from the airport and rounded the stairwell into the babies' area. Seeing the ayis struggling, she suddenly remembered something. Reaching into her handbag, she fished out two specially-designed bottles for feeding babies with cleft palates. Her friend, Dr Frank Le Bacq, from Gympie Hospital had given them to her before she left. Linda had stuffed them into her bag and had forgotten about them until she saw the twins.

'She strode in like Mrs Doubtfire with these bottles,' the twins' adoptive father, Don White, said. 'She's kind of ditzy isn't she? But I have no doubt that the twins are alive today because of Linda Shum. No question about it.'

The following week, Linda took the twins to Beijing where American surgeons, through a fledgling charity called Love Without Boundaries (LWB), operated on the girls to close their clefts. It was the first surgical team sent by LWB to China.

The twins are teenagers now, named Sydney (because there were no way Don was going to name a child Gympie) and Reagan, after the American President who opened the path for Americans to adopt Chinese orphans.

The Shum's sponsored child, Lin Jie, turned four in 2003. She had grown taller since their visit a year earlier but had developed rickets, a sign she was malnourished. Despite many attempts to correct a sensitivity in her mouth (a problem related to visual impairment) she was still only taking sweet milk mixed with baby cereal. Greg and Linda bought a year's supply of vitamin supplements for her but she still wasn't getting enough nutrition and her muscles were wasting from lack of exercise and therapy. During their fortnight in Jiaozuo, the Shums were allowed to take her out of the orphanage and back to their hostel each day for play and affection. She loved these special moments. She adored Greg's tickles, rolling on the bed or taking a nap nestled in the crook of Linda's arm. Linda placed a mattress on the floor to break her fall as she was unable to walk unaided. Linda and Greg called her their grandchild and were heart-broken she wasn't thriving and developing like a normal child. So they came up with the idea to bring her back to Australia for medical treatment.

One night, Linda, Tao Mei and one of the orphanage leaders, Director Gong, set out on a mission to drive to Beijing where Australian embassy officials would assess Lin Jie to see if she qualified for a visa. Apart from Lin Jie, there were six babies including the girls with cleft lips and palates who would later become the White twins. The babies were going to foster homes in Beijing to await surgery. Director Gong flattened the rear seats of the van and draped bedding over them creating a makeshift baby ambulance. There were no baby capsules. The babies were just well-wrapped in quilts. This was the Chinese way. The van with its precious cargo departed Jiaozuo with enough supplies of sweetened milk, bumping along the highway and a few back lanes. Twelve hours later, they reached the outskirts of the Chinese capital.

The babies were safely delivered to the foreign-operated foster homes where they'd remain until undergoing surgery. Linda was invited to stay with the founders of one of the homes, Dr Joyce and Robin Hill. Joyce's son by her first husband is Adam Liaw, the 2010 winner of the TV series *Masterchef*. The Hills, who are Christians, began to foster Chinese orphans in 2000 in a village south-east of Beijing. Two years later, the Hills built a new facility through their charity, the New Hope Foundation, which cared for twenty-six special needs babies. Linda was deeply impressed by how the Hills had converted their home to cater for the orphans and their carers.

Finally, it was off to the huge grey bunker that was the Australian embassy in Beijing for Lin Jie's assessment. After the interview, Linda went in search of a reputable doctor to assess Lin Jie for her visa application. They spent the rest of the afternoon as tourists, joining the throngs first on the expanse off Tiananmen Square and then for a long walk through the grounds of the Forbidden City. Tao Mei and Director Gong carried Lin Jie's stroller up the stairs of the Forbidden City. The sensation of being bumped and jostled delighted the child and produced an afternoon of giggles. Linda hoped more memorable times lay ahead once Lin Jie got her Australian visa.

The medical report from Beijing together with a stack of high-profile references gave Linda hope she might be bringing the little girl home with her in 2004. She wrote personally to Immigration Minister Amanda Vanstone pleading Lin Jie's case. Ms Vanstone didn't respond and Lin Jie's application was rejected. Two more times, Linda tried and failed to get Lin Jie the visa that would have rescued her from life in an institution. An Australian official told Linda he didn't believe Lin Jie would ever return to China once she left.

Before the visa idea, Linda had contemplated sending Lin Jie to a boarding school for the visually impaired in Henan's capital Zhengzhou where blind children trained in massage. Becoming a massage doctor or *Daifu* was considered a respectable occupation for a blind person. However, the school only took children from the age of eight who were able to eat, talk and walk. Lin Jie still hadn't reached those milestones. With a heavy heart, Linda conceded that door was closing.

She realised Lin Jie didn't have the cognitive skills to become a masseuse. A few months later, Lin Jie made her second trip to the capital where Linda arranged for her to attend the

101

Bethel foster home for the visually impaired. At Bethel, Lin Jie was diagnosed with autism. She was never going to live independently.

Fundraising for the orphans was an ongoing challenge. The Shums paid for their own airfares and practical items like baby formula, medicine and vitamins, but they could never afford to support the needs of 250 children by themselves. COAT's role was to manage the sponsorship and any special projects the orphanage deemed necessary. Rotary in Gympie contributed generously and another local company, Network Communications, paid and still pays COAT a twice-yearly contribution. The Shums compiled DVD newsletters for sponsors and supporters while Linda delivered talks to community groups to spread the word and grow the number of sponsorships.

A South Australian company which manufactured Fluffies cloth nappies gave Linda a good deal: $13 for a dozen nappies, delivered to the orphanage. To her delight, she discovered its China factory was in the neighbouring province. As the manager was heading off on leave, he agreed to put 1,000 nappies in the back of his car and drove 800 kilometres to deliver them personally.

Not every transaction was as serendipitous as Fluffies. Aside from the challenge of fundraising and supplies, Linda realised that the burden of handling the orphanage's Chinese bureaucracy now fell to entirely to her.

There were three key officials Linda dealt with: Directors Lan and Gong and Ms Teng. None of them understood why Linda was bothering to raise money for these 'throwaway' children. Director Lan was a former military man who'd been given his cushy government job on retirement. Built like a boxer, he had a matching nuggety personality. He was the rudest of the three. He barely tolerated Linda's presence when she first took over from the international NGO. Over time, it dawned on him that Linda's charity could be a potential windfall for the orphanage. He thought all foreigners were rich. Once, one of Linda's staff overheard a phone conversation between Director Lan and one of the orphanage superiors, Ms Yan. Director Lan told Ms Yan that Linda carried a lot of cash in her money pouch and it was her duty was to get as much of it as possible before Linda returned to Australia.

In reality, Director Lan couldn't refuse Linda's help. As the orphanage filled up with abandoned, disabled children, costs also mounted while government funding did not. Linda knew that if she was to 'survive' in this landscape and improve the lives of the orphans, then she had to maintain a good working relationship with the Chinese officials, even if she didn't agree with them. From the outset, it was a daily battle to convince the Chinese that there were better and more compassionate ways to run an orphanage.

Many developed countries phased out children's institutions – seen as Dickensian and counter-productive – decades ago; but not China. Though there are excellent models of foster care around the country, orphanages are not likely to be phased out soon. Linda pondered how she might convince officials to vary the care provided to the severely disabled children from the first floor who were tied into potty chairs or their beds for most of the day. Even those who could walk had very little to occupy them once the volunteers went back to their homes. In other sections of the orphanage, children sat or lay around watching television, waiting for meal-times. Reminding herself of these scenes kept Linda awake as she listened to the last of the bird calls at home.

'I wanted the kids to clap and sing and play with building blocks and all those things children need to develop their brains,' she said.

But changing habits was a slow process. One of the curious things about Chinese buildings is that if they are seven storeys or under, there's no requirement to install a lift. The orphanage building didn't qualify, so walking up and down stairs provided good thinking time.

'Why don't we start a school?' she thought as she climbed the stairs. 'If we employed even one teacher to throw a ball and interact with the kids, it had to be better than seeing them sitting by the wall, rocking back and forth for stimulation,' she said.

In the 1950s, China had a huge problem with illiteracy which affected more than three quarters of the population.[2] The Chinese government turned this around in the 1980s by mandating nine years of compulsory education. By 2002, 98.58 per cent of children were enrolled in primary schools.[3] A major problem for the orphanage however, was only 10 out of 250 orphans were sufficiently mobile to attend the local school. The biggest challenge for the others, Linda realised, was that they weren't physically capable of getting to school or sitting quietly in a classroom. There were special needs schools in existence but outside the major cities these were rare.

'Normal Chinese schools didn't want dribbly kids who couldn't control their hands,' said COAT's secretary Margaret Mason. 'Government schools didn't cater for that. Nor did government teachers want to be changing incontinence underwear.'

The going salary for a teacher at that time was about 450 yuan ($90) per month. Linda wondered how she might pay for one, possibly two, teachers. She saw a newspaper article about businessman Dick Smith and his global adventures and decided to write to him, asking for a donation as a first step in setting up her school for orphans in China. Dick Smith obliged, sending Linda a cheque for $1,000.

With her first significant donation, she marched across from the children's wing to the administration building and asked to speak with the directors. Director Lan puffed on a cigarette as he sat behind his huge desk.

'That's crazy!' he said wrinkling his face as if something smelled bad. He made no excuses – he thought special needs children were not worth the trouble of educating.

Director Gong also drew on a cigarette. He looked thoughtful. Linda had met Director Gong during her first trip in 1998 and came to know him quite well over the years. He had invited Linda to his village for several meals over the years which for her was a great honour. She learned that his father was a retired coal miner whose family had lived through The Great Famine of 1959–62 by rationing food that they grew themselves. Some days, they had only a cup of rice to feed a family of seven people. Though she considered Director Gong an old friend, he once suggested Linda's charity would be better led by a man. Now, she awaited his response to the idea of starting a school at the orphanage.

'Not all the children can attend,' Director Gong said. 'How can we afford that? What about restricting the school to children with foreign sponsors?'

Linda didn't need to do any calculations. That would leave 200 out of the 250 children out in the cold. She thought that was unfair.

Then, Director Lan made a surprising proposal. 'Instead of paying for one qualified teacher, why don't we hire four ayis instead?' he said.

Mr Lan's rationale was that ayis were cheaper than teachers and there were plenty to choose from in the orphanage. If an ayi could be trained to be a teacher, they could afford more 'teachers'. Stubbing out his cigarette, his eyes widened and a smile spread across his face as he began to enjoy his own idea.

Once again, Linda sighed. It wasn't what she had wanted but she felt she couldn't refuse because as she had been taught, 'the Chinese would rather die than lose face.' COAT was still so new and her charity and the orphanage were not on equal terms. She really had no right to be there. So she accepted his suggestion and a few days later, through a translator, proceeded to interview twelve ayis who were already employed at the orphanage.

Director Lan allowed Linda to make her selection but to demonstrate who was boss, he vetoed her choices. Eventually he himself selected four women, choosing the ayis with musical skills so they could teach the children to perform songs for visiting VIPs.

Once the selection process was over, Director Lan stepped back. Linda planned to approach her regular business and church contacts back in Australia to fund the extra staff. Between them, the four new staff could run two classrooms for the children aged three to six each morning under the lead teacher's direction. Her name was Ms Xia and though she didn't have qualifications, she learned teaching skills from Linda and supervised the other three ayi-teachers. In the afternoons, all four went down to the first floor and provided activities for the older, intellectually-impaired orphans. These children had never had anything like this before. As well as the ayi-teachers, the government provided an administrator whom Linda found, to her delight, had skill and integrity.

Despite many disagreements, in May 2004, government officials, directors and staff gathered for a low-key ceremony.

Linda dragged a red cloth, supposed to be a curtain, off a brass plaque announcing the opening of the COAT School of Hope. There were the obligatory speeches followed by a lavish banquet in the reception hall. Then, school opened everyday from 8 am to 6 pm six days a week.

'It was like magic,' said Linda 'all systems go.'

The school began as a single classroom with large brown vinyl mats for the children to sit and play on and a few boxes of toys. By the end of 2004 there were 13 ayi-teachers and 100 kids taking up the entire third floor of the orphanage. The smarter kids did proper school work including learning Chinese characters, reading and maths. There was also a junior class.

Decades of Linda's early-childhood teaching experience were now channelled into training the first four ayi–teachers. The most schooling any of them received was to Year 10 and none of them had taught before. Linda gave them lectures on how to teach language, mathematics, science, social studies and drama simply by using the resources that were already around them.

'I knew how children learned, so it was easy to use everyday objects to teach them. We bought ten new wheelchairs for example. Each one came in a beautiful box. Stuff the wheelchairs, we loved the cardboard boxes.'

Linda created little islands of learning using one of her favourite teaching tools; building blocks. Plastic and wooden blocks were donated and sent with the volunteers from Australia. She watched the children's faces as shaky little hands clicked two Duplo blocks together. That click, and the rumble of little bricks on the marble floors was a beautiful sound.

'Once they got familiar, I showed the teachers how to use blocks to teach maths, numbers, positions, nouns, adjectives and descriptive phrases to expand their language. Even fantasy! You can build things like toy towns or a house or a family of monsters or planes and you can make up stories, all using blocks.'

The teachers hadn't grown up playing with blocks and toys. The older ones grew up during The Cultural Revolution when there was no luxury or entertainment. Their own children weren't showered with toys either because life was simple then and these were not wealthy people. Discovering play proved a joyful novelty. The teachers lapped it up, losing their inhibitions and learning to relax under Linda's leadership before passing their new skills to the orphans. Even disabled and intellectually-challenged kids got a few hours of school every day. Linda insisted one of the teachers go down to the first floor each day, to untie and bath a girl named Chun Li who was severely intellectually impaired. Linda wanted her brought up to the activities room where she could watch the other children and be given a fluffy toy or a book to hold.

'"But Mama", I was told, "she eats books". My response was that she should be given very old books. She came out of her shell a bit although she never learned to speak. She learned to walk at school and for many years, she was happy. It's not much to ask, that a child be allowed to be happy.'

With the sponsorship money and donations, COAT bought equipment such as chairs and desks, whiteboards, markers, books, Swiss balls, crayons, keyboards and hand-puppets. Linda showed the ayis that even kitchenware could be used as toys. She encouraged the Chinese staff to be resourceful.

'It's like eating an elephant,' she told the ayis through a translator. 'How do you do that? You do it one bite at a time.'

One of the ayis turned out to be a skilful seamstress. Linda paid for an old industrial sewing machine and sourced bolts of good quality cotton and wadding. Using the material, the ayi sewed all the children's clothing and quilts. Every winter the damp, old, stinky quilts which were never washed in the previous orphanage were thrown out. In their place, the children were given fresh, hand-sewn bedding.

A Melbourne company donated a sturdy plastic play gym and other donors paid for it to be freighted to Jiaozuo. When Linda returned on her next visit, she discovered the gym still in a box in the storeroom.

'We didn't want the children to break it,' the ayis said. 'So we [the volunteers] stormed over to the storeroom and put the thing up ourselves. How many times did I have to tell them that children need play and exercise to develop normally?' Linda said.

In her frustration, she complained to Miss Zhao, one of the orphanage supervisors whom she had known for many years.

'How do I make them understand?' asked Linda.

Ms Zhao nodded, a slight smile spreading across her face.

'It's like eating an elephant,' she said. 'How do you eat an elephant? One bite at a time.'

CHAPTER 9

The Story of Orphan Fu Yang

Fu Yang was born in 1991, but he doesn't know exactly where. He doesn't recall whether his parents – who owned a travelling circus – gave him a name. He travelled around the country with them in a procession of trucks and a troupe of twenty people including performers and a support crew. They were hired to entertain local residents in remote towns and villages. For months at a time, he and his parents lived in their East Wind truck, a sturdy brand of vehicle made famous during Communist times. His father navigated China's potholed highways while Fu Yang and his mother sat with him in the front of the truck. The truck carried everything they needed: bedding, cooking utensils, clothing and costumes. At night, his parents moved the bundles aside so that the rear cabin became a bedroom during their long months on the road.

Fu Yang remembers he had an older brother who lived in a house with grandparents and went to school. He wasn't sure why he didn't stay behind and go to school like his brother. He remembers that during breaks, he lived in a large farmhouse in the countryside with his parents. As well as the family, all the circus animals were housed in enclosures on the property as guard-dogs patrolled the yard. While other families kept the odd chicken, geese or pigs, Fu Yang's parents owned an exotic menagerie: monkeys, tigers, zebras, horses and three elephants.

When Fu Yang thinks back to the farmhouse or the truck he and his parents travelled in, his memories sadly, are not of a nurtured and adventurous childhood. The truck was his prison: he ate in there and slept there. He spent hours locked inside the cab. When he was desperate for the toilet, if no-one was around to let him outside, he just wet his pants.

Fu Yang's parents managed everything to do with the circus. His mother was a performer; a plate-spinner, trained to twirl bamboo sticks balancing crockery on the tips of the bamboo. Like all Chinese performers, she learned the craft of plate-spinning as a small child, training in a circus school followed by more years of practice. Fu Yang's father handled the administration and twenty employees. He also helped to erect the tents and seating and fed the animals as they moved from town to town. Many of the children who came to see the circus dreamed of being part of it. When he dared to, Fu Yang dreamed too. He dreamed of running far away from his family's big top.

Fu Yang wasn't like other children. He knew that early on. For one thing, he looked different. He had a facial deformity that caused his eyes to droop over flat cheekbones, as if part of his face had melted. He also had a cleft palate. He was deaf and didn't speak. His language was a game of charades; he mimed actions and when his parents spoke to him, they mimed actions back. He had never been to a doctor but apart from his disabilities, he was physically strong.

Fu Yang's mother was always angry with him. He would notice the way her mouth hardened into a crease as she scolded him. Most days, she beat him with a bamboo stick, hitting him hard on his head, on his thin shoulders and on his back. Sometimes, if he couldn't dodge her, her beatings drew blood from above his drooping eyes. He disappeared quickly, curling up inside the front seat of the truck, crying a strange monotone cry until the pain went away. His father would come looking for Fu Yang after his wife's outbursts. His father was kind and didn't hit his son.

One summer evening when a gentle breeze caressed the corn in the nearby fields, Fu Yang's father woke him and told him to put on his shoes. The boy was five years old and did exactly what his father told him. His father led him into a forest far away from the house. They walked and walked with only the moonlight to guide their way. Fu Yang never questioned anything, he just followed his father. He didn't know why they were walking all this way in the dark. When they reached a clearing, Fu Yang's father stopped and bent down low so he could speak to his son using hand signals.

'I am going away,' his father told him. 'You are staying here. Never tell anyone where you came from.' Then he shooed him away.

Fu Yang recalled running after his father, who signalled to him to go back. He realised his father didn't want him. The boy walked all night, without any money, any food, water or even a last glance from the man he loved.

Even though he had been abandoned, Fu Yang didn't cry. He felt relief to be away from his abusive mother. He curled up near a tree and slept. Eventually, slashes of light appeared between the leaves above him, reminding him of the holes in the curtains of the truck. But he wasn't in the warmth now. He stood up shakily, remembering the previous night's events, and shook the earth off his clothes. Still wearing his cloth shoes, he began walking without knowing where he was going. He crossed a slippery carpet of leaves until he saw a road in the distance. He followed the road until he reached an outdoor market in a township. It was a riot of colour. Hawkers sold vegetables off tarpaulins on the ground. There were butchers wielding choppers onto ribs of meat. Chickens ran about in the open spaces. He had never seen so much food in his life. Fu Yang knew he could eat here. This five-year-old boy was now on his own. He had to work out how to get money and find somewhere to stay for the next few nights.

On that first evening, he found some discarded packaging which had been tossed onto the street. Every evening after that, his job was to find boxes or spaces that might shelter him while he slept. Sometimes there were storerooms or ticket booths that had been left open where he was able to huddle near the coal briquettes and get a good night's sleep.

His other main priority was evading the police. In China, the police are known as the Public Security Bureau. They looked like soldiers in khaki uniforms, always on the lookout for vagrants and thieves. Fu Yang had already seen how they violently dragged beggars into their blue and white vans. It taught him to position his sleeping box carefully beside a wall or close to rubbish so that it didn't look like an obvious shelter.

After several weeks on the street, life began to feel normal for Fu Yang, except that he was always achingly hungry. Once, he found himself amid Lunar New Year celebrations with fireworks and revellers in the middle of a town. Two men were kind and offered him a bowl of food. The men suggested getting away from the smoke and noise and Fu Yang, believing that more food or even money was coming his way, naively followed. When the three of them reached a quiet alley, one of the men took a packet of cigarettes from his pocket and lit one of them. The men tried to start a conversation with Fu Yang. Of course, he didn't hear them and he couldn't respond.

Suddenly one of the men grabbed him around the neck and pressed a glowing cigarette into his hand then jabbed it into Fu Yang's face several times. He felt like the caged tiger from his family's circus: fear leaped out of his chest. He began to scream in his odd voice. He started boxing the air hoping to attract attention. Panicked, the men ran off. Fu Yang was left alone: his burns hurt and his heart was beating wildly, but even more painful was the prospect of hunger.

The boy wandered around like this for several years. He scoured the towns for his livelihood and wondered whether he would ever see his parents again. One day he started begging in the market and managed to steal a warm bun for his breakfast. He noticed a police car driving by and started to run. The police got out of their car and gave chase. When they caught up with him, he was bundled roughly into the van. After driving for about an hour, the van stopped outside the gates of a government building. It was the Jiaozuo Children's Welfare Institute.

With its odd collection of children with disabilities, babies, the elderly and intellectually-impaired, the orphanage felt a little bit like the circus except that they were all together all the time, even at night.

Fu Yang remembers the old residents being mean to him and laughing at his strange face. The orphanage sent him to a boarding school for the deaf but his deaf classmates picked fights with him all the time. There were so many fights that two months later he was sent back.

At the orphanage, he befriended two boys about the same age as himself. One of them was incontinent. This boy sat on a plastic bucket all day. The other child was named Huang Qiang.

He had lobster-like pincers instead of hands and strange feet with only two toes each. Huang Qiang had been abandoned beside a noodle stall at the railway station and told by his parents to wait. He stood as a sea of travellers carrying huge bundles went out and back like the tide. No-one paid any attention to the boy with the lobster-claw hands. Huang Qiang waited. And waited. He waited until the stall-holder closed down her noodle cart and towed it away. Still his parents didn't return. Eventually, Huang Qiang went to look for them. For the best part of a year, he lived, courtesy of the Chinese railways, riding and even sleeping on the third-class carriages. Finally the police caught him and he was brought to the Jiaozuo orphanage.

The two boys missed their freedom and truly hated the orphanage at first, but with winter coming, they knew that at least it was a comfortable alternative to the constant search for shelter or possibly freezing to death on the streets. Fu Yang was now seven years old. At the orphanage, free meals came twice a day. It was usually some bread with corn or millet soup stirred with egg. Never enough for growing boys, but it warmed them and besides, anything was better than an empty stomach. Sometimes a supervisor came to check on them. Most of the time, no-one bothered them.

On winter mornings they awoke to a blanket of snow draped over the courtyard. Rats ran along the top of the wall and down through the toilet to the sewer below. This didn't worry the boys so much, although some of the smaller children were bitten while they slept. The two boys would clamber over the uneven brick wall, careful to avoid the broken glass at the top. They were headed for the neighbourhood market right next door where they could steal as much food as they could carry, which they did. This way, the two boys supplemented the diet of all the orphanage residents except for the intellectually-impaired men who would steal any food as soon as they discovered it.

One day as the worst of winter was over, a group of foreigners came to visit the orphanage. The Chinese cadres call them 'Old Outsiders' or 'Foreign Devils' and thought they were bringing money to invest in China. The children had never seen Caucasian people before. One of the foreigners was a large man with a booming voice. He told the children he was a teacher. He taught the boys how to add and subtract. Fu Yang proved to be a fast learner.

Huang Qiang, the boy with the lobster claws, could not adjust to being in a confined space. Soon after the foreigners left, he escaped the orphanage by climbing over the wall. The directors said he had joined a gang of beggars. Unexpectedly, some of the foreign volunteers came across him in a vagrants' colony one day where he was under the protection of the adult beggars. The volunteers offered to arrange for him to go to school, but Huang Qiang declined the offer. No-one saw him or heard of him again.

Fu Yang was devastated. He had never had a friend before, but he also knew that for his survival, he couldn't follow Huang Qiang into freedom. If he left, who would bring the extra food for the children? Fu Yang was now officially an orphan, a ward of the Chinese state. Even though he faced an uncertain future he had a roof over his head, warmth from the other boys who slept in the same bed and food twice a day. This was his new life.

A decade after his adoption in 2005, I meet Fu Yang DeLuca via Skype from Dallas, Texas, where he's on a break from college. He's now a broad-shouldered young man, sitting next to Dinah, his adoptive mother, a native Texan. At times I can hear his Dad, Louis, in the background. He also has two brothers and a sister. Fu Yang doesn't look anything like his childhood photos. His face has much more structure than it had when he was a child, the result of multiple surgeries. He has long hair tied back in a pony-tail, which his Mum explains will be cut off soon for a charity which makes wigs for cancer patients. The other difference is that Fu Yang speaks now, which he started to do after coming to the US in 2003. As we are on Skype and the communication isn't perfect, his Mum is there to interpret for him and explain Fu's words to me.

Fu – as everyone calls him in the US – first met Linda and Greg Shum at the Jiaozuo orphanage. Greg taught him maths. He recalls that the foreigners seemed particularly concerned about the babies or *wa-wa* as they were called.

'I was really scared, so I tried to hide when I saw them at first,' Fu said.

'They looked so different: white skin, round eyes. I didn't know where they were from and what they were doing,' he said.

He soon discovered that the foreigners were extremely kind and for the first time since he could remember, these people seemed to care about him even though talking with him was difficult. When the orphanage staff got to know him a little better, they worked out how to communicate with him. Like Fu's father, the staff acted out a game of charades, until he demonstrated that he had understood.

In 2003, an American visited the Jiaozuo orphanage and photographed some of the children. He seemed particularly intrigued by Fu Yang's unusual face and he forwarded his images to The Grace Children's Foundation which provides free medical help to Chinese orphans. A proposal was drawn-up offering Fu Yang an opportunity to travel to the United States to see what medical experts could offer him there. Within months, the deaf boy with the strange face embarked on another life-changing adventure, accompanied by a nurse, on his first ever plane journey.

'I didn't even know America existed,' Fu said, talking and signing. 'I had no idea what was happening.'

Many people, including the nurse, assumed that Fu would understand better if they shouted at him. She wrote a note – reminiscent of what was left with Paddington Bear waiting patiently at the station – that Fu was to carry with him at all times: 'My name is Fu Yang. Please call this number if you find me.'

At the Craniofacial Center at Medical City Dallas Hospital, Fu was diagnosed with Treacher Collins syndrome, a rare genetic abnormality that affects one in ten thousand infants. Treacher Collins sufferers have flat cheekbones which makes the skin around their eyes droop. The condition meant Fu's ears and the palate in his mouth had never fully formed.

He remembers the frightening first round of surgery in that bright, clean facility where everyone was so friendly to him. It was so strange after being ignored and seeing nothing but the walls of the orphanage for years.

The medical team's challenge was to create a structure or base for Fu's face so that cheekbone implants could be inserted. Two pieces of bone were taken from his skull and grafted onto each side of his face under his eyes. Once he was sewn back together, his swollen eyes remained shut for several days.

Because he was completely in the dark and still had no hearing, the nurse created a way to let him know whether it was day or night. She made a board with rocks and another one with cotton balls glued to it. When she gave him the one with rocks, he knew it was night-time. The board with cotton balls signified day-time. Fu Yang knew who his visitors were by feeling their arms. One day, he felt a man's hairy forearm by his side. The owner was a photographer who had come to document Fu's medical journey in the US.

Louis DeLuca is a veteran photojournalist for the *Dallas Morning News*. He first met Fu after a call from a friend one day, asking him if he could take pictures of a little Chinese boy who was heading to a Dallas hospital just minutes from Louis' home. It was autumn 2003 in the United States, the heart of football season. Louis was going to be tied up at the Texas Stadium, home to the Dallas Cowboys. Too busy to do this favour for a friend, his wife Dinah stopped him as he voiced his reluctance. 'He's an orphan,' she reminded him. 'Take an hour out of your time and go help him.'

'Apart from the fact he couldn't talk, he was just like a regular kid,' Louis said and he felt an instant connection with the boy.

The plan was to have the surgery over several months and then return to China. However, in December 2003 after Fu's surgery started, the CEO of Medical City Dallas Hospital resigned and all donated procedures had to be put on hold until a new CEO was appointed. The DeLucas stepped in as host family, so Fu could stay in the US rather than going back to China to wait.

Once the new CEO was in place in early 2004, Fu's surgery continued. To capture the moment when medical staff turned on his hearing aid, Dinah and Louis made arrangements for a camera crew to film the event. Everyone waited for the magic moment. However, Fu had been deaf for so long, his brain had to learn what it was hearing. The 'moment' came and Fu didn't even blink.

After his hearing had been fixed, he had an eye-lift to remove the skin over his eyes.

The eye-lifts weren't as successful as the surgeon would have liked because Fu's skin was too taut. But even small procedures were an improvement.

Doctors now turned to the task of repairing his cleft palate. This defect, which affects one in 600–800 births, is where the two halves of the roof of the mouth don't fuse during fetal development. Once surgeons fixed his palate, Fu had cheekbone implants. Then surgeons created a right ear using cartilage from his ribs and a skin graft from his buttocks.

As the bond between Fu and the DeLuca's grew, the head of the organisation which had brought him to America, Nancy Robertson, suggested to Louis that he adopt the boy.

Louis felt numb. This wasn't something he had considered. Louis and Dinah DeLuca are committed Christians but Louis was deeply unsure about the idea of adopting Fu. Today, Louis recalls this story with embarrassment.

'It was unchartered territory for me,' he said. 'We already had three kids. Adopting a special needs child would definitely be a huge step of faith. My job was demanding time-wise and I wasn't sure if there was "room" in our lifestyle for another child, especially one that might require the commitment he would need and deserve to have from us.'

Louis was on assignment in Alabama more than a thousand kilometres from home, when he began fiddling with the car radio dial and came across a conversation about adoption. A woman discussed how adopting seemed to be such an unlikely turn of events, but that she and her husband were thankful they had continued despite their doubts. Incredibly she had used the exact words that were in Louis' own mind: 'There's absolutely no way we could do this. It doesn't make sense. We don't have the money.'

Like Louis and Dinah DeLuca, almost all adoptive parents realise at some stage, adoption doesn't make sense. But it resonated deeply with Louis. 'We eventually did it,' said the woman on the radio. 'And I'm so glad we did.'

Louis found himself wanting to go to the hospital and just 'hang out' with Fu. He decided to discuss the idea of adoption with Dinah. In her practical, Texan way she had already reached a conclusion. 'You know there is no way we can let that little boy go back to China, don't you?' she said.

Fu is now a strapping man who turns twenty-six in 2017 which is also the year he's due to graduate. Not surprisingly, he has followed Louis' trade and studies photography at Texas State Technical College in Waco, a two-hour drive from his home in the Dallas suburbs. He is, by Louis' account, a gifted photographer and an incredible imitator who learns by observing.

One day he was photographing his school football team in a vital playoff game. Louis was covering the same game for the *Dallas Morning News*. Later, Fu Yang showed Louis his best photo and Louis transmitted it back to the news desk. The paper ended up running Fu Yang's photograph instead of Louis'.

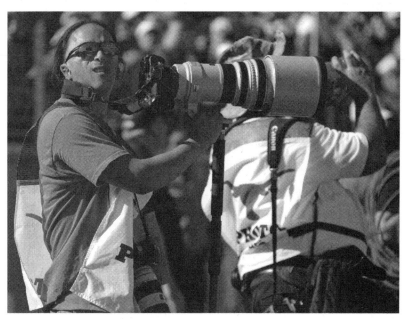

Fu Yang at work. Fu Yang DeLuca has been studying photography and is graduating in 2017. His Dad, Louis, took this photo at a football game. Louis says Fu has a great photographer's eye. (Louis DeLuca)

The biggest challenge for Fu, Louis said, was communication in a world that is hearing and verbal. 'Fu can hear well now with his hearing aid. But his verbal skills are what you would expect from a person who spent the first twelve years of his life not being able to hear or speak.'

'The other issue,' Louis said 'is because of his facial features, he's constantly getting stared at and at times, made fun of. This has obviously happened his whole life and he has dealt with it admirably. But my heart breaks for him when I see it going on.'

'Fu is a survivor,' said Louis. 'His life and amazing story have had an impact on so many people around us. He is very smart. He just wasn't born with the full set of physical tools most of us get at birth.'

'He's a Chinese Huck Finn,' Dinah chimed in. 'He doesn't back down from a challenge, he has drive and a determination that is rare and self-confidence that is hard to explain.'

Dallas Morning News photojournalist Louis DeLuca took this 'selfie' with Fu Yang while the orphan was undergoing several rounds of surgery at Medical City Dallas Hospital in 2004. (Louis DeLuca)

CHAPTER 10

Better Days

In February 2004, three American women arrived in Jiaozuo for an internship organised through the same Christian NGO that originally brought Linda to China. Two of the women, Hope Annis and Michelle West, were childhood friends who had recently graduated from high school. Hope had visited Chinese orphanages during her school years and found the experience to be uplifting and rewarding. She encouraged Michelle to apply for the internship. The third woman, Emily, was in her mid-twenties and had also visited Chinese orphanages in the past.

'The kids were so poor,' Michelle said. 'One little boy didn't have shoes and his feet were swollen and blue from the cold. It was very challenging. It was heart-breaking, actually.'

Michelle remembers the numbing cold of the northern Chinese winter. 'There was no heating,' she said. The children were dirty and their clothes were torn. The young volunteers tried to give the children baths, but the workers were adamant they should not. In the babies' room, there were four or five to a crib.

'They were lined up and when they were being fed they were laid on their backs with a bottle propped in their mouths. If the bottle fell out, then that was all the food they were given,' Michelle recalled. Many of the bigger children were put on potty chairs where they were left all day long.

At first, the orphanage didn't know what to do with the American women. Director Lan sent them to local schools to teach English but around the orphanage, he didn't have much time for them. The girls lived in the orphanage guest hostel during their six month stay. Director Lan insisted they pay for their board which they did. He took $40 per day per woman.

A few weeks after she arrived, while looking down the long hallway of the second floor, Hope spied a door on the left which she hadn't noticed before. The orphanage workers usually turned right to go into the babies' room. The door on the left however, was always closed. Hope had never seen anyone going in so she presumed it was empty. As there were no workers around, she decided to take a look.

The door wasn't locked so Hope walked straight in. It was just like the babies' room across the hall, painted in the trademark institutional colours – green on the lower section, white on the top. There were two windows at the far end, but no decorative children's paintings like the other rooms. It felt like something was missing. In front of her were several blue metal cots, again, just like the baby room across the hall. At first the cots seemed empty. Then Hope noticed a small bundle in one of them. Her heart pounded with excitement and trepidation. She inched forward until she was leaning against the cot's blue iron railing. Peering down, she saw the top of a baby's head with a shock of black hair. She gasped. It was lying there like an antique doll, its skin pale and jaundiced, in complete silence. Then it began to cough, a pitiful, agonising bark more like a sick animal than a child.

Hope found some nappies and slowly pulled the blankets aside. It was a boy.

Hope went to find Emily and Michelle to share her news about the secret room. Soon all three of them were leaning against the blue railing, looking down at the infant who was clearly very sick. Emily picked him up and rocked him. They talked about it for a while before they resolved to take action.

Michelle recalls, 'We all thought, he shouldn't have been left there to die, but no-one was looking after him.'

The next day, they returned to the room unnoticed by the ayis. The sick baby was still there. And there were two others. Like the boy, they too appeared weak and vulnerable. Why was no-one looking after them?

'We all agreed that we would start going into that room and feed the babies. We organised shifts, getting up early in the morning to feed them. And then, more babies appeared. We fed them three or four times a day and it became our whole purpose for being there,' said Michelle.

One of the ayis told Hope the babies were not going to be fed. They were sick and unlikely to survive so they had been left in the room to die. To try to help them was just prolonging their suffering. Without knowing, Hope had stumbled on the orphanage's dying room. There was no doctor in sight. She couldn't see that leaving the children in there was in any way humane. To her, it was just cruel.

When the lab-coated orphanage workers discovered the American girls had found the room, they gathered up all the baby formula and the feeding bottles and hid them. So the girls went to a local department store and used their own money to purchase formula and bottles to keep the feeding regime going. When the workers discovered this, they locked the door to the room so the women couldn't get it.

Hope said tearfully, 'After they locked it, we broke in. Michelle and Emily helped me onto their shoulders so I could climb through a window at the top of the door. I would let them in through the door and that's how we visited the babies every day. We decided that we were going to pick up and comfort all the children so that they wouldn't die unloved.'

Hope discovered a little girl she named Mei Lin in one of the blue cots. When she pulled aside the bedding, she gasped. An angry rash had spread all over her bottom, her back and withered legs. There was also a sac of liquid protruding from the lower part of her spine, indicating spina bifida. 'I could tell she was dying. I thought about it and I didn't want her to die alone, so I took her back to my room in the hostel.'

She intended to cradle Mei Lin in her arms until the little girl died. Then she had second thoughts. Hope was nineteen. The idea of holding a dead child frightened her. So instead, she brought the child to the room she shared with Michelle, turned out the clothes from one of her suitcases and covered the interior with a blanket. Then she carefully laid Mei Lin in the makeshift bed. The next morning Michelle peered down at the child. Her body was cold. The girls began to weep. They cried for the loss of Mei Lin, but felt relief that she was no longer miserable. Hope took the stiff little bundle back to the orphanage and gave it to one of the ayis. She felt regret that she didn't have the courage to hold Mei Lin, but in the thirteen years since her gap year in China, she still believes she and her friends did the right thing.

One of the ayis told Michelle that a man came to take the babies' bodies and buried them somewhere. The ayi said during spring and summer, three to four babies were brought in to the orphanage each day and if they had a serious physical deformity or disability they were placed in the room on the left.

Hope remembers that apart from Mei Lin, another infant died in suspicious circumstances. However, many of the babies began to show signs of improvement with regular feeding and the attention paid to them.

'The experience affected my whole life,' said Hope. 'I know many of those children we saved are still alive today,' She paused. 'I think about it at least once a week although I know I won't ever do anything that meaningful again.'

When the workers realised they couldn't prevent the women from their feeding mission, the room was cleaned and decorated and finally in May, three months after the room's discovery, all the babies, sick and healthy, were kept together and routinely fed.

After hearing about the dying room, Linda encouraged the orphanage directors to open a palliative care facility in the orphanage. Saving babies, rather than letting them die, would make the orphanage look good, she suggested. The special care facility in Jiaozuo opened in January 2005, operated and funded by Joyce and Robin Hill's New Hope Foundation for more than a decade. The Hills were the couple Linda had met in Beijing who ran the Hope Foster Home for special needs orphans. There was no more need for a dying room at the Jiaozuo orphanage.

One evening while Linda was staying at the orphanage hostel, there was a loud knock at the door.

Her eyebrows raised, Linda looked at her sister-in-law, Elva Kayes, before checking her watch. It was nearly 10 o'clock.

'Who is it?' she called out. Someone outside giggled.

'We are students,' said a girl's voice.

Two young women stood at the door. The watchman had told them where to go to find the foreigners. One of the women introduced herself as Lisa. They were local university students and had cycled over to find foreign people so they could practice speaking English. Linda smiled. Somehow, students always seemed to know when the volunteers were in town. Despite the late hour, Linda invited the women to stay for a chat and some tea. They talked about the weather and their studies and their boyfriends. They seemed in no hurry to leave.

Lisa, a slight woman in her early twenties, wore dangly gold earrings and despite the trip on a bicycle, a flowery red dress under her jacket. Her hair was covered in tiny clips, like a little girl. There was a frailness about her, as if she needed protecting. Linda took an instant liking to her.

As the night unfolded she told Linda and Elva in a hushed voice that her grandfather had been a victim of The Great Famine. Henan province was one of the provinces hit particularly hard. After Lisa's grandfather died, her grandmother, Granny Liu, kept her daughter and younger son (Lisa's father) alive by dragging them on foot from county to county in search of food. In some parts of the region, entire villages were wiped out. People were forced to eat bark and sometimes soil. Corpses lay on the roadside, close to where people had attempted to flee. Often they were blocked by soldiers trying to prevent hungry people from flooding into the cities.

Fortunately, Lisa's father and aunty survived. Granny Liu gave the best food to her son, her daughter came next and she took whatever was left. She almost starved. She said her husband had become so weak, he lost the will to survive or help his family. One day, he lay down in a bed of hay and simply 'gave up'.

Lisa was always grateful that her father had been so lovingly protected during those difficult times. She was in awe of her grandmother. Granny Liu still lived with Lisa's family and helped with the work of growing cabbages, cauliflower and corn. Lisa was the eldest of six children; five girls and a boy. Because she was the first child, she was given the privilege of a university education. Her other siblings stayed in the village to tend the fields. One of her sisters was sent away to work in a factory to support the household. She worked seventeen hour days, six days a week for $100 a month, most of which was sent home to the village. As Linda says, the lives of ordinary Chinese people never ceased to be anything but amazing. Some years later she found sponsors for Lisa's sister to help her leave the factory and return to school for a few years.

After that night, Linda hired Lisa as a translator for COAT, working at first on a casual basis. Lisa proved hard-working and loyal and soon, her boyfriend Jackson also began to work for COAT. In 2005 she began a traineeship eventually becoming Linda's full-time manager in China. Tao Mei, the orphan Linda hired in 1998 was unhappy with Lisa's appointment, but over time, Tao Mei's work had deteriorated and she began to feel a sense of entitlement with her role. She had always lacked people skills. Several years later, Linda moved her aside so that she would no longer work with the children. She gave her a job in the office.

Several months later, another pair of students, a young woman named Joyous Li and her boyfriend Xiao Ming, also turned up at COAT to practise English. They were aptly-named. Joyous Li was such a sunny personality. She made everyone around her feel somehow light. And Xiao Ming (which means Little Bright) was singular and reliable.

Linda felt fortunate to have met good people who would come to be part of her growing social enterprise.

In February 2004, a baby boy found by police was brought to the orphanage. At the time several children in the orphanage contracted chickenpox and the new arrival became very sick. Linda's cousin Kay who was visiting at the time and who was a registered nurse, cared for him. The hospital shaved his tiny head and fed traditional Chinese medicine intravenously through his scalp, which was a confronting sight for the Australians. Once he recovered he was diagnosed with spina bifida, although his lesion wasn't an open sac of liquid like many of the babies, but a closed lesion similar to a large mole. When he was twelve months' old he suffered another trauma. Chinese doctors severed the tendons in his legs so that they could be straightened. The surgery rendered his legs useless. Linda was furious about this, but on the other hand, had the infant arrived at the orphanage in earlier years, he may have been taken straight to the dying room. That boy was Wen Xuan, the first orphan I met in 2013 at Zhengzhou airport with Linda. The one I nicknamed Oliver.

In June 2006, Linda took a team of seventeen Australian volunteers to Jiaozuo to lead a series of staff training sessions. They gave talks about science, maths, drama and physical movement. Margaret Mason, who is COAT's secretary, was on that team. She's a former science teacher; an efficient, practical woman with short grey hair and, when I met her, a plain dress buttoned down the front.

'I co-authored a biology textbook in the early 2000s,' Margaret, who's 70 said. 'This gave me a lot of standing in the eyes of the Chinese.'

Margaret had dreamed of being a missionary when she was a girl and she thought going to China would be a great adventure. The early days were chaotic 'like a zoo,' Margaret recalled. 'Linda warned us before we went, it would be smelly, the toilets were grotty, the kids don't get bathed that often.' She was also warned that in the orphanage, they might find children tied to their beds.

Margaret didn't see them tied to their beds, but did observe them tied to potty chairs.

'I had learned about many of the disabilities like cerebral palsy and Down syndrome in text books, so I didn't feel overwhelmed by the scene that confronted me. But my friend Joan, who was a nurse was so shocked with the conditions that she never went back,' she said.

Margaret's friend was overwhelmed by the cruelty and futility of some of the medical treatments which were taking place. For instance, two of the children had club feet. To correct this, they were operated on repeatedly by local doctors. One of the boys, Shan Shan was seven at the time of the volunteer's visit in June 2006. As a baby, he'd been neglected because of his spina bifida and crippled feet, until Linda found an Australian 'Mama' named Marolyn to sponsor him. During a medical procedure in 2006 doctors repositioned (broke) his bones to fix his feet. His feet and legs were put into plaster casts and he was supposed to stay in bed for six weeks. Being a youngster and because there was no supervision, he got out of bed and played in the bathroom. As a result the plaster got soggy. Joan, Margaret's nurse friend offered to re-plaster Shan Shan's feet, but the orphanage staff forbade it. Staff said it that would make the Chinese doctors lose face. Shan Shan had six rounds of surgery which all ended in failure. Linda described his feet as having been 'butchered'. As a result he walks with an awkward shuffle.

Margaret gathered the ayis for a training session. She used a Baby Bjorn to strap a baby to her chest and caressed the child the entire time she spoke. She taught the ayis it was the flow and balance of hormones in the infant's body which enabled her to thrive and develop. Touch and maximum stimulation according to the science, promotes brain development.

To underscore her point, the volunteers went shopping, spending a few hundred dollars at a local department store. They bought mountains of beads, ornaments, string and plastic coat hangers. Margaret showed the ayis how to thread them together to make mobiles to hang above the babies' beds, to get as Linda described their 'happy juices flowing into developing little brains'.

'It was stuff I studied in my first year of psychology,' Margaret said, recalling the experiments of American psychologist, Harry Harlow. For his 1958 report 'The Nature of Love', Harlow, controversially, isolated infant rhesus monkeys from their mothers to show how the deficit affected their social interactions.

Harvard pediatrician Charles Nelson has studied the effect on orphans when their brains are starved of love, touch, stimulation and human contact. He focused on Romania where, at the fall of Nicolae Ceausescu in 1989, there were 170,000 children in state orphanages. In a 2000 study, Professor Nelson found orphans in institutional and foster care had dramatically reduced neural activity and compromised brain development. However, if they were adopted or fostered before the age of two, the children generally recovered.

'On the whole it was just breathtakingly awful,' Nelson said. 'One of the eeriest things about these institutions is how quiet they are. Nobody's crying.'[1]

Though the Jiaozuo orphanage was still the scene of many power struggles over the right way to care for orphans, unlike in the past, there was momentum now. Margaret Mason knew before she walked through her front door back in Gympie, that she would be returning to Jiaozuo. And she has done so nearly every year since that first trip in 2006.

Linda's mantra became 'every day, every child, happiness.'

Everyone who visited the orphanage noticed the transformation. In just three short years, classrooms, therapy rooms and play areas sprouted up. When they weren't teaching, school staff worked in the massage room, stretching and exercising the limbs of children with physical disabilities. Soft mats and walking frames gave toddlers who would have grown up with disabilities an early boost to their muscle and brain development. Everywhere the shelves were bursting with toys, musical instruments and building blocks that Linda wanted the children to access at any time.

COAT was now responsible for the welfare of ninety orphans. Fifty-five children had foreign sponsors and the very sick children were taken care of in the special care unit. COAT paid for eleven teachers in the school and four dedicated ayis to hold, feed and play with the children. In addition to this, COAT paid for smart uniforms and bonuses for the forty-six orphanage ayis to boost their professional esteem and to take their pay to a more reasonable level. During the week, the sound filtering down through the orphanage was beautiful and chaotic and alive. But when the ayis clocked off on Friday afternoons, all the toys, books and equipment were locked away until Monday morning. The children spent long, uneventful weekends loitering in the darkened halls.

'The only way to get better care for these kids was to hire our own staff, train them and pay them,' Linda said. 'We constantly struggled keeping the staff on track and stopping them from reverting to their previous ways.'

One December day Linda discovered the ayi in charge of the intellectually-impaired children on the first floor had gathered up all the newly distributed Christmas presents much to the distress of the children. The ayi stuffed them into a cupboard 'in case they got broken or dirty'. Tearfully, Linda videoed the saga and then dragged one of the directors down to the first floor where she demanded the children's presents be returned to them, which they were.

In 2006, eighteen COAT volunteers descended on Jiaozuo mid-year to start work on a new set of bunk-beds for the intellectually-impaired children on the first floor. After the new furniture came a plan to help the neediest children; those with severe disabilities. These children wouldn't have lived beyond a few years if they'd been born ten years earlier. Life for them meant endless days lying on hard wooden beds. Linda wanted to give them permanent rooms where they could be cared for lovingly. So volunteers painted two of the rooms with bright-blue walls filled with rainbows. They scrubbed the floors, cleaned out the bathrooms and called them The Rooms of Joy.

'All the improvements at the orphanage began as dreams or ideas and every one of them has only been gained after years of negotiations, Western sponsorship and the multiples of teams that came to China, one building on the other,' said Linda.

Chris Plummer, a COAT volunteer from Britain, came up with the idea of starting a foster home. Chris explains, 'We wanted to see a place where the staff actually cared and loved the children and were not just doing a job.' Chris, who is now the UK representative for COAT, was deeply impressed after visiting another organisation in the north-west of China which ran foster homes for children in the local orphanage.

Foster homes were introduced to China in the late 1990s (again, in response to *The Dying Rooms*) by a British social worker named Robert Glover. In studying the UK experience of foster-care, he found that alternatives to institutions were hugely beneficial to the children. In 1998, he moved to China with his family where, after visiting an orphanage, he found not only the children were in a desperate state but so were the staff.[2] He set up the charity Care for Children to work with the Chinese government, establishing foster care projects that took children out of institutions and placed them with local families. Chris Plummer thought something along these lines might work in Jiaozuo.

With the help of translators Joyous Li and Xiao Ming, Chris and a mandarin-speaking volunteer named Annie, negotiated with the directors for some of the children to be moved into a foster-type arrangement. At the time, the Chinese mentality was to keep children in institutions which were cost-effective to manage. Though foster programs were running successfully in several parts of China, they still weren't universally accepted.

The directors agreed to the idea, but they wouldn't allow the children to be taken out of the welfare compound. As a compromise, COAT was allowed to lease the fifth floor of the nearby administration building.

In the orphanage, ten children were monitored by one ayi. The COAT volunteers thought one ayi to three children would provide a better quality of care. The plan was to accommodate twenty-four children, but because there was no lift, all the foster-children had to be mobile.

Chris Plummer recalled, 'Towards the end of the renovations I asked one of the ayis to clean the windows. The next time I looked, she was squatting on the window ledge *outside* the window, cleaning away, oblivious to any danger.'

Sometime between June and December of 2006, Director Lan was discreetly removed. Although no-one was told the precise reason, it was good news to Linda's mind. His replacement was a man named Mr Sun. Director Sun was in his mid-forties, a thin man who was fussy with his food and believed meat caused stomach problems. To begin with, he turned out to be just as grasping as Director Lan.

COAT by now had sixty children sponsored at $40 per month. That worked out at an income of 12,000 yuan, $2,400, a month.

'We took twenty-four kids out of the orphanage for the first foster home,' Linda said. 'The only way I was able to take so many was that I agreed to give the directors the sponsorship money I received for those kids. The orphanage was desperate not to lose it.'

In one sense, the foster home wasn't a true foster-care facility. They had carers rather than foster-parents and it was only in the building next door to the orphanage. But in other ways it was light years from the halls of the social welfare institution and for the Shums it signalled that more might be possible.

CHAPTER 11

Life and Loss

In November 2006 as the end of school term approached, the Shums prepared to fly to China to open COAT's new foster home. Gympie sweltered although summer was still a few weeks away. Greg and Linda had their to-do lists and there was much to fit in. For Linda, there was the added pressure of the end of the school year. Greg had his duties as the church administrator, including the upcoming AGM. And as they were going to miss Christmas at home, they wanted to spend as much time with their grandkids as they could. They liked to take them out one at a time to make each child feel special. There was much to organise, buy and pack for the weeks ahead.

One Sunday during the last minute rush, Greg arrived home and said something strange had happened to his eyes. He lost vision temporarily. As it had been extremely humid, he suspected the heat might have something to do with it. On Linda's advice, he downed a few Aspros. Thankfully, his sight returned and he didn't think much more about it.

Though he didn't know it yet, he was having a series of mini-strokes.

Greg arranged to collect Linda from school the following day. When he got to the staff carpark at Two Mile State School, she found him trying to drag himself over to the passenger side of the car. His legs had given way under his 130-kilogram frame. After the trouble with his sight the previous day, now it was his legs. He wondered whether this was really heat-related. Linda yelled out for someone at the school to call an ambulance. The paramedics arrived, gave Greg oxygen and took him to Gympie Hospital, despite his protestations. Sometime after midnight, he was given the all-clear and sent home.

The following evening at home, Greg began to have a fit of vomiting. Lying on the waterbed, the wave-like motion made him feel dreadful so he rolled onto a foam mattress which Linda placed at the foot of their bed. Despite moving to something firmer, the vomiting proved unrelenting. He vomited for three straight hours.

Once again, against Greg's will, Linda called an ambulance which arrived twenty minutes later. Then, the paramedics said because of his size, they couldn't lift him onto a stretcher. 'He left our home crawling down the hall, throwing up for all it was worth ... through the lounge room, out onto the patio and then backwards like a small child going down the steps. Then the ambos put him on a stretcher and took him to the hospital to die,' Linda wrote in her grief journal years later.

She expected the hospital staff would give him an injection of Stemetil and he would soon return home. But despite four hours in emergency, the medication hadn't worked.

'I had six days to get used to the idea of being a widow. It was the beginning of his end,' she wrote.

Doctors at Gympie Hospital said he had suffered a series of strokes. Over the next few days, Greg's condition continued to deteriorate. He went blind again and then half of his face became paralysed. He struggled to form words, causing him much frustration.

At that stage, Linda and Greg had a conversation about what might lie ahead. They were hopeful the strokes wouldn't progress further and that rehabilitation might bring back a good quality of life, whatever that meant. Greg insisted he didn't want to be resuscitated if he was too far gone. He didn't want to be evacuated to Brisbane either. The specialists in Gympie were direct in their assessment that this type of stroke had a poor prognosis.

'You must go to China. There is much to do,' he told Linda in a halting growl which was all he could muster.

Linda kept vigil by his bedside, joined by a procession of close friends including their pastor, Rick Roberts. Sitting by the bedside as Greg lay in his purple gown, Linda later wrote that the process of death was like the birth of a child: '[There are] many of the same feelings of being in labour; the pain, the passing hours, the wondering how long, the nurses popping their head in the door sometimes, the family waiting and hoping for the miracle of life, the hand holding, the back rubbing, the encouraging words. "That's good darling, you are doing ok. It won't be long now, my beautiful one".'

The vigil was to last two nights and two days.

A doctor from Papua New Guinea was assigned to look after Greg. After examining him, he told Linda that he wasn't able to save her husband. Then he began to cry. Linda was so moved by his honesty and concern. She comforted him assuring him he had done his best and that he wasn't to blame. She gave him a hug. He nodded and went behind a partition to cry privately.

Palliative care staff worked to make Greg comfortable. They suggested inserting a catheter which Greg wasn't happy about.

Linda joked about how Greg was concerned the catheter might curb his style with the nurses. By that time, only one side of his face still worked, but he managed a lopsided smile.

'My wife's a ratbag,' Greg growled to Pastor Rick as Linda chuckled.

It was to be the last time he spoke.

Family and friends had gathered to say goodbye. Son Jason arrived from Cairns, Damien and Debbie came from work. Debbie was Linda's teaching partner at Two Mile State School and they had taught Debbie's eldest daughter, Ebonnie. Linda promised Ebonnie her beloved grandfather would be better soon. We say those foolish things with the best intentions.

They took turns to rub his feet, his hands, his back or just talk to him hoping he could still hear them.

'I prayed,' Damien said. 'Just take him now. Damage had been done to his brain but if he survived, he would be mentally impaired and he wouldn't be able to cope with that.'

'We all took turns to wet the purple gown he wore with tears that could no longer be controlled,' said Linda. She kept vigil with two of the children, Greg's Mum Freda and his sister Elva. She still hoped he would sit up, look at her and say, 'What on earth are you blubbering about!' She longed for that to happen, but of course, it did not. 'Till death do us part' had come all too soon. Eventually he stopped breathing although his heart continued to beat.

Debbie wasn't in the room as she had left to fetch something from home. Linda shouted at her husband, 'Don't you dare leave until Debbie gets back!' Then she yelled at Jesus, 'Don't you dare take him until Debbie gets here.'

For forty-five minutes, Greg's heart continued to beat. Debbie finally returned after being caught in roadworks. Distraught, she rushed over to hug him hard, crying, 'Daddy, Daddy! Don't leave me!'

And though his heart alternated between fibrillating and a regular beat long enough for Debbie to say goodbye, fifteen minutes later, Greg's heart finally stopped.

The man Linda had married thirty-six years ago was gone.

I never had the opportunity to meet Greg. He had a broadcaster's voice, which I came to know (plus a little of his personality) through the video newsletters he and Linda prepared together. He could have easily found a job as a radio newsreader if he hadn't chosen to be a teacher, principal and then a church administrator. Like Linda, he had a natural sense of humour and was easy to listen to. In one of the voice-overs, he cheekily thanked God for the Chinese airplane meal which consisted of only bread and cakes. Linda said apart from sweet things, he was as fussy as a toddler about food. His mother used to pour custard on his vegetables to get him to eat them. Not surprisingly, it turned him off custard for life.

Linda's friend, Pastor Christine Roberts, wife of Pastor Rick, encouraged her to write a grief journal which Linda worked on for almost a decade. Even on the subject of death, Linda managed to make me laugh.

'Etched into my mind was the sight of my man, my big strong man, my lover, my friend, my other half, scrunched into that coffin that was the third cheapest they had,' she wrote. Greg insisted before he died that money shouldn't be wasted on an expensive coffin. 'Get the cheapest one you can!' he'd insisted.

On the day of Greg's memorial service, Linda wasn't sure whether to allow mourners to view his body. Her sister-in-law, Elva, took a photo of Greg (in the coffin) with Linda standing beside him. For some strange reason Elva said, 'Smile!' which Linda did.

'It was a terrible photo. But later on it came in handy with the Department of Transport. Greg had five different vehicles registered in his name. He also had multiple phone accounts. For each one, I had to prove that he was dead with the death certificate. I got sick of the transport people hounding me after a while, so I sent them that photo of me and Greg in the coffin. Do you know, they haven't hassled me ever since?'

Linda put one foot in front of the other after the funeral. Greg had urged her to be stoical and go to China without him so that she could open the foster home. In truth, she wasn't in a fit state to do this.

'I knew there was no way of stopping her going,' daughter Debbie said, 'so my brothers and I didn't even try. We knew it was what Dad wanted, so who were we to question it? We were all grieving, but Mum wasn't in a position to support us in our grief. She had raised us to be strong and confident, so we grieved while she was gone.'

On the eve of the anniversary of Greg's death – 30 November 2015 – Linda posted on Facebook: 'Now that it is 9 years since the heart of my best beloved ceased to beat, I don't think about him as often. I have it down to about 4 times an hour. The pain of loss is not as intense ... I have that down to a gentle ache.'

I have yet to experience that level of grief. In most of our conversations, Linda mentioned Greg often and how he would have felt about something or what he would have said. One time while checking dates with her, I suggested a timeline Greg had mentioned in the voice-over of the DVD newsletters produced prior to his death.

Greg's timeline – because he was talking about something which had just happened – proved correct.

'Don't you hate that?!' Linda responded. 'Greg was always right! How could I possibly doubt him nine years after he went to the other side. Sorry for my muddled brain ... I try hard, but I am not often right ... just ask Greg.'

I never saw Linda depart from her deference to Greg although I knew their relationship wasn't perfect. Whose is? She will forever be his cheerleader. My parents are exactly the same. They would never put the other one down. I found when Linda was really sad about something, she disappeared for a while. The emails went silent, no posts on Facebook. There would be a few quiet days to collect herself before the old sense of optimism returned. As for Greg, I felt his presence hovering about as Linda and I conversed, whether she was in Gympie or Jiaozuo. Sometimes during Skype conversations, all four of her dogs started up a barking chorus. We paused and wondered what had set them off. It was as if Greg was around the corner, making his way up the path from the house. Thankfully, he didn't punch me to get my attention.

Linda mentioned that two children in a room of six in a persistent vegetative state have died in recent years. Actually, let's be honest, she calls them Veggie Kids. She uses outdated terminology to describe disability: mentally deranged, crippled, retarded. They are the words she was brought up with, although she never means them in a derogatory way. She goes searching for the right word, but the old-fashioned ones come into her mind first. From everything we know, she said of the children, they are 'vegetables'. Linda had brought them into the foster home despite the fact very little could be done to heal them. Every day, they are lovingly hauled out of their beds by the ayis, propped up on bean-bags or strapped into wheelchairs.

When you see the Veggie Kids lying on their bean-bags for the first time, perhaps your instinct, like mine would be to run away and cry. They sit or lie, mouths gaping, contorted face muscles, floppy heads, empty eyes staring ahead. The Veggie Kids rarely respond to touch or the sound of a voice. They will not recover and they have no future. But they are cared for.

One of the ayis holds up the head of a pimply-faced girl named Jie Yi. She was seventeen when I saw her in 2013, an age when a healthy teenager expects freedom and new horizons to be just around the corner. But not this teenager. She was a prisoner in her own body and there was no key. I wondered, rather guiltily, whether there was purpose in lying on a bean-bag all day?

Not all the severely disabled kids were in a hopeless or helpless state. Golden Dragon was the proud name given to a boy who wasn't strictly intellectually impaired but didn't talk nonetheless. When I first met him, I thought he was much younger than he was. He was brought to the orphanage in 2007 when he was nine, which seemed so cruel. Nothing was known about his story. His body was contorted like a gnarled tree but he dragged himself, without anyone's help, from the floor to the toys to the dining table. Golden Dragon had epilepsy but as a child it was never treated. He became progressively brain-damaged because of seizures he's suffered all through his life.

Bev Gigney, who ran the COAT foster home some years ago, discovered Golden Dragon by accident soon after he was brought to the orphanage. 'I found him in one of the rooms, hidden away,' she told me. 'He was just skin and bone.'

Golden Dragon had been bound to his cot and there were scars on his wrists. At the time he weighed just 10 kilograms, about the same as a toddler. When Bev went to untie him, she found he had an oozing pressure sore 8 centimetres long on his hip bone. The orphanage ayi told her he was tied to the bed to stop him falling over during seizures. Bev needn't concern herself with him, said the worker, because he's worthless.

Both Linda and Bev were furious when they heard this. They marched into the orphanage and untied his hands and feet. Then Linda burst into Director Sun's office, throwing the ties onto his desk. Director Sun promised Linda that Golden Dragon wouldn't be tied up again.

But a few days later, Bev went back down to the orphanage. There was Golden Dragon – once again tied to the bed.

On this occasion, Linda took the matter to the female official, Miss Teng. She gave permission to take Golden Dragon from the first floor to the foster home, where twenty-four of the orphans lived. Bev personally took charge of him. She began by feeding him small morsels; mashed banana and bits of hard-boiled egg. She also gave him an enema, and from the content of his bowels, she felt convinced he had been purposely under-fed. Bev dressed his wounds and gave him something to eat every hour.

'After seeing him, some visiting groups have said to me, "wouldn't it have been better to leave him? The ayis said he was worthless, why bring him here to the foster home?" And I said "No". He's a person. There is a human inside. You cannot leave children like that,' said Bev.

Three weeks later, Bev lifted Golden Dragon out of bed and dressed him for the day, propping him up against a cushion on the sofa. She disappeared into the kitchen to prepare his food. When she returned, she found Golden Dragon had somehow walked or crawled over to the table and put himself into a seat, ready for breakfast. Bev had to spoon-feed him in those first few months. Later, a large high-chair with a tray was found for him. Bev put pieces of banana on the tray and over a year he learned to feed himself.

'I wish we could save them all,' Bev said. 'But we have to save the ones we are able to save, even if it's one child at a time. If you don't love them, you know, they don't wake up.'

Golden Dragon had the face of an old man. He drooled so much that he wore a bib, devised by one of the foreign volunteers; a hand-towel with a hole cut into the middle for his head to fit through. Golden Dragon turned nineteen in January 2017 although he was the size of a nine-year-old. His erratic

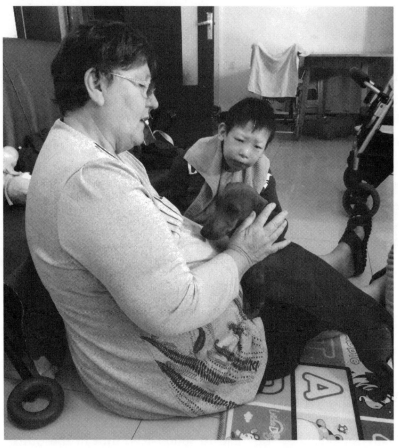

Linda plays with Golden Dragon and her dog Fan Fan in October 2015. Golden Dragon was discovered tied to his bed on the first floor of the orphanage. He was placed in one of COAT's Jiaozuo foster homes where he lived until his death in January 2017 – at the age of nineteen.

arms swung everywhere and his hands were permanently crumpled into fists. He was good at pressing buttons, though.

'He went for telephones, microwaves, the toys. He went missing a couple of times. Then the ayi noticed the lift going up and down stopping at all the floors. After that, whenever we couldn't find him, we knew exactly where he was.'

Although Golden Dragon didn't speak, he understood and followed instructions. He could shuffle and crawl. But he was incontinent. He was never going to live an independent life and he was too old to be adopted.

'The point was,' Linda said going back to our discussion about life and death, 'he was happy and he had dignity.'

Golden Dragon died in January 2017 a few days after his birthday and just prior to moving to the adult welfare centre. His medication was no longer able to prevent the terrible seizures. A small community of Linda's Facebook followers mourned his passing. Linda was thankful he didn't have to endure the trauma of leaving the foster home.

I began to ponder what constitutes a worthwhile life? At what stage do we consider life no longer worth living? In Atul Gawande's excellent book *Being Mortal*, Professor Susan Block, a psychiatry and palliative care specialist says we need to start end-of-life discussions to gauge 'what level of being alive is tolerable'.[1] Her father, with a spinal cord tumour, was willing to live if he was able to eat chocolate ice-cream and watch football on TV.

And what about orphans or the Veggie Kids? Who decides what constitutes a meaningful life if a child itself cannot? I had a photo of Jie Yi, another severely brain-damaged teenager who died recently. When I met her, the ayi turned her face towards mine, so she would look more natural. Her broad pimply face and dark eyes stared vacantly back at me. Going through puberty seemed so unfair.

'She would just lie there,' Linda said of her last few months. 'She kept getting pneumonia. The ayis took her to hospital and she'd get antibiotics. When she was better, she came home to lie on the bean-bag again.'

Linda paused.

'They saved her each time because the hospital staff didn't want to lose face with the foreigners. So the last time she had pneumonia, I told the staff to keep her here at the foster home. Keep her here but make her really comfortable.'

In the last year, Jie Yi was having seizures every twenty minutes and medication made no difference. So the final time she had pneumonia, she didn't go to hospital.

'She died here,' Linda said. 'Peacefully.'

I reminded Linda about her opposition to abortion and voluntary euthanasia, which wasn't surprising given her Christian faith. She thought for a moment.

'The other Veggie Kid who died recently was Chun Tao. Her only joy was eating. Come meal-time, she'd opened her mouth like a bird and the ayi fed her. In the end, she didn't want to eat or drink. She wouldn't even open her mouth. She gave up.'

It was my turn to sigh.

'When Greg was dying,' she continued cautiously, 'he lay there paralysed. He wasn't able to divert the saliva into his stomach, so it filled up his lungs instead. All the doctors' could do was to calculate how long it would take for his lungs to fill up.'

'I could have kept him alive,' she said. 'On a machine.'

In the quiet of that moment, there was a hum and metallic clatter from a nearby construction site. It reminded me that we were in China where too many children are abandoned out of poverty or the stigma of a physical or intellectual impairment.

After the longest pause, Linda gathered her thoughts. 'I didn't want to keep Greg alive that way,' she said.

'His death really influenced my views about life and death. I believe children, because they are innocent go directly to heaven.'

'What is heaven?' I asked.

'Greg used to say that heaven is more than harps and clouds. It is our eternal destination, so we should look forward to it,' she said. 'Losing him changed my world.'

In late 2012 after a medical check-up, Linda was diagnosed with breast cancer. The diagnosis caught her off guard but without hesitating, she dealt with it in the only way she knew. Apart from her immediate family, father Charles whom she was full-time carer to, her three children Debbie, Jason and Damien and their nine children, she had more than 200 orphans and staff relying on her in China. Linda could not afford to take time off to have chemo or radiotherapy. She immediately opted for a double mastectomy at the earliest possible date. A matter of life and death ticked off the list.

After all she had been through, how did she cope with having cancer?

'I went through the breast cancer without any fear,' she said. 'That's because the worst thing that could have happened to me, had already happened. I had lost my soul mate. After that, could anything really be as bad?'

CHAPTER 12

Shenanigans

Death and grief come at inconvenient times. Linda responded to Greg's death in several ways. The most obvious was that her speech was affected for several months. Whenever she tried to talk, the voice that emerged wasn't her own. She laboured through sentences, stumbled on easy words and then sputtered to a halt like a dying car. When her mother Molly died, she stuttered for a year. She also went into a state of depression.

'When you grieve,' she said, 'the solar plexus twists and you need to have hours of unrestrained sobbing to relieve it. You have to precipitate that storm of weeping so that it doesn't happen in a public place, because if it does, it renders you incapable of driving or anything else. I wrote about my grief in a journal in case it was ever useful to anyone. Because if you don't understand what's happening, you will think you are going mad.'

Despite her fog of grief and subsequent depression, Linda was certain of one thing. As Greg insisted on his deathbed, Linda should go to China as they had planned to open the first

COAT foster home for the Jiaozuo orphans. The plane tickets had been booked. Everything and everyone depended on her being there. Though it was less than two weeks since Greg's death, she resolved to travel although her close friends knew she was suffering deeply and should not go alone.

Her friend Margaret Mason, COAT's secretary, saw the depths of Linda's depression over the years. 'Once, when we travelled home from China together, Linda lost her passport on the plane. It was nearly two years after Greg died and Linda went into a complete meltdown, sobbing uncontrollably. She was already on antidepressants and took Valium to help her sleep. When that didn't work, I had to sing her to sleep.'

As Linda slept, the flight-crew called ahead to Australian immigration officials alerting them that a passenger had lost her passport mid-flight.

'The following morning,' said Margaret, 'the passport turned up on a seat. It had fallen out of her bag.'

On another occasion in Gympie, Linda woke to find herself at church. She had somehow driven herself in the car, for quarter of an hour, without any recollection of it. On another occasion, she woke up standing near a gully below the dam on her property. After those incidents, she handed the car keys to her dad.

The sleepwalking happened while she was in China too, said Margaret. 'She used to give me her keys so that she couldn't unlock the apartment door and go out wandering in the middle of the night. Everything just became too much.'

On a visit to Gympie, Linda collects me from the Sunshine Coast airport. As we walk through a lush, tree-filled carpark, I am stopped in my tracks. Her car is a white SUV, completely covered in photos of the orphans' smiling faces and the words: 'Sponsor's needed' 'Change the life of a child' and 'Chinese Orphans' Assistance Team,' in case the acronym is lost on anyone. I am now sitting in the passenger seat of the most attention-seeking car I've ever seen, heading to the home of two of Linda's closest friends, Christine and Rick Roberts.

Chris as she is known, and Rick, were former pastors at Linda's church. Rick had been a close friend of Greg's. Chris is in her sixties with soft, fair hair and serene, almost worried eyes. Rick is a few years younger. It's hard to tell what he's thinking. Together, they exude calm next to Linda's effusiveness and welcome us into their scrupulously tidy home. I get the feeling it would have been that way had we dropped in completely unannounced. With a mug of tea in front of each of us, Chris' brow was slightly furrowed as if she was about to deliver worrying news.

'Let's face it,' Chris said fidgeting with the tightly-held mug of tea, 'I didn't want to go to China. It wasn't a part of the world I wanted to visit. But Linda was in no fit state to go by herself.'

In her role as a senior pastor of the Gympie Christian Family Church, a spiritual counsellor and a minder of souls, Chris knew she could keep an eye on Linda despite her fragile state. In her direct way, Chris said she wasn't 'called' to China, but she was called to Linda.

'It wasn't an easy time,' she began. 'I knew when the volcano was about to erupt or she was going to lose the plot. It was a heart-wrenching time and it meant I would be away from my family at Christmas, but there you go,' she sighed, remembering her reservations – and her own grief brought on by the death of her friend and the church's administrator.

From the outset, Chris found the entire China experience confronting. First there was the journey itself. By 2006,

China's aviation network had evolved since Linda's first visit in 1998. Chinese airlines used brand new Airbuses instead of cast-off Tupolevs from Russia or ancient Boeings. The new generation of planes were clean, the flight network was efficient and prices reasonable. Yet Linda and Chris still travelled to Jiaozuo via an indirect route; flying first to Hong Kong where they stayed in a dreary hostel on Nathan Road, meeting the man who arranged their Chinese visas, taking a train to the Chinese border staying at the railway hotel in Shenzhen (which at least had a comfortable bed and a 'real' toilet, Chris noted) followed by a character-building twenty-four hour train ride on a hard-sleeper (as opposed to the more comfortable soft-sleepers) from Guangzhou to Zhengzhou before finishing off with a five-hour ride on the public bus on the highway crossing the Yellow River before reaching the city of Jiaozuo.

'Why would you choose to travel that way?' I asked, turning to Linda.

Rick was the first to talk. 'Every spare dollar went to the kids. She didn't want to waste it on expensive international flights.'

Chris continued her story. Looking out across the landscape from the public bus, she imagined scenes from the movie, *Mao's Last Dancer*, about the life of Australian–Chinese ballet dancer Li Cunxin discussed in Chapter 4. She remembered the desperate poverty of his home village, something few Westerners could imagine. Now she was glimpsing a similar scene.

'Oh, it was dingy, ramshackled, dirty … and there were just so many people,' were her initial impressions. 'Then we crossed this bridge and there was a traffic accident. The cars involved stopped, but no other vehicles stopped. They just kept making more lanes of traffic. Six lanes of traffic became twelve. It was a nightmare.'

After the challenging journey, the two women barely had time to unpack their belongings in the orphanage hostel when they were summoned to a banquet with the new orphanage official Director Sun. Director Sun had replaced Director Lan, the man who had been the cause of so many conflicts with Linda and COAT. Linda barely knew the new chief. Chris' attention was diverted by the enormous banquet in front of her. It was enough to feed a choir, and yet there were only ten people around the table. She struggled to process this after seeing such poverty during the ride into Jiaozuo. As a newcomer to the country, Chris thought most of the food in front of her was completely alien. Who on earth ate braised chicken's feet?

'I just thought, I can't eat this. But Linda kept telling me I had to, or the officials would be offended! I was just dazed. All I could think of was, What am I doing? What have I done? As for Linda, she was still numb with grief. She was on autopilot,' Chris recalled.

There were more challenges ahead. In setting up the foster home, Linda arranged for Christian volunteers, including a family, to come to Jiaozuo to take charge of the foster children. The idea was they would stay in the foster home for a few months to build a caring, family atmosphere with the twenty-four orphans. The volunteers hadn't been to China before nor did they have any experience in foster care. Instead of creating a homely atmosphere there was instant antagonism between the adults.

'I heard all this shouting one day,' Chris said, 'These two Australian women were having an all-out brawl in the corridor. One of them didn't like the lucky Chinese character poster (which said 'Fu' meaning good luck). She wanted it taken down. I reminded them we had to respect Chinese culture. But it was pretty volatile.'

In the early days, COAT couldn't have existed without foreign volunteers. I asked Linda whether in hindsight, this had been a mistake. In recent years, 'voluntourism' has fallen out of favour, as professional humanitarian commentators point out that the short-term nature of the work doesn't always benefit and sometimes harms the children. Linda concedes she was very green at preparing the volunteers to work in a country like China.

'If I had done a better job in preparation, I am sure that the difficulties we had with some of our volunteers would not have occurred. I had experience running a classroom, not an organisation in a foreign country where there were so many restrictions.'

Apart from witnessing personality clashes among the volunteers, Chris Roberts was about to be given a lesson in orphanage politics.

In building up COAT's China operation, Linda received advice and support from her local manager, the former bright-eyed student translator, Lisa. Lisa had come to the orphanage hostel one night nearly four years earlier, hoping to practise her English. She proved such a committed worker that in 2006 she was promoted to COAT's China manager. Linda also hired Lisa's boyfriend Jackson as the foster-home project took shape. The couple got married just after the home opened. Linda arranged for them to have a room on the staff floor of the orphanage which they gratefully accepted as they had nowhere else to live at the time.

Lisa was always present during any negotiation or discussion with orphanage officials. With Linda's encouragement both Lisa and Jackson became Christians.

Shortly after the opening of the COAT foster home in December 2006, Chris Roberts couldn't believe her ears one day when the new boss, Director Sun, bowled up to Linda in the corridor and told her that she needed to front up with more funds. Lisa translated his abrupt message from Mandarin. His words tumbled out arrogantly and Linda stammered her response. Her husband had died less than two weeks ago. She was doing her best under the circumstances, she had said quietly.

'That's your problem,' he replied, flicking his hand dismissively. 'The orphanage needs more money.'

Director Sun knew Linda was planning to buy a minivan for the foster home. 'If you're doing that, you might as well buy one for the orphanage,' he demanded.

Chris observed the awkward scene without making any comment. When Director Sun turned to leave, she felt the anger rise in her chest.

'I felt like we were these gullible Westerners,' she said shaking her head. 'But what could Linda do? She complied. She had to.'

Every step Linda took, particularly in those vulnerable days after Greg's death, she feared challenging or upsetting the Chinese would cause her to lose the twenty-four orphans who'd been transferred to the foster home. From their clean, comfortably, happy rooms, they could be sent back to an institution. She couldn't face the thought of that. In those days COAT wasn't permitted to have its own bank account because it wasn't officially registered in China. This didn't happen until 2013. However Linda had a personal bank account, so she withdrew 36,000 yuan ($7,200) in cash in order to pay for a 7-seater Daewoo minivan for the use of the orphanage.

Linda and Chris emerged from the bank, carrying wads of carefully counted banknotes, bound up in thirty-six small bundles. On the way back to the orphanage compound they decided to buy some supplies at Jiaozuo's equivalent of David Jones, a luxury department store with the charming name 'Dennis'. Dennis' policy was that handbags must be left at the front desk with a store attendant. Of course, that wouldn't have been the responsible thing to do given the women were carrying so much cash. So Chris, holding the banknotes, waited for Linda outside. People stared at the nervous foreign woman cradling a bulging bag as if it were a precious baby. The money arrived at the orphanage safely and within days Director Sun had his new vehicle.

'That money would have come from donors in Australia and all over the world yet it was used to buy a van for a state-funded orphanage,' Chris said. She was outraged.

As COAT's former treasurer, Greg had been a prudent manager of its finances, even starting an investment fund which in 2005 held $80,000. Half of it was used to fit out the foster home but donations and sponsorships continued to accrue. Now, Linda also had the proceeds of Greg's life insurance policy and his superannuation at her disposal. She decided in order to create a true foster-home environment for the children, she would have to create even more distance from the orphanage, away from the social welfare compound and into a premises out of the clutches of Mr Sun and his cohorts. The foster children would still be wards of the Chinese state, she couldn't change that. But she felt greater independence from the orphanage was paramount.

Jackson and Lisa helped Linda find a suitable apartment in a newly-finished gated complex for Jiaozuo's middle-class residents. It was called Gold Mountain Villas. Buying a property in China in 2007 was like stepping off a platform into a bungy jump. For starters, it was impossible for foreigners to get a mortgage, although in those days Chinese apartments, particularly in a small city like Jiaozuo, were cheap in comparison to Australia. Using some of the money from Greg's life insurance policy, Linda agreed to purchase the apartment for 90,000 yuan ($18,000).

In those days, it was customary to pay in cash for property, so Linda and Lisa went to a Bank of China branch. There, they withdrew a Gold Mountain of Chinese banknotes. The largest banknote in China is 100 yuan, so a machine counted the money into ninety bundles of 1,000 yuan which the clerk re-counted several times. Then he tied the bundles into neat packets which Linda stuffed into a shoulder bag. She left the bank nervously, looking like someone who was just about buy an apartment outright. It was stiflingly hot that day, not unlike a humid Gympie day, so the property agent nominated a restaurant which had air-conditioning. Feeling like an ATM, Linda, Lisa and Jackson took a taxi to the appointment. The taxi-driver, Mr Cai, happened to be someone they used regularly – and therefore a familiar face – but soon the chatter in the taxi went quiet as they found themselves heading down a dark laneway which just didn't feel right.

At the end of the lane, Mr Cai said he couldn't take the taxi any further. Now it was a journey on foot. Linda sweated profusely, a combination of nerves and the heat. She asked Mr Cai to escort her to the restaurant which the agent had nominated. When they reached the restaurant (or more accurately, a shop which sold drinks and instant coffee), it was boarded up and appeared dark inside. Fearing the worst, Linda whipped out her camera and took photos of her surroundings so she might have a record if things turned bad.

Eventually a woman heard their knocking and after some scrutiny, ushered them in, turning on the lights and thankfully, the air-conditioning. Ms Lu, the agent, appeared smiling brightly in her high heels, gold-chained handbag and a short tight dress. Linda nudged her shoulder-bag of money across to her as Ms Lu sipped a green fizzy drink. The young woman began to count the money by hand. Lisa helped her but even then it took almost half an hour. Satisfied that everything was in order, she whipped out a booklet and wrote Linda an official receipt which is an important document in China as the red stamp on a receipt makes it a contract. I remember once when I was a correspondent being given a receipt for a bribe. We filmed at a museum housing dinosaur relics in a small Chinese city and the museum cadres insisted we pay a fee. No pay, no story.

'What will you call this?' I asked the official.

'It's a filming fee, of course,' he replied. He wasn't smiling so much when he realised we filmed the money changing hands.

Apart from presenting Linda with the receipt, Ms Lu took her fingerprints, also in official red ink. In return, Linda photographed the agent's identity card, which Mr Cai also examined closely to ensure it wasn't fake. Counterfeiting wasn't only an issue with Gucci handbags in those days.

Finally feeling a certain sense of relief at the conclusion of the transaction, Linda and her chaperones said their farewell. Now it was Ms Lu's turn to feel nervous. She didn't feel comfortable going to the bank by herself carrying all that cash, she admitted sheepishly. *Would Linda and her friends mind escorting her to the local bank branch?* They did, and eventually Linda was the proud owner of a Chinese apartment. A year later with the help of her son eldest son Jason who travelled to Jiaozuo with her, she bought a second, much bigger apartment which is where she lives whenever she's in China. It cost almost double what she paid for the first one (170,000 yuan or $34,000). Thankfully by 2008 she was allowed to pay via direct debit.

In Gympie one afternoon, Linda was in very low spirits as she arrived at a meeting to sort out her finances in the wake of Greg's death. During the meeting she got a call from Director Sun, the new official-in-charge who'd demanded she buy the orphanage a van. It wasn't good timing. She was depressed and the financial advisor sympathised with her distress as she took the phone-call. After nine years in China, Linda spoke passable Chinese, although she couldn't understand all Director Sun said. The message was in his tone, which was shrill but also seemed quite serious and involved COAT. There had been an incident at the foster home, he said. A resolution was required. He wanted her to come to China immediately.

Bev Gigney, the Australian volunteer at the foster home, also telephoned Linda.

'Lisa's been arrested,' Bev said, completely calm. Linda trusted her implicitly. She exhaled slowly. Lisa was a key staff member, her manager in China. She trusted her too.

'I think you need to get here,' said Bev. 'Quickly.'

As Linda still didn't feel confident to deal with Director Sun on her own, it fell to Chris Roberts to travel with her to China for a second time. Chris bemoaned the fact that most people go to China for the beautiful scenery or attractions, perhaps the Taihang Mountains, the Yangtze River, Shaolin Temple, The Great Wall or The Forbidden City. To this day, Chris Roberts hasn't seen one of them. After Chinese visas were hastily arranged in Brisbane and plane tickets bought, Chris and Linda travelled from Brisbane via Melbourne to Zhengzhou, a thirty-six-hour journey. At least it was the express route and not the overnight train from Guangzhou. Of course, there was still the bus ride to Jiaozuo to follow. Improvements in the highway meant that the journey only took four hours now compared to the previous six.

In Jiaozuo, Director Sun, who, with his receding hairline resembled Mao Zedong in his later life, paced the floor of his office, jabbing the air as he spoke. Sparks of saliva flew from his mouth. 'Against my better judgement,' he shouted in his high-pitched, reedy voice, 'I allowed you to open the COAT foster home.' Now she was bringing shame to the orphanage by the behaviour of HER staff. 'It is a disgrace,' he said, his index finger now wagging in the air. Then he threatened to close down both the school and the new foster home.

By now, Linda had learned the full story. Her two most trusted Chinese staff, Lisa and Jackson, were in deep trouble. Still jabbing the air as he spoke, Director Sun repeated that, HER staff personally caused the whole problem. Now Linda had to fix it. That day was a blur, but everybody at the meeting began to talk on top of each other. Then Linda stopped. She realised that someone whom she respected and loved, Lisa, a sweet, young Chinese woman who had shown her nothing but loyalty since their meeting in 2004, was in police custody.

Bev Gigney, who was in Esperance, Western Australia, when we spoke recalled the incident clearly. Jackson, Lisa's husband, had gone to have a shower near the foster home where twelve girls and their ayi slept. Jackson and the ayi, Miss Xu, had been seen flirting together for a while. After his shower, temptation got the better of him and he decided to act.

In the silence of the darkened dormitory, he and Xu Ayi exchanged a kiss.

A teenage orphan heard them, raised the alarm and immediately ran to fetch Lisa. A commotion ensued as Lisa reached the foster home and learned what her husband had done. She shouted at Xu Ayi and blamed her for initiating the tryst. Eventually, Jackson calmed his wife down, the orphans were settled and after more angry words flew across the halls, people returned to their rooms and the lights went off again.

'It was funny,' Bev said. 'Everyone went back to bed, but I had this inkling that it wasn't settled. Something didn't feel right.'

People had returned to their rightful beds. Everyone except the reliable, demure administrator, Lisa. She waited until everything was still and the children and Xu Ayi were quiet in the dorms. Then she silently made her way upstairs to where Bev's room and the dormitory were located.

Bev heard a loud rattling coming from the kitchen. She realised Lisa was rummaging through a cutlery drawer looking for a knife. As fast as she could, Bev rushed outside to the hallway. There she collided with Xu Ayi, as she fled the dormitory trailing blood. Lisa followed a few steps behind her.

'Xu Ayi locked herself in the office. By the time I got there, Lisa had just lost it. It was completely out of character for her. She was wildly lunging with the knife, trying to stab the ayi through the door.'

Bev phoned downstairs to Tao Mei, the adult orphan who had been Linda's first employee in China. Tao Mei immediately telephoned the police. Then Bev managed to open the office door, grab hold of Xu Ayi's pyjama sleeve and drag her into her bedroom. She could see blood on the young woman's feet but the wound didn't look serious. She left the ayi and went in search of Lisa.

They met eye-to-eye seconds later in the hallway.

'Get out of my way. I'm going to kill her!' Lisa screamed.

'You are not going to kill her,' Bev replied calmly, standing between the wild woman in front of her and the wounded woman in her room.

Lisa brandished the kitchen knife. 'If you love me, you'll get out of my way so I can kill her,' Lisa said.

'Because I love you,' responded Bev as gently as she could, 'I am not going to let you kill her.'

As she and Bev faced each other, the hand holding the knife slowly descended.

For whatever reason, after the initial commotion, Xu Ayi had opted to sleep the opposite way around in her bed. Fortunately because of this, only her legs and feet were cut. Had she slept the other way, she might have been stabbed in the chest or the face.

Bev looked at the crazed woman in front of her. As Lisa's temper subsided, she leaned over and offered Bev the knife.

Xu Ayi now rang her husband, Xiao Wei, on her mobile phone. He went to muster his friends and shortly afterwards, burst into the foster home accompanied by half a dozen men. Now it was Xiao Wei who threatened to kill Lisa.

Once again, Bev positioned herself so that she stood between Lisa and, this time, the six men. Fortunately, they didn't have weapons.

A team of dishevelled police arrived. They arrested Lisa, who was now quiet and dejected, and took her away. Xu Ayi made a dramatic departure to hospital with Xiao Wei and the Gang of Six.

As the volunteer-in-charge of the foster home, Bev Gigney was left to pick up the pieces. Reflecting on the incident, Bev said it marked a turning point for her.

'When I visited Xu Ayi in hospital, I didn't know that the right thing to do was to take lots of milk and eggs and healthy things to help her recover. The husband got very upset about this and wanted to kill me as well as the teenage girl who raised the alarm. I realised after the incident that it wasn't good enough for me to live in China without knowing the language. So after that I went to study Chinese in Xi'an for six months.'

Bev is the same age as Linda. They turn 70 in 2018. She and Linda call each other 'heart sister'. After studying Chinese, Bev remained for several years in Xi'an, the city close to the Terracotta Warriors, and set up the Doves Wings Foster home for the orphans of Xi'an.

Despite the fuss and the blood, the ayi's injury turned out to be a small wound requiring four stitches.

After the night of the long knife, it was time for Linda, with Chris' help, to pick up the pieces.

'You can't keep the children safe,' Director Sun admonished her, 'Your employee is dangerous!' He kept jabbing the air, as if there hadn't been enough drama already.

'If something *more serious* had happened,' he said, avoiding the word death, 'I would have been held responsible.'

Linda was deeply dispirited. She could not deny any of what he said. Jackson and Lisa had behaved appallingly.

'He was going to close us down,' Linda said. 'I had to sort something out.'

One of the junior translators working for COAT, Joyous Li, guided Linda through the difficult days following the stabbing. After many hours of negotiation, Director Sun, Linda and Chris came to an agreement. Lisa and Jackson would have to leave COAT. Lisa was to spend fourteen days in jail and Linda would cover all her legal costs. After that, Lisa and Jackson would have to leave Jiaozuo and find somewhere else to live. After Lisa served her fortnight, the couple relocated to Shenzhen in the south of China near Hong Kong where Jackson's aunt owned an apartment where they could stay. Although distressed by the events, Linda forgave the couple, despite the trouble Lisa had caused. She gave the couple enough money to set themselves up in Shenzhen. That was the end of the affair. Or so she thought. Xu Ayi remained in hospital for at least a week despite having just four stitches in her leg.

'She was a very good actress,' Chris Roberts said. 'I think she was under instructions from her husband.'

To Linda's surprise, an official from the local court insisted the case be heard privately in the hospital room. He arrived wearing an everyday suit instead of the blue uniform of a court official. Apart from interpreting, Joyous Li gave Linda support and advice so that they could finish this business without any harm being done to COAT's work. Soon afterwards Joyous Li and her fiancé, Xiao Ming, took over as Linda's most trusted employees and today, they run COAT's China operations. Xiao Ming is a member of the COAT committee.

When the judicial proceedings started, Chris Roberts felt confused by what unfolded. From the outset it appeared the outcome was a foregone conclusion. 'I think the victim and her family saw this as an opportunity to get money off this big Western woman,' Chris said. 'And the court case, if you can call it that, was only about the money.'

Linda, Joyous Li, Chris Roberts and the husband sat down to discuss compensation. Xiao Wei demanded 50,000 yuan ($10,000) compensation. Linda wasn't a seasoned haggler, even when it came to buying fruit from the street hawkers. She proposed 30,000 yuan ($6,000) whereas Chris felt 10,000 yuan ($2,000) was more reasonable. Linda knew the husband had lost face because another man kissed his wife. It later transpired that he had recently been in jail himself, which was how he knew his way around the judicial system. Eventually it was agreed that Linda would pay Xiao Wei 30,000 yuan and the matter was closed.

At this point, Chris said she wanted to punch the husband. Linda took packets of Chinese banknotes from her handbag and in front of the court official, handed them directly to the schemer.

Then, she mustered all her powers of Christian forgiveness. 'May God Bless you and cause you to prosper,' she said.

'He already has,' Xiao Wei replied cheekily, throwing a bundle of cash to his bed-bound wife. In front of the foreigners, the couple counted the money, disrespectfully holding one or two of the notes up towards the tube lighting to check for counterfeits.

After the case ended, Chris was desperate to return home to her regular life in Gympie. She didn't understand China. She felt angry and upset for Linda, who had paid the compensation and Lisa's costs out of her own pocket. China was becoming one of Chris' least favourite places.

'We had to go and visit that woman in hospital every day. We took her food. We brought her gifts to make her comfortable. We tried everything to placate her husband,' she said shaking her head.

'For what exactly? She had a scratch on her leg and four stitches for goodness sake,' Chris Roberts said. 'And she lay there like the Dying Swan.'

CHAPTER 13

Putting Out Fires

The stabbing marked a decline in the relationship between Linda and Director Sun, the senior official in charge of the orphanage. This was set against the backdrop of huge changes taking place in China as a result of the impending Olympics in Beijing.

When the announcement of China's successful bid came through, tens of thousands of people flooded into Tiananmen Square to celebrate. The whole nation rejoiced in this grand act of recognition. It wasn't simply going to be a spectacular Olympics as one commentator put it,[1] it was 'a statement from 1.3 billion people who (were) seeing their place in the world.' China was fully aware that the games were an opportunity to demonstrate its competence and showcase its rapid economic growth and modernisation to the world.[2]

In the lead-up to China's proudest moment, a raft of business and social regulations were overhauled.

'For so long the West seemed to thrive on making policies about everything. Now China was doing the same thing,' Linda said.

'Within a month, we suddenly had all these notifications that we had to comply with. We had to install fire extinguishers and hold fire drills. We had to pay pensions and insurance for the staff. It was curious because we weren't even officially registered.'

'The Olympic Effect', as Linda dubbed it, vastly inflated COAT's budget. At the time of Greg's death in December 2006, COAT's China operations cost a grand total of A$13,500 per year. By 2014 it had blown out to more than $400,000 chiefly due to staff wages and insurance. It wasn't only Linda's operations that felt the change. All over China, the cost of living was rising. Between 2000 and 2009, the average annual income in the cities almost tripled to more than 17,000 yuan ($3,400).[3]

'People were better paid, they could afford good schools, open a business or buy a home. All of this filtered down through the whole economy,' Linda said.

The Olympic Effect also changed how people felt about themselves and their country. Linda noticed Director Sun and other orphanage officials seemed to have more bravado than previously. There were murmurs in the halls of the orphanage that letting foreigners provide care to abandoned children made China lose face. Foreigners had previously exposed the reality about the state of China's abandoned children. Now China was keen to show this was no longer a problem. After the first national census of orphans by UNSW's Professor Xiaoyuan Shang and her colleagues, China was moving towards a basic living allowance for orphans which came into effect in 2010. In addition to this, throughout the 2000s, foreign adoptions were a lucrative source of income bringing in US$3000 a child. Wasn't China now capable of looking after its own orphans?

After the December 2006 opening of the foster home, one of the girls there contracted Hepatitis A, a virus that affects the liver which is usually spread as a result of poor hygiene such as lack of hand-washing and flies around food. Two other children contracted it, although it was debatable where exactly they picked it up from as they still visited the orphanage every day for schooling, play and therapy.

The orphanage doctors insisted Linda pay for the cost of treating the infected children, which came to 30,000 yuan ($6,000) for two months' hospitalisation. She was furious about this as she knew the hygiene standards in the foster home were far superior to that of the orphanage. In the foster home, there was a hand-washing policy after going to the toilet and before eating. Fly-screens cut down the number of flies. In the end, the volunteer Mum Jenny isolated the girls in her own bedroom. The Chinese doctors arrived each day to give intravenous medicine to the girls, making a show of not touching anything in case they became infected with the disease themselves.

Director Sun imposed harsher rules on the volunteers. For example, they couldn't invite friends to visit without his permission. The foster home became a battle of wills.

'I wanted to get more kids out than we could fit into the fifth floor. I wanted to get out from under Sun's roof to where he had less control over our everyday movements. He was driving me nuts with his petty policies channelled from Beijing.'

Linda began a series of negotiations with Director Sun to open additional foster homes away from the orphanage. She negotiated the Chinese way by inviting Sun and other government officials to a good local restaurant where they feasted on abalone, smoked-duck and hand-made noodles. Then she invited them all to a dinner at the new apartment she'd bought in Gold Mountain Villas. She fitted out the sixth floor apartment for sixteen non-mobile children from the orphanage. They had to climb the stairs by gripping the rails and pulling themselves up. It was a long process, but Linda's eldest son, Jason, was visiting at the time and he did whatever heavy lifting was required. Eventually with a bit of help, all of the children managed to reach the sixth floor.

A girl named Ting Ting who was ten and born with cerebral palsy was in the first group. Linda had met her in the first orphanage when flies swarmed around her dirty face. She was left by the orphanage workers in a potty chair all day. Ting Ting was just one of many 'beacons' for Linda. If this child could have a joyful dignified life, it was worth every drop of sweat.

Linda bought desks and turned the lounge area into a school room. She designed the curriculum herself, hired a teacher and taught her how to cater for children of all different levels. The teacher proved excellent at her job and taught the children manners, how to dress and feed themselves, how to care for their belongings, to appreciate books and respect each other's equipment. She even managed to toilet train some of them.

The children, according to Linda, were 'over the moon' in their new home. They had immediate access to books and toys and a place at the head of their beds to put their own clothes and belongings. In the orphanage, everything was communal and toys and books belonged at school. Linda employed two ayis to supervise them and once again, invited Director Sun to the home so that he could witness the orphans in their clean clothes and see their smiling faces.

In 2008 the second, larger apartment in Gold Mountain Villas was filled with nineteen children including Wen Xuan, the boy in the wheelchair whom I met at the airport. They were cared for by a volunteer Mum named Joy who ensured the children ate a healthy diet and drank plenty of water, which was something the orphanage kids rarely got. Orphanage staff didn't like it when they drank too much water because it usually meant more washing and cleaning up after them. The volunteer Dad, Noel, made high chairs for all the children so they could sit with large trays and learn to feed themselves. The sponsor of a little girl with muscular dystrophy, Bai Hua, sent her a spoon with a curved handle and a plate with a suction cup so that it didn't slide off the tray. Volunteer Mum Joy mashed her food up at first and slowly Bai Hua learned to feed herself. Within a few years, she was able to eat regular meals.

'That would never have happened if she had remained in the orphanage,' Linda said. 'She thrived by having a "family" for the first time.'

Then Linda leased three more apartments in Gold Mountain Villas. The last one she turned into a school, hiring four teachers and providing all the teaching materials and furniture.

'It felt great,' Linda said. COAT had seventy-five orphans living in foster homes. 'I was determined to get as many kids as possible living in the community. I wanted to get right out from Director Sun's power.'

Linda and Greg's dream for the children was now unfolding in front of her. The costs of leasing and fitting out the apartments, hiring new staff and buying more equipment was soaring. Linda needed $35,000 per month. She felt confident, as long as she had three months of funding, that she could manage to stay on top of everything COAT now managed.

In June 2010 the Jiaozuo orphanage relocated once again, this time to a shiny, modern, ten-storey building in the eastern section of Jiaozuo city after a five-year building program initiated by the Chinese government. Called the Blue Sky Implementation Plan, it was devised after former Chinese President, Hu Jintao visited a Beijing orphanage in 2006 and made one of the few statements about orphans ever uttered by a Chinese leader.

'They are the weakest and neediest group in our society. They need the most care and love. Party committee and government at all levels must put these special children in their hearts – improve their care and education. We must mobilise the whole society to share in care and love for the orphans. We must bring them to the same level as other children, to live and grow happily under the same blue sky of the motherland as us all.'

The new welfare compound was located on a major road, the People's Avenue. The feeder lane leading up the gatehouse was lined with small willow trees and peach blossom bushes. A small lake surrounded by drooping willow fronds stretched in front of the courtyard and there was plenty of open space for the children as well as a brightly coloured playground with a log-cabin cubby house. On the front of the building was a logo with a person growing out of a hand, like a sprouting seed and a motto in Chinese: 'Everything for children. Always have consideration for children.' Joy of joys, the building was ten storeys high, tall enough for a lift. The orphanage had entered the 21st century.

The COAT school was re-located to the fifth floor of the new building. Invited to Director Sun's new office, Linda expressed satisfaction with all of the progress so far. Director Sun's office was less grandiose than his previous room in the old compound. This one was small and practical, lit by neon tubes overhead while pipes and wires poked out from the wall nearest the window to accommodate the air-conditioning.

Linda complimented him on the new orphanage, noting its excellent location on a major thoroughfare. There were wheat fields all around them, but soon, they too would be replaced with high-rise buildings. She told Director Sun she felt certain the children would be happy in their new home.

Apart from the school, COAT was given a free lease on the tenth floor of the building where Linda planned to fit out six small foster-home apartments, each for six to ten children with their ayis. There was also going to be a small residence for long-term volunteers and short-term visitors. Her plan was to move as many children as she could afford to, out of the orphanage and into foster care.

As Linda explained her ideas with her logistics manager Xiao Ming translating, Director Sun picked up a pen which he began to roll around his fingers. It was a little disconcerting. Then he returned it to the ornate pen-holder in front of him and leaned back in his large, faux leather office chair, by far the grandest item in his office. He smiled and for a change, looked directly at Linda.

'A decision has been made,' he began. Xiao Ming translated his words. 'The Ministry of Civil Affairs has decided that COAT is no longer to run the school connected to this orphanage. We are capable of operating the school now. The orphanage is now in charge.'

Linda felt as if her chair had fallen through the floor. She was stunned but also didn't really believe it at first. Was this yet another power play? Would the plan see the light of day? Was it really happening? Linda felt powerless. Everything – including the first foster home – had been relocated to this new building including all the equipment in the school which COAT had paid for. COAT was funding almost twenty staff at that stage. What would happen to them? As it transpired, the government agreed to take over their wages.

The only thing Linda would have any control over was the apartment school in Gold Mountain Villas with its twenty-four students and four teachers.

She felt helpless. And furious. After twelve solid years working to improve the lives of the Jiaozuo orphans, was this how it was going to end?

After the school was handed over, Linda ran a smaller operation with two volunteers looking after the foster homes on the tenth floor of the orphanage building and the apartments in Gold Mountain Villas. By this time, she was spending longer stretches in China as she'd retired from teaching. At the time Linda was forced to hand over the school, COAT was opening more foster homes, so it wasn't difficult to absorb the forty-eight staff, but what, she wondered, had changed in the minds of the officials? After operating successfully for six years, why did government officials want to take over this tiny school which, in the grand scheme of things, was not that significant? Linda thinks it was a straightforward issue of 'face' so that the orphanage could demonstrate to its highest officials that they didn't need the help of foreigners.

I wondered whether she had felt like pulling out at this stage?

'I have never felt like pulling out. I've felt frustrated and sometimes disappointed, but it's a given that I will never pull out. Not until I die.'

Over the following months, COAT volunteers began to notice significant changes to how the school was run. Children began returning to the foster homes at odd times. Sometimes, the teachers were absent for the entire day. Linda's admin staff discovered that the new teachers hired by the orphanage were actually office workers from the orphanage so they weren't trained to teach the children anything.

The children did drawings and watched DVDs in the classroom. The new teaching staff found the special needs orphans irritating and decided that it was enough to keep them quiet and occupied. The school which Linda and Greg Shum, donors, volunteers, staff and ayis had built up over the years became little more than an unruly child-care centre.

What truly broke Linda's heart was that after all this time investing in the education of children whom the orphanage at first insisted couldn't learn, the children were indeed falling well behind in their studies. Even the faster learners were found to be no more advanced than Grade One.

Yuan Lihai was a street-vendor who rescued abandoned children and cared for them in her home. She began to rescue children in the 1980s after a local hospital paid her a few dollars to dispose of an infant's body. The boy had been born with a cleft palate, which could have been fixed by surgery. She discovered that he was still breathing. He became the first baby she took into her care. Over the years, she housed and nurtured more than 100 abandoned, disabled children. Although her home was unregistered and received no assistance from the government, children were sometimes brought to her at the recommendation of welfare authorities.[4]

Ms Yuan's home, less than 200 kilometres from Jiaozuo, was a squalid shack, but it was all she could afford. Nearly forty children lived there suffering from various conditions including albinism, mental illness and cleft palates. Some of the children couldn't use their hands, so they simply ate their food off the dirty carpet. Toddlers slept on straw or filthy bedding. When babies died, Yuan Lihai asked an old farmer to bury them discretely in the surrounding fields.

When a fire broke out in Ms Yuan's home in January 2013, witnesses say the flames spread quickly through the structure until it was completely engulfed. Seven children under the age of six died.

Social media went off like a firecracker. One lawyer blamed the lack of a coherent welfare policy saying, 'The government should be responsible for the care of orphans.'[5] The fire also sent waves of panic through China's welfare administrators. Questions were asked about why officials had tolerated, and in some cases facilitated, Yuan Lihai's care of children.

Within a few months, the central government in Beijing responded with an edict called a Notice on Further Strengthening Work with Abandoned Babies 2013. It reiterated the importance of regulating the care of abandoned children by NGOs. This included COAT. After hearing this, manager Joyous Li telephoned Linda in a panic. She said officials were threatening to send all orphans back to their original welfare institutions because foster homes were now considered dangerous.[6]

Linda hadn't heard Joyous Li so anxious before and was horrified at the thought of losing her Chinese kids. She knew the big hand of Beijing had the power to shut COAT down completely.

All she cared about, was that the children in her care – who came from seven different welfare institutions around China – would not be sent back to their original orphanages. She wanted them to stay in her foster homes and continue to thrive and get an education.

After the fire, Linda boarded a flight to China in April 2013 to try to save her orphans and what remained of COAT. She was prepared for the worst while hoping for a miracle.

Once again, she sat down in Director Sun's office. There was a flurry of meetings with government officials who arranged inspections of COAT's facilities. They examined fire prevention, evacuation procedures and everything to do with safety.

'We passed with flying colours,' said Linda.

Then, in a large meeting room just behind the dormitories of the older orphanage children, Director Sun and a group of officials lined up on one side of a conference table with Linda and COAT's secretary, Margaret Mason, and other volunteers on the other. It was like the start of a joust. However, the resolution was that COAT could keep its foster homes on condition that it take back the administration of the school. The government would fund two qualified teachers but COAT had to foot the bill for the other seventeen teaching staff.

'I knew we couldn't afford it,' said Linda. 'but it was that or go home to Australia and leave the kids with nothing. I couldn't do it. So I said "Yes!" We were given a lease on the seventh floor to turn it into a "good school", Director Sun said.'

Apart from setting up the school, again, COAT was also going to be officially registered. No other foreign NGO in a regional Henan province had been registered before, so this was breaking new ground.

Director Sun proposed a respected man he knew of to become COAT's local director. Linda had no idea who this person was, so the following day she sought out former director Mr Gong to see if he might be interested. Mr Gong was in his early sixties and had retired from the orphanage a few years ago, but he had known Linda since meeting the Christian volunteers at Zhengzhou airport in 1998. Mr Gong was not initially enthusiastic about Linda's idea.

'He said if anything went wrong, because we were foreigners, he would be the one that would go to prison or even be executed because that's the Chinese way.' However after further thought he decided to take the risk because of their long friendship and the trust they shared.

Director Sun accepted the proposal. Linda chose Michelle Baumgartner, a colleague from Bundaberg in Queensland as education co-ordinator. With her mother, Carolyn Wood, Michelle would take charge of staff training to get the school into shape. Director Gong chose the new name of the school and foster homes and Linda approved them. He said the word 'dream' was currently a word that was in vogue. In fact 'The Chinese Dream' was a phrase coined by President Xi Jinping in his inaugural speech in 2013, so having 'dream' in the title would be looked upon favourably by government departments. Now COAT in China was part of a registered Chinese company with an official special needs school known as Linda's Dream Children's Home.

'We would have to worry about finding the money to pay the wages later,' said Linda.

Within a year, the school was running so well, it expanded to another floor to include babies and intellectually-impaired children, eventually including *some* of the forty-four children tied into beds on the first floor of the orphanage. These were the children 'rocking for self stimulation, masturbating, making meaningless noises, smelling badly from staying all day in their own mess,' Linda said. At least some of them would now have the chance to be untied, given a shower and brought to 'school' in the day-care classes.

'We want them all to get a turn to come to school,' Linda said of the orphans on the first floor. 'It was just another battle to be fought.'

After the ceremony to celebrate the official registration of Linda's Dream Children's Home, a commemorative photograph was taken in the courtyard playground. In the photo, Linda sits on the ground, surrounded by her happy children, although unusually for her, she is dressed completely in white.

'Of course, no-one told me before the photo was taken that wearing all white is for funerals in China,' she chuckled.

CHAPTER 14

Jiaozuo Today

'Sleep well?'

Linda's head appears around the door. It's October 2013 and I'm in Jiaozuo.

My bed wasn't designed for 'contemporary luxurious comfort' as I noted on an advertising billboard. It was hard, but notwithstanding that, the sleep had been good.

Linda hands me her specialty, a Lindaccino; a frothy, instant coffee, half boiling water, half milk. It goes down really well. In a land where espresso machines are not a priority in every home, you have to learn to adapt. *When you enter a village you should follow its customs* as the Chinese saying goes, which means I should probably opt for green tea. But some daily habits are hard to break.

We arrived on the public bus from the airport during the late afternoon on the previous day, crossing the bridge over the Yellow River, hurtling past villages until the countryside became suburbs. Then we were in this vast, but empty city, built several times too large to allow for growth. Wen Xuan, the boy I called Oliver, fell asleep, so there was no repeat of the motion-sickness he suffered on the outbound journey. At one stage we were all made to get off the bus at a petrol station in the middle of nowhere. Wen Xuan's wheelchair was in storage under the bus, so he clambered into Linda's arms. I was slightly perturbed when the bus drove away. Apparently it was just doing a circuit and after refuelling, we lumbered back on board.

Joyous Li and Xiao Ming met us at the bus station. It was strange to finally meet them in the flesh as they had so far been characters in someone else's story, but I knew the formality would evaporate over the coming days. Xiao Ming dropped us at the entrance to Linda's building in Gold Mountain Villas before returning Wen Xuan to his foster home at the orphanage compound across town.

Gold Mountain Villas did not deserve its name. There was rubbish in the laneways which had the smell of over-ripe fruit. While some of the flowerbeds had been turned into vegetable patches, others were scruffy and abandoned. The buildings needed a fresh coat of paint. Advertising posters were pasted everywhere across the top of each other. And people parked their trikes and scooters in any available space. Electrical boxes spewed out their innards and the wires overhead revealed spaghetti junctions. I wondered how you would find anything in a blackout. As the building was only six storeys tall, there was no lift. At the top of each flight of stairs, a clap of the hands or stamp of the foot activated sensor lighting. It didn't always work so you'd have to stamp and clap like a Flamenco dancer. As we puffed our way up, a light appeared at the top of the stairs. And then the metal safety door swung open. Facing us was a beaming middle-aged ayi. We were inside Linda's large, warm apartment which also served as a foster home to eight of the older boys.

Every orphan comes with a story. There was a lanky, eighteen-year-old named Li Hong, who was healthy and disability free. His father was a criminal on the run who took Li Hong and his sister with him then left them in the care of a sex worker on the other side of China. When his father was caught and jailed, the siblings returned to Henan to live with their maternal grandparents. The grandparents didn't want to care for them so the children become wards of the state, although the grandmother never allowed either sibling to be adopted. Xiao Li is a smiley eleven-year-old with cerebral palsy, Tu Tu, also eleven, has a cleft lip and palate as well as learning and emotional difficulties, while Little Chang was a boy from a local family who had brain damage. He needed to attend a special school and was rejected by public schools over the years. He lived here during the week and attended the COAT school, returning to his family on weekends.

As I looked closely at the boys' faces, I noticed two who appeared in virtually all the videos since Linda's first visit to Jiaozuo in 1998. They were babies, then toddlers, and now here there were, nearly adults. Pang Li, now sixteen, contracted Hepatitis B at birth. It's an infectious and inflammatory disease of the liver, transmitted by exposure to body fluids. He's one of 120 million carriers in China (one-third of the world's total) and while he doesn't show any symptoms, Hep B victims face huge discrimination because there's widespread ignorance about how it's spread. When he was seven, doctors wanted to keep Pang Li in permanent isolation. The staff were terrified at first and washed all of his clothes and utensils separately until they were educated about how to deal with it.

Shan Shan, also sixteen, has spina bifida and suffered though numerous failed operations to correct his club feet when he was a child. Now nearly an adult, he dragged his heavy feet as if they were concrete blocks.

'*Ni Hao Nai, Nai!*' 'Grandma! How are you?' the boys greeted her.

Linda was the only foreigner living in the complex which wasn't surprising because I'd only ever seen one, maximum two other foreigners in Jiaozuo. 'Local people thought I was very rich to afford such a large apartment outright,' said Linda, giving me a tour of her 'penthouse' which she gave to COAT as a gift. It was certainly spacious even by Western standards, although not especially flash. I thought the team from *The Block* might be able to work some miracles here. The Chinese kitchen amazed me. It was about the size of two shower cubicles, with a portable double-burner, a microwave and a rickety tap over the sink. The fridge had to go outside where there was a dining table, shelves for the vegetables and fruit, and a living area. There were also four narrow dormitories where the boys slept in bunk-beds. Linda kept the upstairs section (two bedrooms, a bathroom and a terrace) for herself and visitors like me.

The apartment served as one of eight foster homes that COAT managed. Eight male orphans (aged ten to nineteen) lived there with their ayi, whose job it was to cook, clean and keep the boys in line.

Linda taught me her way to prepare instant coffee. We were the only ones drinking it. The boys and the ayi drank tea or hot water. Though you can buy Nescafé in China, it's still considered a luxury item and so Linda brings hundreds of sachets from Australia each visit to ensure she doesn't run out. By far the most important piece of equipment in a Chinese kitchen is the boiling water dispenser. For a Lindaccino it's a sachet of cappuccino powder into a mug. One-quarter of the cup is filled with boiling water. Then she snips the corner off a palm-sized plastic bag, which is how the local milk comes. It's worth learning the Chinese characters for 'fresh milk' because the sweetened yoghurt container looks exactly the same. The only difference is a red Chinese character in front of 'fresh milk' which says '*suan*' meaning sour. The secret to a decent froth given there is no machine is a vigorous stir with a wooden chopstick. Et voila, the Lindaccino is complete.

I was acclimatising to China. Not normally a fan of instant coffee, the Lindaccino became a treasured ritual that I looked forward to. Two years later when Linda went on a strict diet by order of her Gympie doctor, she stopped making Lindaccinos for herself. Instead she began to eat her coffee; sprinkling it over oatmeal, a handful of fresh mulberries and a splash of milk.

For the boys, breakfast at the apartment was hard-boiled eggs with leftovers from dinner: noodles with meat and vegetables if there was any left, cold bread (bought for dinner) and rice porridge. They seemed to love the tasteless rice congee, dispensing with spoons and slurping it noisily from bowls. The boys got a daily serve of sweet yoghurt, and unlike me, they all knew the correct package to take from the fridge. No Cornflakes, Sugar Pops or Weetbix in sight. By the time Linda and I arrived at the table, breakfast had usually run out after the boys had eaten and gone to school. This was a good excuse to have breakfast out and get a taste of the world outside.

Linda's apartment is in a private compound for Jiaozuo's rising middle class. Gold Mountain Villas consists of twelve blocks of units placed around children's playgrounds, convenience shops and what was once a large man-made lake. Linda thinks someone might have drowned in the lake as it has been drained, permanently. This created a huge smooth space on the lake-bed a metre below ground-level. By 6 am every day of the week, the lake bed is filled with different groups doing some form of communal exercise to music from a ghetto blaster. Middle-aged women dressed in wine-coloured *kung fu* outfits, practice *tai chi* in a corner of the lake. Their leader wears a set of pale pink pyjamas. She is incredibly flexible and graceful and her team is in perfect sync. It's so much more calming than the earnest bootcampers who take over the beach near my home. In the West, keeping fit involves so much effort. But the scene unfolding here is so Tao. Even an oldies exercise group is here, swinging their arms like windmills, patting their bodies all over and walking backwards. By 8 am people start to pack up their belongings and head off on their bicycles and scooters. The lake-bed is empty until late afternoon when it belongs to the schoolchildren.

On the western side of Gold Mountain Villas (for some reason, one is always more compass-aware in China, because that's how everyone describes where things are) is the neighbourhood food street known as Auspicious Cloud Street. By 8 am, the street is humming. Life and commerce spill out of hole-in-the-wall production booths. Everywhere you look, people engage in industry. No one loiters. There are no beggars. Jiaozuo people like to make things. They aren't snobbish like people from Beijing or Shanghai. They are proud of where the city has come from and excited by where it is going.

A new beauty shop called 'Hermia' celebrates its opening. Sixteen beauticians line up outside the front of the shop and take part in calisthenics. They are dressed in their uniforms: pink jackets and black pants for the managers and white lab coats with nurses caps for the beauty workers.

Workplace exercise was brought in by Chairman Mao during the Communist era. In 1951 when the average life expectancy in China was only thirty-five, Mao urged people 'to strengthen [their] body to protect [their] homeland'. Exercises were devised for the masses and broadcast over the radio. Known as the People's Radio Calisthenics, the program has undergone updates since its inception. Briefly dropped in the lead-up to the 2008 Olympics, it's back with a vengeance.[1] Many companies insist their workers exercise in front of the workplace just as they do at Hermia.

Music roars from the shop's loudspeaker. It is synthesized, has a disco-beat and a stern vocalist calling the moves. Out in front, the manageress leads her team in an elaborate routine which is exhausting just to watch. She has a no-nonsense pageboy hair-cut and knows every step. And though cars and scooters honk as they pass by this scene, not a single hair is out of place. Nor are the buttons on her smart pink jacket ever undone.

Outdoor exercise undertaken by beauticians on Auspicious Cloud Street in Jiaozuo. (Author photo)

We watch the calisthenics from the side of the road. The beauticians go back to work into their pink shop and the street begins to unfold in front of us: a Lego city coming to life. On either side of the road, people work hard at preparing food. Every kiosk, stall, or hole-in-the-wall has a specialty and China's army of ordinary people, the *Lao Baixing* or Old One Hundred Names, work the woks, burners and rolling pins. Apart from *bing* (a sesame-topped flat bread), they prepare fresh *baozi* (steamed buns with pork in the centre) in round silver steamers stacked up into a tower as tall as a man. Other shops make *jiaozi* (dumplings stuffed with meat, vegetable, prawn or a combination), fresh, floury, hand-pulled noodles and *youtiao*, a twisted length of dough, puffed up in a deep-frying wok. Everywhere you can smell purpose.

One morning we sit down at a brown stall. The tables are brown, it sells brown soup with bits of brown-skinned beancurd and sliced brown shiitake mushrooms. The soup (apparently it's very popular for breakfast) comes out in a plastic bowl which is covered with a plastic bag, either to ensure cleanliness or save on the washing. I tentatively pull apart the disposable chopsticks, hoping they don't stock 'recycled' ones.

Hygiene, especially at roadside food stalls, is still an issue in most parts of China. In the brown shop, there is a single cold-water tap at the back of the stall and the dishwasher is of the human variety. I confess to Linda that I am not very fond of the brown soup. She eats everything in front of her, uncomplaining. Then amid all the brown, I see a man in blue, a blue lab coat. He's a human factory, rolling oblong slabs of dough the shape of a large domino. He presses the dominos together, rolls them a bit more, then he cracks an egg between the two.

'Could you do that with two eggs?' I ask. I speak fluent Chinese when it's to do with food.

Daily food preparation on Auspicious Cloud Street where people are so industrious. These round snacks are *baozi*; steamed buns with a pork filling. (Author photo)

The author having breakfast at the brown stall. While she didn't particularly enjoy the brown soup, she loved the double-egg dough pockets. (Linda Shum)

'Two eggs inside one pocket? Easy,' he says, cracking a second egg.

The dough pocket goes for a bubbly swim in the giant wok. When it's the colour of a croissant, he turns it over. Using long, wooden chopsticks, he plucks it out and rests it on a sieve. This is definitely what I tell my daughter is 'sometimes' food. But the double-egg bread pocket beats any other fast food I've had. The perfect breakfast on the run.

'How much for 500 grams of strawberries?' I ask a vendor.

She pauses, which means she is about to double the price.

'30 yuan' ($6) she replies.

'How about 15?'

'Ok sure.'

Over the next week, this strategy yields results. Five days later, I managed to get half a kilo of strawberries for 8 yuan. ($1.50)

Linda never bargains when she goes shopping. She believes people should just tell her the correct price. If the vendor asks for 30 yuan ($6) when she should have paid 8 yuan, she always hands it over. But she's had to bargain at other times. The director of the orphanage asked Linda to bring medicine from Australia for his wife's rheumatism. Though Director Sun doesn't normally trust her, Linda complied and brought the rheumatism medicine for Mrs Sun. Over the years, Linda has also bought the equivalent of a container load of infant milk formula for the grandson of the Chinese director of COAT, Director Gong. He still asks, even though the boy is now five. In China, imported baby formula is gold since the tainted milk scandal of 2008 in which six babies died and thousands fell ill after consuming melamine-contaminated formula. Both directors offered to pay Linda for her trouble, but she didn't accept it. Instead she asked to take three little girls out of the orphanage for placement in her foster homes.

That's a better bargain that the strawberries.

Linda doesn't have a Chinese driver's licence. She would have to sit a multiple choice exam (in English) and spend around 5,000 yuan ($1,000) to get one, but really, given China's road safety record, I think it is a smart move not to. This doesn't mean she doesn't drive though. She has bought several vehicles for the orphanage and for COAT, but for getting around herself, she first purchased a maroon-coloured electric trike.

Linda's trike had a passenger seat. I was the passenger. And here's the tricky part. Although she didn't have a driver's licence

Linda Shum taking an urgent phone-call on her way to the orphanage. She uses the 'bicycle' lane which accommodates slow-moving vehicles including electric cars, scooters and trikes. (Author photo)

and the roads are pretty terrible, you don't need a licence to own or operate an electric bike, trike, scooter or car. E-vehicles are considered bicycles, presumably because they can't go faster than 40 kilometres an hour. Apart from the roads and highways, it's legal to use the e-car on the pedestrian crossings to cross the road.

Recently, Linda decided to upscale the trike to an electric car (think Mr Bean) just before e-trikes were banned by the Jiaozuo government in 2015. Bans happen periodically. For a while, bikes and trikes were legal, e-cars were not. Still, there are hundreds if not thousands of them on Jiaozuo's roads today. Linda loves her gold dodgem car. If she happens to see a policeman, she just smiles.

The Alert Driving website declared that, 'China's Drivers [are] among [the] worst in the world.' There are more than 150 million private cars in China and 300 million drivers[2] many of them (literally millions) with very little driving experience. These days, China is the biggest producer and consumer of electric vehicles in the world. 35 million are sold each year slashing around 42 million tons of carbon emissions.

Chinese authorities frequently release video of grisly road accidents in a bid to scare people. The evening news once aired a story, which wouldn't be allowed on Australian TV, featuring a car hitting a man who was running across an expressway. The running man flew into the air and somersaulted like an acrobat before falling to earth and hitting the windscreen of a second car. It was replayed in slow motion over and over again. Today it would be called a GIF.

Once, Linda was in her electric car, driven by her granddaughter Ebonnie, who was fifteen. They were nudged by a bus, enough to dent both vehicles. Within minutes, the whole of Jiaozuo had stopped to have a look. The bus driver and Linda began to haggle (which Linda doesn't normally do) over compensation.

'I told him 500 yuan ($100) or nothing. I just didn't want the police to come,' she said.

After handing over the money, Linda drove away with Ebonnie. That's what you do in China when you are a foreign driver. It's doubtful the bus company ever saw the cash. That's a month's salary for some people.

Outside the gates of Gold Mountain Villas one afternoon, a row of brand new scooters are for sale.

If I were living in China, I asked myself, *which one would I choose?*

I settled on a scooter covered in a black and white cow print.

'Go on!' said the young woman handing me a brochure. 'You should definitely buy that one. It looks so nice. It matches your clothing.'

That fancy e-scooter was $675, but there was no way I could bring that home.

I told the sales lady, 'I don't think they are legal in Australia.'

'Do they use scooters in Australia? I've heard it's a very beautiful country. I would like to visit one day.' It was a familiar refrain. Virtually every Chinese person I met said that.

Then the sales lady sighed.

'Australia is a big country with a small population. We have too many people in China.'

Everybody says that too.

The Jiaozuo orphanage is 8 kilometres — thirty minutes by e-trike — from Gold Mountain Villas. The commute became one of my favourite parts of the day. Linda was a cautious and courteous driver, calling *Ni hao* to the gatemen before merging into the bicycle lane on the edge of the six-lane main thoroughfare, The People's Avenue. As the e-trike picked up speed, I caught glimpses of different Chinese scenes: corner

The author poses beside an electric scooter on sale outside Gold Mountain Villas. She eventually decided against buying it. (Linda Shum)

markets, rich kindergarten children waiting for the schoolbus, a man with a pair of turtles wrapped in such a way as to suggest they were not pets. And then there were the people in motion; on carts, in cars, on buses, and a solitary man on a mountain bike wearing bike shorts, the first time I'd seen this in China.

We came to a notable corner block with the Holi-land cake shop on the ground floor – with its six-tiered wedding cakes on display. Above that, a large neon sign advertised The Love Hotel: $6 for two hours. From then on, I called that part of town the 'have your cake and eat it' corner.

Everywhere there were families out on scooters. Three people on one scooter. It became a game: father, mother and daughter. Then mother, father and son and various permutations. Soon, I began to notice that many of the families didn't have just one child; many of them had two. This was before the one-child policy officially ended in 2015. I'm guessing that the policy was applied more liberally here, given it's a smaller city.

Less than a decade ago, much of Jiaozuo was rural. Even today, in between the building sites are fields. The fields used to grow wheat or corn. Old grindstones impossible to dump make good seats for the food stalls. Now instead of corn, the fields grow pylons. Like many places in China, Jiaozuo city has boxed up its past, tied rocks to it and let it disappear under the quicksand of industrialisation.

As we moved through the orderly streets, all around us daily necessities were being transported. Country women with wrinkly faces on e-trikes ferried strawberries and plum tomatoes from the surrounding villages. On the pedestrian islands, young women wearing make-up handed out flyers advertising luxury linen and deluxe furniture. Lots of people on scooters also chatted on their mobile phones while waiting for the traffic lights to count down the seconds to green.

When I first told a Chinese friend I was going to Henan,

he told me Chinese people often told jokes about it. Henan people had a reputation as scammers and fools. CCTV, China's state television network, once featured a gang of criminals portrayed by actors speaking in the Henan dialect. I discovered that many bad headlines did indeed emerge from the province: scandals involving tainted blood and HIV, the foster-home fire and fraud. It's true, Jiaozuo people are not as affluent and lack the brashness which characterises the new rich of China's megacities. They look and sound a bit rougher and their spoken Chinese has an earthiness to it. But they retain a kindliness and slight naïveté which has virtually disappeared in the big cities. Often on Auspicious Cloud Street, Linda and I were offered free drinks and food simply because people wanted to make us feel welcome. No-one in Jiaozuo ever tried to rip me off.

After a day out in the city, we returned to face the six flights of stairs, the ayi and the boys in foster home Number One. Dinner was waiting; thick white noodles and minced pork flavoured with dark, rich vinegar. Linda says she likes her food tasty. From a shelf up high, she took down a packet of Australian Parmesan cheese (she's brought twenty packets with her from Gympie) and sprinkled it liberally all over her noodles, pork and vinegar.

Exhausted, I excused myself. Before closing the curtains, I peered across to the apartment opposite where a family ate dinner at a small table, the television on in the background. Here was another two-child family. Why was this staring me in the face, when downstairs were a group of boys relinquished by their parents? As I threw back the duvet on my hard bed I could hear construction somewhere in the distance. It reminded me of something I'd read: that in the space of two years, China had used more cement than the United States used during the entire 20th century. Too. Much. Detail. I drifted off to what sounded like elves' hammers working deep into the night.

CHAPTER 15

Uninvited Visitors

The orphanage occupied the first three floors of the welfare building where about 200 children live. On the fourth floor was the Show Hope Special Care Centre which Linda made a point of mentioning we would not get permission to go into. The rest of the building consisted of dormitories for the orphanage staff, COAT's foster homes and the COAT school, *Xi Wang Le Yuan*, which translates as the Place of Hope and Happiness. Anything to do with orphans usually has 'hope' or 'dream' in the title. That day, we were standing in front of the lucky 'chubby babies' posters at the entrance to the infamous first floor.

'The doors are normally locked,' said Linda wiggling the door handle. 'I'm supposed to get permission, you know.' She looked at me as if she was expecting an answer. But just at that moment, I heard a small click and the heavy door swung inward. My journalist heart beat faster. This was the feeling I used to get right before getting into trouble during my years as a correspondent. It was usually at the point where our TV crew had seen or recorded something that was illegal to tape. For a moment we'd feel a warm glow, that we had happened on 'gold' as we called it. It was usually something you didn't have permission for. This was how I felt the moment the door to the first floor opened.

The annoying heavy plastic curtains inside which acted as a fly deterrent proved a small but final hurdle to our entry and then, we were inside. Inside a Chinese orphanage. I pinched myself. This would never have happened if I'd been travelling with a camera crew. We were like thieves who'd climbed through a wide-open window.

Linda was keen to show me the orphanage so that I could see the contrast in conditions there and in her foster homes. She was allowed to visit the orphanage anytime she liked, as long as she notified staff. If a place opened up in her foster homes, for example after a child had been adopted overseas, Linda took a stroll through the dormitories of the orphanage to go 'baby shopping' as she called it. She'd select a child or several children to bring them upstairs to live in one of her foster homes.

'Sometimes I've walked through the orphanage wards and noticed particular children that I simply couldn't walk past. Wen Xuan was one of those. It's like a little spark that shoots from them, to me, and back again. Then I have to negotiate carefully with Director Sun to get my way.'

In the past, she would choose some of the severely disabled children because she felt that orphanage staff were abusing them. Other children were brought to the foster homes because they'd been singled out by a visitor who chose to sponsor them. If Linda was told to pick two children, she couldn't help herself and selected six. Around the time of the Olympics, Linda was told by the orphanage director that she could only have the ugly orphans.

'They (officials) wanted the pretty children to be able to perform for visitors and television programs. The director at that time was always amazed when he visited the foster homes and discovered that we didn't have any ugly children at all. He used to ask, "where are the ugly ones?" I told him that love makes them all beautiful,' she said.

On the day of our impromptu visit to the orphanage in March 2015, Linda had a mission although it wasn't a baby-shopping trip. She wanted to find a sixteen-year-old girl named Lin Jie who was blind and autistic. Lin Jie had come to the orphanage in 1999 after being abandoned by her parents. Linda had found her leaning against a radiator and neglected by the staff, when she was six months old. The Shums became Lin Jie's sponsors so that the orphanage workers would pay greater attention to her.[1] Lin Jie had been living in a foster home for blind children in Beijing since the age of four. Then, out of the blue, just a few days before, Lin Jie was 'returned'. The Beijing foster home said they couldn't help her anymore so she was sent back to her orphanage of origin.

From the hallway, we entered the first doorway into a large dormitory to our left. By now, a vision of *The Dying Rooms* documentary was playing on a loop in my head and I was expecting to see the full horror of how I'd imagined a Chinese orphanage to be. Either that, or a deafening journalist alarm was about to go off and I would be hauled away and deported from China.

But it was nothing like I imagined.

Natural light poured in from windows on the far side of the dormitory. Cute cartoon characters – monkeys, chickens, cats and dogs – adorned freshly-painted eggshell blue walls. The lower wall was tiled and spotlessly clean. Those horrible institutional walls, green paint on the lower half, white on the upper half, were gone. This didn't seem so awful. It felt like we were in a ward of a children's hospital. But you soon realise that places like this are like an onion. The longer you look, the easier the layers peel away.

Against the wall with the windows were rows of beds with iron railings. There wasn't a mattress in sight. Some beds were covered in plastic sheeting for the bed-wetters. Quilts were stacked at one end of the bed. It all seemed tidy and clean. The beds were grouped into four, perhaps to give the kids companionship or to make it easier for carers to manage. Not that there was anyone supervising or looking after the children at this moment. That job was left to a wall-mounted TV playing a Chinese soap opera with Russian subtitles. Apart from the sound of the actors and melodramatic music from the TV, there was silence.

Was it normal for a roomful of children to be so silent?

Twenty children stared at us in surprise. The children were probably aged five to teens. There were no babies. Most of them were boys with physical and/or mental disabilities. After eighteen, children are supposed to go to the adult welfare home across town.

I didn't know whether it was the right thing to do to approach the children. I didn't know if that would bring unwanted attention to our presence. So I just stood and waved, not daring to take out my phone/camera. We moved a little closer to the beds. I noticed a faint smell of urine and it made me stop. It wasn't so much the smell that held me back, it was fear. I could sense that there was something wrong with many of these kids and I wasn't sure how to feel. They didn't know me, so should I approach them or just observe? Linda however, gently went up to one of the children and stroked his hair.

Then, something caught her attention. Her mouth went into a straight line and she stiffened.

We stood in front of the first row of beds and could see all the children in the room from where we were.

Several of them were playing with lengths of cloth. How curious I thought naïvely, that a kid would be given something like a rope to play with in bed. And then slowly, my line of thought unravelled with the length of cloth in that boy's hand. It wasn't in his hand, it was around his wrist. He was tied to the bed.

I searched the room looking for more pieces of twisted cloth. Some of the children were rocking back and forth which is what they do when they need stimulation. A boy hit the child next to him. There was no response. I continued to scan the room, counting eight children who were tied by their hands or their feet to the iron railings of their beds.

Linda had already seen what took a while to register with me. That's why the doors to the outside world were always locked. Was this how China took care of 'the weakest and neediest group' in society, as the former president had said? Did tying children to the railings of their beds really happen in 2015? (It was still happening in 2017 as I finished this book.) My eyes were drinking in the miserable scene. Now it was obvious that some of the children were blind, others had deformed limbs, several appeared intellectually-impaired.

Linda's face was like a storm cloud: grey and broiling. I hadn't seen her like this before.

She didn't need to see children tied-up to become livid. She was already upset that morning after hearing of Lin Jie's 'return to sender' like a misplaced package. We decided to leave the children to their daytime television and continue searching for Lin Jie. We went up to the second floor to see the babies. This time, the door to the rooms was locked. Linda knocked vigorously, calling out to the ayi to let us in. The ayi recognised Linda instantly and showed us in to have a look at the infants, some of whom had only arrived in the past few days. Linda often came to see the new arrivals just in case she could find places for them in one of her foster homes upstairs.

On the infants' floor, the rooms were painted pastel pink and green with wide, clear viewing windows like a newborns' nursery in a hospital. Despite the cold outside, the heating was on here, there were clean quilts and sheets on freshly-painted cot-beds and thankfully, no TV. And, of course, there were babies; at least ten of them, both male and female. Linda counted four who had the flat facial features of Down syndrome. She showed me how to look at their feet and find the gap between the big toe and the first toe; a tell-tale sign of the condition. The ayi stood and watched. She seemed impatient for us to leave.

All of the babies appeared to have a physical or developmental disability. One of the little ones probably had microcephaly because the head was so much smaller than the body. Linda did not pick the baby up in case the ayi objected. In the orphanage, the ayis are in charge, not Linda. She did the rounds of the room, stopping to stroke a face or straighten some bedclothes. She made sure to touch every child bending down to tell them quietly how very special they were.

Little bundles with faces blinked at us. Strangely, as before, the room was eerily silent. I cooed at a baby boy who had probably never seen a foreign face before. His face quickly wrinkled, his mouth opened wide and an ear-piercing wail filled the room.

It was a good cue to leave. We waved goodbye to the ayi, and as she turned her back to walk away, our attention was diverted to a play area, the length of a basketball court, opposite the dormitory. Linda said it was a therapy room and pointed out the balls, toys and little trikes scattered about. Strangely, all the lights were turned off. Perhaps it wasn't being used, I thought. But I was wrong. I saw the outlines of three little people, alone in different sections of the play area. They were barely moving. One side of the building was in the shade, so the windows, which were fitted with bars like a prison, didn't let in much light. Below one of the windows was a boy of around eight years old. Two long pieces of rope tied his wrists to the metal bars. He could shuffle a bit, but given he was tied up, he couldn't move very far. Closer to where Linda and I stood peering through the viewing window, was another boy. This one – naked from the waist down – was doing a wee. Elsewhere, puddles of urine caught the light and shone like pools of oil. There was no ayi in sight. This is how the therapy room looked when there were no foreigners or high-powered visitors scheduled to drop in.

Despite the disheartening tour that morning, we both knew conditions were much better compared with what Linda had encountered when she first came to China in 1998. Nowadays, the Jiaozuo orphans were kept warm, had clean clothes and were well fed. But if they remained too long in that state, in that orphanage, the lack of stimulation, toys, cuddles, affection and therapy could have a lasting affect on their lives.

Linda called for an ayi to help us find 'the new girl'. She led us into a dormitory and called out the girl's name.

'Lin Jie!' There was no reply.

After searching the room, she yelped *there!* and led us to a lanky girl with short hair and a big smile. She wore pink trackpants and a padded grey top dotted with little strawberries. Curiously, I remembered it was strawberry season and recalled the country women driving their electric carts into Jiaozuo to sell their berries on street corners. Did Lin Jie's mother bring cartloads of strawberries to sell in the city? Did her parents ever pine for the child they had abandoned on the steps of the county police station? Or was it a relief not have the burden of a blind, autistic child? An imperfect child. Frustratingly, we will never know.

'Here is your *Nai Nai* [Grandma],' the ayi told Lin Jie as she guided her towards Linda.

'Nai Nai,' Lin Jie repeated. Her arms jerked about and though she was skinny, she looked otherwise healthy. Linda held her arms wide and wrapped them around the thin child whom she once feared would starve to death.

'That's right, I'm your Nai Nai,' Linda said gently in Chinese.

Given Lin Jie's autism and the fact that she hadn't seen Linda since she was four, she wouldn't remember her Nai Nai. But she clearly enjoyed being embraced by this big, foreign woman and wasn't in any rush to let go.

'Nai Nai,' Lin Jie repeated.

For the longest minute, neither of them let go. Linda wept quietly knowing that despite all her efforts, she had not found a loving home for Lin Jie. She had snatched her away from death, but the girl's future was still unresolved. The adoption window was already closed.

After the reunion, Linda and I continued our impromptu tour, heading to the third floor toddlers' room. It was mid-morning now and the children were napping in their cots or sitting up doing nothing. A '*Fu*' poster, the character for 'good luck', hung from the ceiling. I caught the eye of a little girl sitting on a plastic-covered mattress on a cot beside the window. Dressed in overalls she had a boy's haircut and a sweet toothy smile like a chipmunk. Watching us intently, she beamed as we edged closer to her. She was the only one in the room with eyes that were full of life and she seemed far too big to be stuck in a cot all day.

In that room, there was a nest of shelves on the wall stuffed with brand new soft toys. I was itching to take my phone/camera out, but I was in China on a tourist visa and Linda had earlier warned me that the orphanage staff were sensitive about visitors taking photos. As I considered my options, I spied Linda briskly heading to the toy shelves. At this point, I threw caution to the wind and took out my phone. Chipmunk Girl began to giggle and clap. She knew something out of the ordinary was unfolding.

In the manner of a teacher in confiscation mode, Linda pulled all the soft toys off the shelves. Most of the toys still had tags attached to them. It dawned on me, cynically I know, that they might even be props for the benefit of visitors. Linda walked resolutely towards the children. Little Chipmunk sat back with an enormous grin. Santa Shum was coming her way.

'There you go,' Linda said, handing a giraffe and a bear to the first child before moving to the next. She allowed a little boy to choose his own toy. His expression veered between delight and surprise. It was Chipmunk Girl's turn next. Linda deposited an armful of toys into her cot. She quickly grabbed three. By the time all the kids had been given at least one toy, and I had taken dozens of photos, I suggested that we leave. If the ayi discovered what we were doing, she wouldn't appreciate the breach of protocol. Nor would she like to see those pristine toys being messed up by the children, although to be honest, most of the kids had no idea what to do with these fluffy objects in front of them.

I glanced back at the toddlers. It was like a switch had been pressed and they had suddenly come alive as a result of the rare interaction and these strange new things in their laps. Chipmunk Girl didn't notice me leave. Linda shouted to the ayi announcing our departure and as I shut the heavy orphanage door, I noticed the posters of happy, lucky, chubby children which read: 'Bring wealth and treasures', 'Harmony between people and families will make everything successful, bring more luck and long lives'. Then the door shut with a definitive bang as if to say, 'Now don't come back.'

After the impromptu orphanage tour, while we headed to Linda's office to check emails, she bumped into Director Sun in the hallway. She asked him to come down to the first floor where we had seen the disabled children tied to their beds. I wondered how she'd communicate all of this to Director Sun with her limited Chinese, but in truth, pointing to children who were tied up didn't require much translation. Linda's emotion was as plain as the millet soup so loved by the kids at the end of each meal.

After complaining about the treatment of the children, she ushered Director Sun across the hall to the viewing window to show him the boy in the therapy room with his hands tied behind his back. The child, who was intellectually impaired, apparently had a reputation for smearing poo all over the floor, that's why his hands were tied. Linda targeted an ayi, a woman with a long face like a horse whom the volunteers called the 'the buck-teethed' ayi.

'Ayi, why don't the children have any toys to play with?' Linda demanded in front of the director, causing a chain reaction of embarrassment and loss of face.

'We can't give them toys,' the ayi said, smiling out of embarrassment. 'They don't know how to play with them. Whenever we give them toys, they break them.'

It was a response Linda had heard too many times over the years, although she was disappointed to hear it resurface.

She turned to Director Sun.

'This is 2015,' she fumed. It was rare for her to lose control with an official in public like this. 'Imagine if this appeared in the Western media? This is a breach of the children's human rights.'

In 2007, Linda and Director Sun were the guests of honour at a Christmas party for the orphans, when a child, a perfectly healthy boy, tried to clamber up onto Linda's lap. She told Director Sun the baby, who was twelve months old, had been found at the age of five months at the cafeteria in the university. 'His parents are students,' she told the Director, 'so the baby is probably intelligent.'

'Why don't you take him home and give him to your wife as a Christmas present from me?' she said half joking.

Days later, she discovered that Director Sun had done what Linda had suggested and his wife was delighted with her new son.

'I don't think that boy was ever officially adopted,' Linda said, 'Because that would have cost 35,000 yuan ($7,000) but the boy was taken off the adoption list and Sun and his wife have loved him and cared for him ever since. He's nearly ten now.'

'I think this shows that the man has a heart and that he has changed since the early days.'

Sometimes however, that compassion is hard to pinpoint. Linda's time in China taught her that the Chinese view of human rights extended only to the children's basic physical requirements; whether they had adequate food, clothing and shelter. If children were tied to their beds, it was for their own safety. Nurturing or cherishing was not a priority. Because of the severity of their conditions, the children on the first floor were unlikely to be adopted. As such, in stark contrast to Linda's view of human rights, they were not regarded as individuals worth investing in.

The Chinese concept of face prevented Director Sun from responding to Linda. He didn't like being ambushed and he clearly didn't like being told by a foreigner that the lack of care in his facility was a breach of human rights. The Chinese felt they were always being belittled by foreigners over the question of human rights. Director Sun appeared deeply humiliated, but he didn't say a word to Linda.

As a result of our impromptu visit that morning, Linda's 'baby-shopping' visits to the orphanage were refused for six months. She was temporarily barred, the unspoken punishment for bringing a foreign journalist into the orphanage.

How did they know I was a journalist? I asked. I assumed the orphanage thought I was a volunteer like the other foreign visitors. I didn't mention writing the book to anyone in Jiaozuo and was careful about taking photos and notes in public.

'I told my staff and Director Gong that you were writing a book about me,' Linda said.

I felt like Director Sun now; angry yet unable to find the words to respond. I knew what this meant. It would be the last time I visited the first floor.

CHAPTER 16

Outreach

Although it's March, snowflake and Christmas tree decorations cling to the walls of the playroom of the COAT school, the Place of Hope and Happiness. Twenty children of all ages are gathered for the morning fruit break. Some of them push stainless steel walking frames, others sit patiently in their wheelchairs. A group of toddlers are under instruction from the school's principal, Xing, who is teaching them how to roll and balance a hoop. She's waiting for them to concentrate but nobody is focused on learning right now. Nor are they much interested in fruit. There's chattering and commotion in the hallway and everyone knows what that means. A group of visitors has come to *xian aixin:* donate loving hearts.

It's a contingent of around twenty adults and thirty children from a wealthy private kindergarten. The pre-schoolers wear fussy uniforms completely unsuitable for small children: blazers, shirts, pullovers and cravats to complete the affect. The adults are wearing the kindergarten's T shirt. The logo shows a little girl in a wide-brimmed yellow hat, looking suspiciously like *Madeline* from the Ludwig Bemelmans books. Apart from armloads of gifts, today's visitors have brought a newspaper reporter and photographer with them.

The reporter introduces herself in broken English as Miss Xuan, from the *Jiaozuo Morning News*. I point Linda out to her, explaining she's the Australian founder of the school. Though she nods, Miss Xuan isn't interested. This is a publicity exercise for the kindergarten, a photo-opportunity so they can be seen to be performing good deeds for unfortunate orphans.

Like a game of Chinese checkers, the kindergarten delegation takes up one side of the room while the COAT schoolkids wait on the opposite side. There's an uncomfortable silence as the children stare each other down, not knowing what to do. What do the orphans think, as they face these rich little children, with their sweet haircuts and pigtails, bearing armloads of chips, lollies and toys? They are exactly what China has been working towards these past decades, the one-child generation, the faces of 21st century China: future 'high quality' global citizens who will never know hardship.

The orphans don't have sweet hairstyles. Joyous Li does the haircuts and they are practical. Four of the orphans are dressed in the same animal-print overalls which were clearly a bulk purchase. Some of the orphans are very cute though. The little Down syndrome girl only wants to give cuddles. There's the boy, Ziguang, featured in the Channel 7 story. He was abandoned because he was missing a left hand. Fortunately, Ziguang is leaving to go to America soon. 'He's so lucky!' the teachers exclaim. But what about the rest of the orphans? They go to school, they laugh and play. But the truth is, most of these children will not graduate to lead independent lives.

And these rich kids, what were they told before they arrived to peer shyly at these strange children who walk like they are dancing, and who have odd-shaped heads or uneven (or missing) eyes? Do the rich kids know this is where they could have ended up if they'd been born imperfect? Would any of their parents know the shame or the pain of giving up a child to the state?

There in front of me, was a snapshot of China's past and future.

❦

Suddenly, a little girl resembling a Cabbage-Patch doll, nudged by her teacher, walked forward holding a blue rubber ball in her outstretched hands. Other kids from Team Kindergarten (with an enviable staff to child ratio of 1:2) waved from the safety of their side of the room. Then as if a silent signal had gone off, the rich kids rushed over to Team Orphan, arms extended with their gifts of space-hoppers, bouncy rubber sheep, building blocks and everything else. In the chaos, popcorn and chips flew all over the room.

Linda looked on disapprovingly. She didn't like it when the orphans were spoilt like this because it gave the impression every visitor comes bearing gifts and snacks. But she herself invited volunteers to come to play and care for the children. Linda wanted the orphans to be more visible in the community because it might change people's minds about abandoning children. But is this visibility or is it like a petting zoo? As I watched the kids in their wild happiness, forgetting who was rich and who was abandoned, I realised I was wiping tears from my eyes.

It was speech time. Linda decided to give the visitors a short history of COAT, why the children were there, how they got to go to a wonderful school and a little plea for help from this wonderful kindergarten. Some of the kindergarten teachers took out tissues and dabbed their eyes. Linda continued, saying it was a daily struggle to make ends meet. *What?* I made a note to ask her later what she meant by that.

All the adults on Team Kindergarten – including the reporter and photographer – rummaged in their pockets and handbags and arms stretched towards Linda's large open envelope, parted with a few thousand yuan between them, which wasn't a bad effort for such an impromptu whip-around.

The pandemonium continued after Linda's speech as the children played together, jumped on the trampoline (the rich kids really liked this) and hoovered every last crumb of the snacks. Ziguang, dressed in one of the animal print overalls, offered me a handful of sodden Chinese Twisties.

Before the kindergarten delegation left the room, the teachers put the children into a line, stood behind them and turned on the enormous ghetto blaster they had brought with them.

An anonymous disco tune started up and the children began an elaborate dance routine complete with shower-turning actions, star-jumps, side-steps and ball-changes. It was exhausting just to look at and quite complex considering the kids were pre-schoolers. It was a valiant effort, but why didn't Team Orphan do something to show off for the visitors? It was so … unequal.

A big, jazz-hands finale marked the end of the visit followed by wild applause and laughter before Team Kindergarten made a swift exit, taking the ghetto blaster, children, reporter and photographer, and leaving all the toys and the pretty cardboard hearts decorated by the teachers, with messages of love for the orphans.

When we were back at her apartment, I asked Linda whether she'd been serious telling the kindergarten delegation it was a struggle to make ends meet.

'Well it has been,' Linda said. 'Every month we survive from hand to mouth. This month we only received $10,000 in donations, but we need double that for the wages. Last month I got a one-off gift which helped. But quite frankly, I'm coming to the end of my tether.'

From time to time, COAT received grants from the Chinese welfare lottery. The terms were that this could only be used to purchase equipment, not to pay for staff. The Australian embassy in Beijing donated funds to set up the school library and then gave another grant to set up a day-care room (called Little Learners) for babies and intellectually-impaired children. The Australian Chamber of Commerce in Beijing donated proceeds from their annual ball three years in a row and Westpac Bank also donated generously. But most of the money propping up COAT came from Linda's advocacy, through little old ladies and gentlemen from all around Queensland, from a few Gympie-based companies, from her speeches and from international sponsorships through the COAT website. She's been doing this for twenty years. Funding a small NGO without corporate sponsorship sounds like an exhausting job. The way Linda described it, it was a constant nagging feeling, like a recurring dream, not painful enough to be called a nightmare, but just a regular reminder, that you never have enough.

At Linda's insistence, Director Gong (her Chinese director) began making phone calls to lobby local Chinese companies and government departments for donations. This was only possible after COAT's official registration in late 2013.

Director Gong didn't much like the idea of approaching businesses to ask for money. He felt it was like begging and wondered whether it would look good for the orphanage and more importantly its administrator, the Department of Civil Affairs. He didn't object to the idea of applying for grants from the Chinese government. In fact, despite the complexity of the application process, he proved very good at this. A grant could deliver 500,000 yuan ($100,000) some of which could be use for wages. This in turn would relieve the orphanage of any pressure to help COAT.

One day, four of us piled into Director Gong's clean white VW Jetta on a lobbying expedition. Linda sat in front next to Director Gong and I sat with Xiao Ming in the back. Director Gong was extremely proud of his car. Although it was two years old, it was spotless inside and had a special hanging air-freshener that kept it smelling like a brand new vehicle. There was pride in Director Gong's voice whenever I asked him about the car. It was like his second grandchild. As he took the wheel he lightly touched the wiper controls and the indicator as if it were a special good luck ritual. But as we pulled out of the orphanage compound, Director Gong didn't have any intention of using the indicators as we force-merged into the traffic. In fact, Director Gong didn't slow down either. He simply beeped the horn as a warning of the Jetta's impending arrival. Then, once he reached the targeted lane, he suddenly braked, then jolted to a 10-kilometre-an-hour crawl, before speeding up again to keep up with the flow. Whenever he approached other cars, he honked the horn for three sustained bursts to alert them to his presence.

I was curious to see whether the drivers around us were shaking their fists at him. On the contrary, everyone drove like Director Gong, with one hand permanently on the horn, one foot on the break, and sitting *on top* of the fastened seat-belt so as not to set off the seatbelt alarm.

It was a short drive along the People's Avenue to the government quarter; a series of tall, grey buildings with the red hammer and sickle insignia of the Communist Party stamped on the front. Linda and I often passed this part of town on our trike trips to the orphanage. I didn't expect that we would ever get a look in. We were waved inside by a tall guard on a rostrum at the gatehouse and went into the most imposing of the buildings, with a hollow square cut out of the middle. We were here to find Ms Lou a director in the Department of Civil Affairs which oversees the orphanage. Despite the impressive exterior, on the inside the building was poorly finished. The walls were slashed with huge cracks with wiring and pipes sticking out as if they had been afterthoughts. It also seemed far too dark for an office. The orphanage was like this too. I wondered whether people thought they were saving electricity to leave the rooms in darkness.

Surprisingly for a senior departmental official, Ms Lou worked in an open plan office divided by flimsy blue partitions. She had a push button telephone on her desk and, seeing there were four of us, took us around the corner from her cubicle where there was a small sofa. There were internal railings behind the sofa, presumably to stop people climbing out of the windows. The windows overlooked a massive concrete park where a huge flagpole took centre stage. It seemed a little ostentatious for Jiaozuo.

'Do you like coffee?' Ms Lou asked hopefully, nodding vigorously when she said 'coffee' in her halting English.

'Yes please,' Linda replied, knowing to say the right thing if she was to get approval to fund raise. Delighted with the response, Ms Lou had it covered. From a drawer in her desk she produced a small kettle. She disappeared for a few minutes and then plugged the kettle into a rickety power point behind the desk. As the water boiled, Ms Lou arranged the coffee paraphernalia: ground coffee beans from a tin, a drip filter, sugar, coffee creamer and four mugs.

'I like VERY STRONG coffee!' Ms Lou said with a chortle, agreeing to make ours weaker after the creamer she added barely changed the colour.

The coffee ritual easily lasted an hour. There was no attempt to hurry things along or get to the point of the discussion. It was as if we had really just dropped in for the coffee. Finally after there was nothing more to say about the brown liquid in our cups, Director Gong mentioned that Linda was keen to approach local businesses to boost the funding of her school. In her senior position, Miss Lou had to approve the move.

'Hmmm,' she said suddenly appearing official. She went to sit back at her desk with four of us still squeezed on the sofa. She suggested Director Gong and Linda avoided cold calls but approach business organisations first for their recommendations. She wrote some telephone numbers down on the back of an old calendar page, which she gave to Director Gong, and then we were all getting up to leave.

'You like the coffee?' she asked with a wide smile as we were leaving.

I remembered the value of a compliment in China, 'You make very good coffee,' I replied with a double thumbs up sign. I hated when I did that, but sometimes it just happened.

Suffice it to say, Ms Lou was very chuffed with my compliment and she wished us a good day.

Our next stop was the top floor of the *Jiaozuo Daily News* building, where we met an old friend of Director Gong's. Editor Wang was in his mid-to-late sixties. He led us to his corner office which was small and stuffy, filled with newspaper mountains stacked immaculately around an enormous desk. Director Gong, Linda, Xiao Ming and I crammed into the room and he closed the door. Although smoking is no longer allowed in public offices, he clearly had some clout because there was a full ashtray on his desk and the room stank of his *Man Bo Lo* (Marlboro) cigarettes. However, he kindly agreed not to smoke, when Linda and I declined his offer of a cigarette. Bringing out a thermos, he carefully unwrapped a paper pouch of tea leaves, which he sniffed to ensure its freshness. He put a pinch of tea into each of four plastic cups and filled them from the thermos.

The next two hours crawled by. I hate meetings at the best of times, but in China, there never seemed to be a sense of urgency to them. The first half hour was taken up with pleasantries and introductions. I was described as Linda's friend from Australia. Xiao Ming was very skilled at answering on our behalf for some of the conversation, but eventually, Linda and I were forced to answer the obligatory questions about Australia, its immense richness, its generous size and small population.

When there were no more pleasantries to exchange, Editor Wang finally asked what he could do for us that day.

It was Director Gong's turn to talk. He began by telling Editor Wang about Linda's work with COAT and the orphanage, her anxiety about rising costs, the difficulty in keeping up with salaries and the little orphans who, after all, were China's responsibility. Finally he gestured towards Linda. I couldn't pick up all of what he said, but he seemed to be describing various health problems. I thought he mentioned diabetes.

'What is he saying?' I asked Linda quietly. 'He's telling Editor Wang I have no breasts, too much sugar in my blood, high blood pressure and I can die at any moment,' she whispered. 'He left out the macular degeneration and neuropathy.'

I glanced at her. She had a sad, puppy dog expression, as if she were playing to his words.

And then the penny dropped. Director Gong was pitching a sob story to Editor Wang. He was working the newsman.

I regarded Director Gong with a new sense of respect. Previously I'd wondered about his contribution to COAT as he snoozed in his large swivel chair in the office. Though he hadn't initially been on board with the idea of lobbying businesses, the meeting ended well and Editor Wang called in one of his news photographers to seal the agreement with a snapshot; his newspaper agreed to produce a half-page spread on the school and the work of COAT.

Linda's awful year started in March 2015. She went to see the orphanage boss Director Sun and put it to him straight. Costs were going up. There was extra funding coming in for projects and items that the children needed, but COAT was not meeting its funding commitments for salaries. They had less than half the monthly bill of $20,000 coming in.

In August 2015, Linda's beloved father, Charles McCarthy, died, two weeks before his ninety-second birthday. She hadn't expected to have to cope with Charles' death as well as a funding crisis in the foster homes and the COAT school. Staff were asked if they would accept a 50 per cent cut to their salaries until the funding crunch was solved. Though some of them were on quite low wages, even for China, they accepted this as they had no choice. Even the COAT administrators, Joyous Li, Xiao Ming and Director Gong, went on half-pay.

Linda, Director Gong and the committee started to mull the options. They were down to forty-five children in the foster homes (because of several overseas adoptions) and were not allowed to take any more children from the orphanage to try to stem some costs. Once the accounts had been done, the focus became on reducing staff numbers from forty-eight to thirty-eight. But who would make the choice about who would stay and who would be made to go?

One member of the COAT committee suggested the staff evaluate each other. They were all given forms to rate the performance of their colleagues. However, all this revealed was who among them was popular and who wasn't. One of the ayis, whose husband worked as a driver for the orphanage, was accused of stealing clothing from the COAT storeroom. There was no evidence. She was just caught holding a bag as she closed the door to the storeroom. It was like bad old Communist times again; dobbing in your workmate to ensure survival.

October 2015 was when the staff contracts were due to be renewed. Director Gong sought advice. It was unlawful to continue paying staff only half their pay so that had to stop. However, he discovered that once a woman reached the age of fifty, she could be forced to retire. As a result, if she were sacked, she couldn't sue for wrongful dismissal. Director Gong had found the answer, however unpalatable. Ten ayis over the age of fifty could be safely 'removed' after being compensated with all of their back pay and a full month's severance. It didn't matter how long they had worked at COAT.

On her sixty-seventh birthday while she was back in Australia, Linda went on Skype to speak with all the women who'd been made redundant. 'It was mayhem at a distance,' Linda recalled. 'Everyone was angry and upset and talking over each other. I was upset too.'

'I said what I had to say: we don't have the money, thank you for the years of service, thank you for taking 75 per cent and 50 per cent of your pay. By law this is the only way we can do it. You are our best workers, but it's inevitable. If we have enough money and the crisis passes, I hope you'll consider coming back to work for us.'

Then after the cuts were made, life at the foster homes continued as it had before. A little slimmer on staff perhaps, but with no more cuts. In fact, as a result of Director Gong's work to secure funds from the Chinese lottery, the kitty soon began to grow again.

CHAPTER 17

The Story of Ms Tian

M s Tian was fifty-three when we met in 2015. She has worked as an ayi at COAT since 2007. Despite her youthful ponytail and thick fringe, you could see her poor country roots in the hollow cheeks, earth-brown skin and lines fanning out from the edges of her eyes. She had spent nearly half her life tending fields until after she had married. Then she found work indoors. As an ayi she earned a respectable 2,000 yuan a month ($400), although in Chinese society, looking after orphans and disabled children isn't considered prestigious. After a few years however, she realised that she enjoyed working with the children. Though she didn't immediately explain why, her widening eyes gave a hint that she needed the orphans as much as the orphans needed her.

We sat in one of the foster homes located in the orphanage building which was quiet as everyone was eating lunch. Ms Tian had eaten already.

Wrapped up warmly in a khaki-coloured coat, Ms Tian was about to head home on her scooter after the night shift. The only bright colour on her came from her socks. They were red and white striped, shouting from under the hem of her trousers like the smallest act of rebellion.

From her handbag, she took out a photograph of her twenty-eight-year-old son, Lang Lang. The young man had a kind expression. His hair was spiky and he had high cheekbones. He looked sophisticated and knowing. He was definitely a city boy. He didn't resemble his mother at all. I asked if he was married yet. It's the second most common question in China after inquiring whether someone has eaten. Personal questions like marriage, children, how much you earn and how old you are, are never considered rude in China. I found comments about my weight less easy to laugh off. To my question about Lang Lang's status, Ms Tian shook her head sadly.

'Not yet. But he should marry soon,' she said. Like all Chinese mothers she was anxious. He was her only son and according to Chinese custom, he should be married before thirty. In China, family, marriage and children are everyone's business. 'Lang Lang shouldn't wait too long,' that's what all Ms Tian's friends kept telling her. And of course, she longed for grandchildren.

She grew up with four other siblings and always dreamed of having more than one child herself. 'When he does get married,' she said quietly, 'I want him to promise that he will have two children. He is allowed to. Soon there will be no more one-child policy.' When we met, the Chinese government had already indicated that the strict birth control policies were about to change and that from January 2016, families could officially have two children. Ms Tian struggled to articulate her feelings. The fact that the policy was going to change seemed difficult for her to accept.

Lang Lang was born in 1983, three years after the one-child policy became official and a year after a new provision was added to it. *Document 7* gave China's provinces and regions power to adjust the policy to local circumstances through a set of exclusions. The more liberal approach was also extended to China's ethnic minorities including Tibetans and Uighurs. In reality, *Document 7* made the overall policy more complex and difficult to understand – whether you were inside China or not. It's why it wasn't a blanket one-size fits all rule. One of the first things I noticed in Jiaozuo, for example, was that there seemed to be many two-child families out on their scooters and this was before the rules changed in 2016. In cities like Beijing or Shanghai, it would be rare to see two-child families.

The one-child policy led to the establishment of an entire family planning bureaucracy. It was like a police force. In 2015 there were more than half a million employees from the central government down to the township level, and more than a million cadres (government officials who are usually members of the Communist Party)[1] working in family planning clinics and offices in the villages. In addition there were millions of individuals who were 'devoted to both policy enforcement and family planning generally.'[2]

At the time Ms Tian and her husband began thinking about having a child, China was moving towards a market economy following the death of Chairman Mao. Some of her friends began to flex their entrepreneurial muscles and started small businesses in addition to holding down their regular jobs. Soon, they were flaunting cash and wearing colourful new clothes. Despite the change, the Party still exerted control in key areas namely where an individual lived and worked. To be an official member of a household you had to possess a *hukou*. A *hukou* was like an internal passport giving the owner access to education and social security benefits. The Party knew how many births there were in each household and that gave them a new power of human veto. In this way, the Party's tentacles reached more deeply into the lives of individuals – particularly women. Imagine having your obstetric and gynaecological details policed by the local clinic. Imagine having to get a permit to have a child. Imagine being told your pregnancy is illegal.

Ms Tian recalled the sense of euphoria at Lang Lang's birth. Despite having no more than a primary education, she was lucky enough to find work as an ayi after he was born and her husband held a secure, government job which gave them housing for a peppercorn rent. Ms Tian was twenty-three and like most of her friends, knew little about contraception. She was surprised to discover that before Lang Lang turned one, she was pregnant again.

Like many other Chinese couples, she and her husband desperately wanted a daughter to complete their family, but she was not entitled to a second birth permit. It would be, in official speak, an 'over-quota' or 'out of plan' birth. Family planning officials cautioned her several times to abort the fetus, but she couldn't bring herself to comply because she badly wanted the child.

Two of Ms Tian's close friends had married men who worked in the transport department like her husband. Because of their government positions, they were duty-bound to uphold the one-child policy. They could have been punished financially if they didn't comply. Another option could have been to pay the birth fine, which was set at the equivalent of two years' salary. Rules and punishments, like the one-child policy itself, differed from location to location. In the case of Ms Tian's friends, neither couple could afford the fine when they fell pregnant a second time. In the end, both wives felt they had no choice except to submit to abortions and give up their hopes of a second child.

One of the women, named Mei, was a native of Sichuan, the western province where the spicy food comes from. She decided to flee Jiaozuo and seek sanctuary in her hometown to avoid detection and punishment. Women who did this were known as 'family planning fugitives'. When officials discovered she had run away, Mei's husband was made to stand down from his job and warned that if his wife refused to give herself up, he'd be forcibly retired. As a result, Mei terminated the pregnancy while she was still in Sichuan. She returned to Jiaozuo with a certificate to prove she had submitted to the abortion, only to discover she'd be issued with a 2,000 yuan ($400) fine. This was a heavy burden on a family living on a government salary. Once the fine was paid however, her husband was reinstated.

After Mei's experience, Ms Tian who was by now eight months' pregnant, came to the conclusion she had run out of options.

'My husband took me to the hospital one afternoon,' she said with her eyes closed. 'There were three other women sharing the room. They were all like me, having late-term abortions.'

'At around 8 o'clock in the morning, a male doctor came in. He was holding a long syringe and plunged it straight into my belly, where the baby was.' She spoke as clearly as if it had happened a week ago. She didn't look at me, but looked down at her hands as she pulled at the tops of her fingers.

'Several hours later, I had to go to the toilet. There was a stinking toilet cubicle in the room and I managed to get there in time.'

She squatted down. To her surprise and horror, she felt something hard poking out of her vagina. It was the crown of her baby's head. Her child was about to be born.

A hospital attendant helped her as she staggered into the birth room where people in surgical masks stood around. In the middle of the room was a stainless steel surgical table surrounded by lamps. She thought she was going to be helped onto the table, but instead, the attendant guided her towards a plastic bucket.

'It didn't take long after that. The baby came minutes later,' she said in an urgent whisper as if she was worried that she wouldn't be able to finish her story. 'My baby was born.'

She remembers the baby dropped down first, followed by the placenta a few minutes later.

'I was surprised just how quickly it all happened.'

At this stage, Ms Tian's husband came into the birthing room to help his wife get up from the bucket. An orderly directed him to help his wife to a nearby bed. Ms Tian's face was taut and her voice became low and clear as she recounted the awful events.

'I heard the baby cry twice,' she said. 'It sounded like a frightened animal, a high-pitched squeal. It was like a knife going through my heart.'

With her husband steadying her by the elbow, she turned towards the sound of the cry. Both of them saw the doctor lift the bucket onto the table. He tipped an enamel jug filled with water into the bucket, immersing the baby. The crying stopped.

The orderly instructed Ms Tian's husband to take the bucket into the courtyard. He told her later there was a large tub outside and that it was the husband's job to dispose of the baby in the tub. Ms Tian's husband carried the bucket outside. He found the tub, but couldn't bring himself to treat the baby's body like food slops. So he left the bucket and its contents beside the tub and went back to his wife.

The next morning, Ms Tian awoke feeling dazed. She looked at her floppy belly, and felt a wave of guilt followed by a wave of grief. These two emotions buffeted her like a typhoon. Afterwards she wanted to think of the baby only as a 'thing'. This 'thing' which had given her such secret pleasure was gone now. She understood. But the next moment, her chest ached as she thought of the child she had lost. It was not a thing. In a few weeks' time it would have been born naturally. She became desperate to know the sex of the baby that wasn't to be. She begged her husband to see if the bucket was still outside in the courtyard but when he checked, it had disappeared. Ms Tian asked the orderly whether he knew the sex of her child.

'It was a girl,' he told her.

By now, Ms Tian's forehead creased into rows like newly-planted fields. She tried to hold back tears. I thought about giving her a hug but her body was so stiff that I ended up awkwardly patting her shoulder. I could not imagine what she had endured. Losing a baby or a child is tragic enough. Having a healthy baby yanked out of your body because of an official target is incomprehensible.

Ms Tian sat up and straightened her clothing. 'It's done now. It's in the past,' she said.

'Last week my husband said if our little girl had been born, she would have looked like me. I think about her all the time,' she said, her head bowed. 'We have a saying in Chinese that a daughter is like her mother's little coat. She brings comfort and warmth.'

Ms Tian seemed lost in her thoughts again.

'Losing my daughter has been my greatest regret,' she said before her eyes began to fill with tears. 'I will never understand for the rest of my life, how a doctor – someone who is supposed to save lives – could do such a thing as that,' she said bitterly.

The flow of tears never came. Instead she pulled on thick woollen gloves over her cracked hands. She lifted a hood over her schoolgirl hair and declared that she was heading home.

A few months after our talk, Ms Tian was to lose her job due to COAT's funding crisis. Life could be hard in China.

CHAPTER 18

The God Factor

In Jiaozuo one Sunday morning, bundled up against the wind, we followed a line of elderly people on foot, on scooters and trikes heading down a lane lined with car repair workshops. At the end of the lane was a warehouse and in the warehouse was a church.

On either side of the entrance stood men dressed in choir gowns, waving us in. This was Linda's church when she was in Jiaozuo, run by the Three Self Patriotic Movement, China's government-sanctioned Protestant church. It was hard to find a pew. There were at least 300 people already seated with more arriving every minute. We were the only foreigners. Finally, we found space and I managed to get a good look around. It was so unlike a traditional church. We were sitting in a modified factory with a stage at the front, surrounded by high windows. Plasterboard in the shape of a lancet had been tacked over each window to give them the look of a church. Seven church windows were printed on a backdrop at the back of the stage, the centre window decorated with a large, maroon, perspex cross. In front of the screen was a space big enough for a choir, and a lectern with a microphone.

People continued to trickle in all throughout the two-hour service. All around me were predominantly women, middle-aged and elderly, standing with arms opened wide above their heads and their eyes tightly shut. The warehouse church didn't just have a piano and a pianist. It had a brass band, a large choir and a group of seven spiritual prayer leaders decked out in matching rainbow-coloured scarves. The music was extremely loud and reverberated in my chest. They repeated the same verses over and over again. It was Hillsong with Chinese characteristics.

All around us in this neighbourhood church was evidence of a spiritual revival that is deeply worrying to the central government in Beijing. In April 2016, President Xi Jinping warned that China has to be vigilant against foreign religious influences. His warning came after a long crackdown on churches with more than 1,700 of them across the country having their crosses desecrated or removed.

'We must guard against overseas infiltrations via religious means and prevent ideological infringement by extremists', he was quoted as saying.[1] Many of the churches affected by the crackdown were unofficial or 'house' churches, but the message was clear: Big Brother in China doesn't refer to the man upstairs. In spite of this, today there are an estimated 100 million Chinese Christians.[2]

In recent years, Linda has been increasingly open about her faith while in Jiaozuo. She even gained permission to tell Bible stories to the orphans. I would have been nervous in her situation, but she simply quotes a famous Chinese underground pastor, Samuel Lamb: 'The more persecution, the more the church grows.'

'My goal isn't to convert the people of Jiaozuo. My goal is to bring love. If you do that,' Linda said, 'everything else falls into place.'

From 2015, Linda stopped using foreign volunteers to take charge of her foster homes. Though she didn't discourage volunteers from short-term visits, she no longer invited families or individuals to be mum-and-dad managers. More than a dozen volunteers over the years made contributions. Some thought they were 'wonderful Christian people out to save humanity,' said Linda. But behind the scenes she found herself dealing with a range of un-Christian behaviour, including petty jealousy, infighting, and a lack of cultural sensitivity towards the Chinese. In one case, volunteers defied Director Lan's edict that COAT personnel were not to preach the gospel or openly pray in tongues. Another volunteer refused to take a severely intellectually-impaired child offered to COAT by the orphanage because, the volunteer told Linda, the child was an innocent and therefore 'didn't need salvation'.

Linda often used words like 'lovely' and 'wonderful' to describe the many Christians she came across. But she could be extremely harsh about those who propagated the Christian message but failed to practice it themselves.

'Christians seem to be the worst ones for offending each other,' Linda said. 'It is the bait of Satan and I am as guilty as the next one of taking the bait. I am working on being a better Christian and not taking offence, but it may take me a while longer to master it,' she said.

I felt uncomfortable whenever she mentioned Satan. It was the first time I'd heard about him since Sunday school. But Satan aside, she made a good point.

'So many Christians set a bad example to others by the way they live their lives – cheating on tax, doing cash jobs, breaking the speed limit, lust, greed or disrespecting our parents, wives or husbands. So often people look at Christians and say – and rightly so – that they are a bunch of hypocrites and no-one wants to be like them, so people don't go to Church.'

Linda has written two self-published novels. She prefers fiction as she can mix and camouflage reality without causing offence.

One of Linda's novels is *Timothy, Honoured of God*. I guess you could call the genre spiritual or supernatural fiction.

It begins with the story of a young boy, nicknamed Stinky, from rural Queensland whose parents neglect and mistreat him. The family is poor. Timothy is a miserable kid. He tries to end his life but is rescued by a strange ghost-like man who turns out to be his guardian angel. The angel teaches Timothy self-respect. He teaches him how to care for himself and eventually, how to read. From here, the rest of the novel unfolds really quickly. Timothy meets a Chinese woman who's looking for sanctuary in northern Australia so she can give birth to a second child in contravention of China's one-child policy. Soon Timothy is travelling back and forth between Queensland and China Narnia-style; by walking through a forest to reach the other location. Timothy has picked up Chinese without any effort. By now he is an adult and returns to regional Queensland where he becomes a doctor so that he can rescue others who are in dire straits as he once was.

COAT's secretary, Margaret Mason, who's also a devout Christian (from the Uniting Church), thought the book was highly enjoyable and more than a thousand copies of *Timothy* have been sold to raise money for COAT.

But the supernatural/paranormal turned out to be a controversial subject. After mentioning my daughter read the first Harry Potter book at the age of seven, Linda thought I should exercise caution. While she saw *Timothy* as a religious fantasy story, J.K. Rowling's Harry Potter series made her uncomfortable. She could barely read past the first book because she was so concerned it might encourage people to 'flirt with the occult'. Linda dislikes, what she calls, the 'normalisation' of witchcraft:

> It amazes me that so many people reject the idea of an Almighty God with flights of angels who are sent as his messengers and to protect people. I believe everyone has a 'guardian angel' who protects us and when our time is up, they show us the way to heaven.
>
> You told me that you didn't like my book because you couldn't agree with angels flitting about and arranging the paranormal, but you are happy to read Harry Potter with paranormal extraordinaire.
>
> People, are very quick to believe in ghosts and karma and spirit guides and other paranormal signs. But that is what Satan wants... to deceive.

'Linda,' I said slowly, 'I don't believe in the world of Harry Potter! But I am entertained by it.'

In 2016, a woman turned up at COAT's office in China. She introduced herself as Ms Duan and said she came from Puyang, a city about 220 kilometres from Jiaozuo. Her church had urged its followers to do more for charity. Ms Duan had heard about the foster homes in Jiaozuo through the media and she thought she would like to sponsor an orphan. This sort of impromptu philanthropy didn't happen often. Joyous Li brought out the paperwork and sat down with Ms Duan. After some discussion, she decided to sponsor a seventeen-year-old girl named Ting Ting.

Ting Ting (which means graceful) came to the old orphanage when she was nineteen months old. By this time, her developmental milestones would have been lagging as she began to show symptoms of cerebral palsy. It's unlikely she was diagnosed. Her parents just knew she wasn't normal so, whether because of their financial situation or inability to cope, they abandoned her.

Though she was often found sitting on a potty chair in the old orphanage yard, the Shums found she loved being cuddled. She clearly needed love and therapy so she was among the first group of children brought to the foster home in 2006. Though she grew into a smart, happy child, over the years she watched as many of her 'siblings' were adopted by American families while she was the one who stayed behind. But if Ting Ting suffered bouts of self-pity or sadness, it was never apparent. She was always smiling and eager to practise her English on visitors. Not surprisingly, Ms Duan struck up a natural rapport with her. Each month, the older lady travelled four hours by bus to be at the orphanage to hand over her 200 yuan ($40) sponsorship money which went directly to Ting Ting, via the guiding hand of Joyous Li.

Ms Duan was in her fifties with a smooth, calm face and an upturned mouth. She was a senior nursing supervisor in a hospital. On one of her visits, Ms Duan noticed Linda's walking stick and asked her what was wrong. Linda tried to be humorous. She listed her ailments: neuropathy (a nerve dysfunction resulting in numb feet), diabetes, macular degeneration, and a few others apart from the double mastectomy following the breast cancer diagnosis in 2012. She later came to regret mentioning her health issues in such a flippant manner.

Ms Duan was a committed Christian. She belonged to an official protestant church called the Shining Light Church. Ms Duan invited Linda to come and visit one weekend. Linda wouldn't have to pay for a thing. She loved an adventure in China and she was curious to experience a new church and connect with other Christians. So she said yes. Her director of China operations, Xiao Ming, insisted on driving her because he didn't want Linda sitting for eight hours on public buses. He decided to bring along his six-year-old daughter, Mei Lin. With all the arrangements in place, Ms Duan, out of kindness, took a bus to Jiaozuo so she could show Xiao Ming the route. They set off together in the van, leaving the orphanage and the orderly streets of Jiaozuo, heading out towards the highway and then weaving north through the hazy towns and villages of rural Henan.

Linda loved watching the countryside roll by. She loved observing Chinese life by the roadside and in the fields. She also looked forward to getting some rest during the four-hour drive as she had developed a painful bladder infection and didn't feel completely well. She started a course of antibiotics which she'd bought over the counter in Jiaozuo hoping the infection would pass quickly. Despite her lack of verve, it didn't take long before she and Ms Duan struck up a lively conversation, with Xiao Ming translating, and she quickly realised that she wasn't going to get any rest on this trip at all.

Ms Duan began by probing Linda's knowledge of the Bible. Linda loved speaking with Chinese Christians and enjoyed helping them to interpret the scriptures. However, she soon realised, Ms Duan had an inexhaustible list of questions and as their conversation deepened, her queries became increasingly challenging.

With her permanent smile and demure manner, Ms Duan had the patience and tenacity of a python. Her eyes never blinked as her questions bore down into the correlation between God, belief and healing. As a nurse, Ms Duan one assumes, had at least a modicum of medical knowledge, but soon her line of questioning began to ring alarm bells with Linda. In Ms Duan's worldview, disability and illness were caused by sin that had been buried and not dealt with. The purpose of going to church was to uncover that sin and then pray for healing. Linda gazed out of the window, admiring the soft, early afternoon light; an unfolding watercolour of a Chinese country scene. She longed to immerse her thoughts in the scenery, but she didn't want to be rude.

Ms Duan wanted to know more. If a person has a sickness or a disability, is that because there is sin in their lives or because their parents had sinned? And if a person is prayed for and they are not healed, is that because they may still be carrying sin in their life or because they don't have enough faith?

Fortunately, Linda had with her the e-Bible on her iPad and quoted Ms Duan numerous passages, translated by Xiao Ming in the driver's seat who was very interested in the conversation. Xiao Ming liked to pray and read the Bible but he and Joyous Li, his wife, like Director Gong, COAT's Chinese director, were Communist Party members – it was a condition of their employment after the stabbing incident involving the former administrator Lisa. For some Chinese, though not Xiao Ming and Joyous Li, being a Party member isn't only semi-compulsory, it makes you an instant 'influencer'. It can open all sorts of doors. Being part of the machinery is also a form of accountability and loyalty. You can't betray your country, the thinking goes, if you vow to serve the Party. But if you are a party member, then you can't call yourself a Christian.

Ms Duan considered the Old Testament's Book of Isaiah to be her favourite part of the Bible. She particularly concurred with passages discussing the wickedness of man: 'Ah sinful nation, a people laden with iniquity, a seed of evildoers, children that are corrupters…'

Linda's jaw dropped. 'Good grief!' she said out loud. And then under her breath, 'Ms Duan is an over-achieving fundamentalist!'

Linda tried to respond as patiently as she could. 'Sin, illness and disability aren't connected,' she offered, gently but firmly.

Ms Duan, it transpired, was singing from a different hymn book.

The Shining Light Church was some way from the Puyang city centre. The church was more like an enterprise, occupying a complex of low-rise buildings on neatly-kept grounds. It had one enormous hall, several smaller auditoria as well as six floors of dormitories fitted with communal *kang* beds. A *kang* is a platform bed which is heated from underneath. They are popular in northern China where winters are bitterly cold. You put the bedding on top of the heated section so it's like sleeping with an electric blanket. One of the *kang* was big enough to sleep twenty people.

Sharing a *kang* and some quilts with Xiao Ming and his daughter Mei Lin, Linda felt groggy from her infection and the day had been mentally exhausting. She fell into a deep sleep without any problems.

The next morning she felt refreshed and ready to return to the lion's den. Everywhere she went in the church complex, she was treated like a new toy. Her over-protective host, Ms Duan was proud to be the one to have 'discovered' her.

Breakfast was held in a high-ceilinged Soviet-style canteen, where everyone lined up with trays to collect their portion of steamed buns and a watery, sweet liquid made from yellow bean. Linda glanced around the hall. As in her own church in Jiaozuo, most of the people were older women. They wore city clothes but looked quite poor. There were people on crutches and with walking sticks. Others were in wheelchairs or had arms or legs in plaster or bandages around their heads. Like the tour groups converging on the Catholic shrine of Lourdes in France, everyone had come here out of desperation and each one was hoping for a miracle.

It was Saturday morning. Ms Duan took Linda, Xiao Ming and Mei Lin into one of the auditoria where a large gathering listened intently to a preacher on stage. The audience was clearly absorbed. Some of them nodded intently and others scribbled into small notebooks like diligent students. Xiao Ming said the session had been going non-stop since Friday night and was due to continue until the end of the weekend, incorporating a full church service on Sunday morning. This wasn't a special, out-of-the ordinary function; the all-weekend church session took place every weekend.

Xiao Ming was not sure what to think. He knew not to say much, just to translate for Linda, but during a quiet moment he spoke up.

'Why do these people spend so much time at church?' he asked. 'Surely they have families and a life to get on with.' Linda agreed. In her opinion, God came first, then your spouse, children and lastly church. In that order.

The preacher looked at the searching faces around the hall. Dressed like a Mormon in a neat blue suit, he pushed his glasses further up his nose before launching into the heart of the Shining Light Church's doctrine: 'Your sin is what is causing people around you to get sick and invites trouble into their lives. All you have to do,' he said earnestly, 'is to ask God what sins you have committed.'

He raised his hands and looked up to the ceiling.

'And then we confess.' His eyes drifted down and he swept his head from left to right. '*That's* when we will be healed.'

A loud, unintended, 'Huh?' slipped from Linda's lips. Some of the pilgrims nearby looked up from their notes and stared at her. She coughed to appear as if she'd been clearing her throat. She couldn't believe what she was hearing and longed to haul the man off stage.

After the preacher had finished his sermon, he asked participants to join smaller guided discussion groups. There was silence as a thousand people rose up to contemplate their sinful lives. Linda followed one group into a conference room, feeling a sudden stab of pain in her toes.

'It is not a sign of anything,' she told herself, wincing.

Her group of fifteen sat around in a circle with the leader, a woman in her sixties named Miss Huang (meaning 'yellow'). Miss Yellow was stick thin and smooth-faced with wavy, salt and pepper grey hair. She had a scratchy voice which occasionally dropped out as if she were recovering from laryngitis. Miss Yellow scoured the faces of the group before singling out an elderly woman with her hand up. She urged the woman to stand and share her story with the group.

The woman, called Aunty Wu, slowly rose to her feet. She was grandmotherly, pensive. Pushing hair away from her face with quivering fingers, she exuded anguished shame. Speaking in a quiet, low voice she said she had suffered serious stomach issues for most of her life. Despite searching for many years, she was never able to find a reason for her illness. And so she continued to suffer for many years. Then one day, she came to The Shining Light Church where she believed she finally discovered the cause of her misery.

As a girl, Aunty Wu continued tentatively, she realised that her father had treated her brothers better than he had treated her. In fact he sometimes behaved as if she didn't exist. She was hurt by this realisation, which started to cloud her thoughts. She stopped and looked down.

'As I grew older, I began to hate my father,' she said. 'I became more and more jealous of my brothers. And that only added to my misery.'

Her head was bowed, like a guilty confessor.

Later in life, she cooked delicious food and special treats for her mother but never for her father. Wickedly, she said, spitting out the words, she had shunned him.

Aunty Wu's shoulders hunched forward as if she could absorb no more shame.

Both of Aunty Wu's parents were now dead. She very much regretted how she'd treated her father and felt convinced that her parents' deaths had been her fault because she'd never apologised for what she did. She had remained unrepentant.

'I have to make sure bad things don't happen to me,' Aunty Wu said. 'Unrepented sins will cause bad things to happen.' And though God reminded her of that sin, she said, it was too late to take it all back as her parents were now dead. Aunty Wu said she woke each morning, damp with sweat.

Finally, she lifted her head, signalling her story was over.

Miss Yellow nodded her head approvingly as if she had heard this story, or similar ones, many times before. Linda, on the other hand, couldn't withhold her silence any longer.

Reaching for her iPad, she read out the part in the Bible where Jesus and his disciples came across a blind man. The disciples asked Jesus whether the man had been born blind because of his own sins or the sins of his parents. Jesus replied, 'No'. It happened so the power of God could be revealed through the blind man.

'Whatever "sin" occurred, Aunty Wu doesn't need to repent,' Linda said, addressing the gathering. 'It's in the past. It's water under the bridge.'

Someone shouted out, 'You can't hide your sins from God! He won't forget!' A man from the circle stood up. He waved an accusing finger in Aunty Wu's direction.

Miss Yellow nodded vigorously again. 'Despite what our foreign friend says, Aunty Wu's sin hasn't gone away,' she said.

Miss Yellow asked everyone in the group to write down the sins God knew they had committed and spend some time thinking of a way to correct the past. In short, she was asking them to write a 'self-criticism'. During The Cultural Revolution, self-criticisms were used to force confessions about ideological failings and 'crimes', but the concept has never really died out in Chinese culture.

Linda told herself to let it go, but she couldn't. She got up from her seat again. 'This is so sad and so wrong. We should not live in such fear! God is bigger than that,' Linda pleaded.

'I told them that they didn't need to live with that guilt because Jesus came, so now we have "Amazing Grace". No matter how wretched we are, Salvation is easy for us ... we do not have to struggle to get it.'

Linda continued to argue her point. During the dinner break when everyone returned to the canteen, the dialogue continued. A stocky woman with the air of a factory foreman introduced herself as Miss Wang (meaning King). She was an English teacher at a local secondary school. Like the group leader Miss Yellow, Miss Wang too seemed to have trouble with her throat and had a voice like a grater. Thinking that as a teacher she must be intelligent, Linda tried to reason with her about this misguided belief that sin causes illness and disability.

'It was like hitting your head against a brick wall,' Linda said. 'For us both.'

On Sunday, followers of the Shining Light put on a service on their second campus, where no officials were attending, in a church with a dress circle and a fifty person choir dressed as angels with large red bows. Then Linda, Xiao Ming and Mei Lin climbed wearily into the van for the journey back to Jiaozuo. As the door was about to slam shut, from around the corner a hand appeared and wedged it open. It was the hand of Miss Wang, the gravelly-voiced English teacher begging Linda to pause for a while. Linda grimaced. By now, her bladder infection was causing her much discomfort. She just wanted to be in the van with the others, and to sleep off the pain. In her scratchy voice, Miss Wang warned Linda that unforgiven sins were the cause of a person's physical suffering and the underlying cause of Linda's own, many physical problems.

'She sounded so urgent and desperate,' recalled Linda, 'like if I didn't agree with her, I was going to be sick and unhappy for the rest of my life. She wanted me to repent there and then before I left.'

Linda didn't dare reveal to Miss Wang that she had a bladder infection. She just thanked her and said goodbye.

Puyang and the Shining Light Church receded in the rear window. For the first time in days, she felt she could breathe freely again. Linda's thoughts turned to Ting Ting, the seventeen-year-old orphan with cerebral palsy whom Ms Duan sponsored.

Ms Duan told Ting Ting that, contrary to medical opinion that cerebral palsy can't be cured, she could be healed by coming to church to confess her sins.

Linda refused to allow Ting Ting to go.

'I told her you can attend church after you turn eighteen next year.' Ting Ting believed in God, but Linda wasn't sure whether she fully understood what Ms Duan was promising. In a few months, Ting Ting would be an adult, with little preparation for life on the outside of the orphanage. Hopefully Ms Duan would latch on to another sinner before then.

CHAPTER 19

Babies For Sale

We set off leaving the clean, wide streets of Jiaozuo city for the countryside. We were on a visit to Joyous Li's hometown. Packed tight like an overstuffed refrigerator, our grey minivan bumped along the highway, ducking and dodging its way around the cars, trucks and semi-trailers on National Highway 107. The tollway runs from Beijing all the way to Shenzhen in southern China, a distance of 2,698 kilometres. But that day in March 2015, we were not travelling so far. Electricity pylons, bare trees and wheat fields flashed by. The townships became sparser, giving way to earth-coloured villages in the distance.

In the minivan was Linda, Joyous Li, her husband Xiao Ming the driver, their daughter Mei Lin, Director Gong and me. Director Gong insisted that he come along for the trip when he heard we were going. It was because Linda told him I was writing a book about her and now he had become suspicious. He took the front seat next to Xiao Ming. They were having their own conversation about something that was in the news. I listened briefly, but it sounded boring. Then Director Gong turned around to us.

'America is very bad,' he said shaking his head as if he'd just caught a whiff of rotten meat.

Nobody in the van reacted. So he continued. 'At least the American President and the government are very bad,' he said.

'Why is America bad?' Linda asked in Chinese.

'Because it doesn't respect China. For so many years and despite China becoming so powerful, they don't respect us. It's in the news this morning. Yet again, President Obama takes Japan's side.'

Director Gong was referring to the ongoing island dispute with Japan in the East China Sea. China's maritime claims have been a creeping concern in global diplomacy, pushing many Asian nations to bolster ties with the United States. Australia also supports complete freedom of navigation. However the Chinese media lambasts any nation that doesn't appear to trust the Middle Kingdom's motivations and Director Gong was a true believer.

He peered around to see whether anyone agreed with him. Nobody did. We were on an informal outing and no-one was interested in a debate about nationalism or the perceived wickedness of America and Japan. I opened the window to let some cool air in. Taking a cue, Director Gong returned to his conversation with Xiao Ming.

Joyous Li is a vivacious woman in her early thirties. When Chinese people name their children, there is symbolism and meaning attached to this. Her Chinese name begins with her surname Li, which is a common Chinese surname meaning 'strength'. It is her name and not her husband's. The other part of her name (in the West, we would call this her first name) means 'joyous' or 'happy'. The name suits her down to the ground.

When she speaks English, she stresses the ends of her words as if they are really important. 'That-a is very –ya… good –da.'

Her mouth is always slightly open, ready to become a toothy laugh at any moment. Her eyes twinkle behind Coke-bottle spectacles.

Happiness is a pre-occupation in China. So is wealth and good fortune. Every door or entrance is framed by red paper posters which are put up during Spring Festival, China's official new year. The posters contain rhyming couplets spelling out good wishes. As well as couplets, there's often the Chinese character 'Fu', meaning 'good luck', written in gold on a shiny, red diamond-shaped poster. Sometimes the character is placed upside-down. It's a Chinese double entendre, when you tip something upside-down, like a magician's cup, it signifies arrival. So the meaning of the upside-down character 'Fu' is that 'wealth' has 'arrived' in the household.

When I first met Joyous Li and Xiao Ming in 2013, they were expecting their second daughter. The couple met at university and became volunteer translators for COAT in the mid-2000s. These days they are senior members of Linda's management team and her right-hand man and woman in China. Joyous Li administers the foster homes and Xiao Ming is responsible for the overall management of the homes and school. Their relationship with Linda goes much deeper. They call her 'Linda Mama' and they deeply admire her.

On that smoggy, cool spring day, the grey minivan reached the tollgate as we exited the expressway. Though there was a uniformed inspector collecting tolls, a recorded voice as well as an LED screen told us we needed to pay 50 yuan ($10). Xiao Ming handed the money to the inspector and as the boom gate opened to a recorded voice saying, 'Thank you and have a safe journey', the man in uniform saluted us. The exit ramp curled around into a small industrial township. We passed an enormous furniture factory, and a small Bank of China branch. Then there were rows of kiosks: a little restaurant, shops selling rope, pipes, tools and ceramic basins. At the basin shop we turned left onto a dirt road with a sign above it pointing to 'Li Village', the same character as Joyous Li's name.

It was hard to tell how big Li Village was and there wasn't a field in sight. The main street rolled out, cracked and unloved in front of us. The road was lined with eight fitness stations. In China, it's the elderly who use them. They love their outdoor exercise. Many of them practice Tai Chi or fan dancing. These fitness stations have become popular all over China, indicating perhaps, that most of the village inhabitants were elderly.

'When I was born here in 1983 Li Village was really rustic with dirt roads. The farmhouses were made of mud and brick,' Joyous Li said, marvelling at the change. It had been five years since her last visit. I glanced at her in the back of the van with her daughter asleep on her lap. Joyous Li was living up to her name, grinning from ear to ear.

In an excited voice like a hungry bird, she called out to her husband to turn right at the first lane. 'The third one on the left,' she chirped.

The van turned and we found ourselves heading towards a maroon metal gate. Standing in front was a fit-looking woman with short hair framed around a tough, round face. She wore black woollen leggings showing off muscular legs, short boots and a dazzling blue coat. Before she recognised the occupants of the approaching van, she looked quite intimidating. I imagined her dressed as a village cadre in a blue Mao suit, wearing a cap with a red star, barking orders in name of Chairman Mao.

When she recognised Xiao Ming in the driver's seat, something in her changed. She waved and shouted excitedly. 'Oh my, oh dear, you are here!'

It was Ms Gao, Joyous Li's mother. The smile mellowed her metallic expression. Now she looked like a trendy granny but one you still wouldn't want to mess with.

I jumped down from the van onto the muddy ground. It was good to inhale fresh air albeit tinged with the aroma of manure and dirty coal. After introductions and hugs, Ms Gao brought out a large bunch of keys as if she were a jailer. I was excited. I had heard so much about Joyous Li's early life although I was under strict instructions not to probe her family while we were here. I had come along to observe, not to dig up the past.

The metal gates in front of Joyous Li's childhood home clearly hadn't been opened in a long time. A tin of WD40 would have come in handy. But after a few good pushes, the gate creaked inward revealing an overgrown courtyard and a derelict cottage.

Joyous Li's home looked like something straight out of a Pearl Buck novel, a glimpse of old China, even though most of the events in the following pages occurred in the late 1990s. The entire two-room cottage was the size of my living room at home in Australia and yet six people including her Grandma had lived here.

The mud-brick walls were plastered with certificates she and her elder sister had received at school. Joyous Li reached out to touch them, peeling and yellowed.

'I was actually a very good student,' she said, grinning broadly.

There was still crockery, broken into pieces, on the rickety, square dining table. Part of the ceiling had caved in over the bedroom/kitchen and there were cobwebs everywhere. It seemed hard to imagine that this was once all her family had. But this was the story shared by the majority of families in Li Village. After years of hard work and suffering, contentment, progress and even a little wealth had crept up on them all.

Joyous Li was born in 1983 three years after the one-child policy came into being. But though she was the second daughter, her parents, who were highly respected in the village, were never troubled by family planning officials. At school, Joyous Li had learned all about China's national priority of population control. Outside the classroom, she witnessed how the policy was enforced, particularly when other families disobeyed the regulations.

'I was very nosy and used to follow the action in the village whenever I could,' she said. 'If someone had a child without permission, this was known as an "out of plan" child. Once I saw village officials arrive with a big truck. The family couldn't afford to pay the fine for the illegal birth, so officials took all their furniture and belongings: televisions, cabinets, chairs, tables. Another time when we knew of a woman who got pregnant, the husband and wife went into hiding. The officials just broke down the door of their home and took everything.'

It didn't always go according to plan for the village cadres. 'If the couple was clever about this, they would move their precious belongings into a neighbour's home. The officials didn't have the right to break in and take anything from an innocent family,' she said, smiling.

Even after the one-child policy came into force in 1980 all the families in Li Village seemed to keep having children; two, three and four. She remembers once, seeing officials arrive at the home of a family with a second, unauthorised child. They rammed trucks into the doorway to break it down.

'After two or three goes with the truck,' she recalled, 'the roof collapsed! The family had already escaped to the city. A few years later they returned and by then had earned lots of money. They rebuilt the house, filled it with brand-new furniture and lived very happily after that,' Joyous Li said with a sense of satisfaction.

Joyous Li had an elder sister, but of course, what her parents really longed for was a son. When Joyous Li was five, her mother finally gave birth to a boy. Firecrackers were set off from the top of their gatehouse to celebrate the birth. The baby boy was named New Sun. He was adored by all, but particularly by his mother.

Joyous Li remembers this time with much fondness. She was eager to explain that a key part of her family's satisfaction came from their social status which was boosted by having a son. It also ensured the family had a lineage and that Mr Li retained good *guanxi* or personal connections with the village leaders.

Joyous Li's father was a farmer. Instead of bringing up the family on a meagre farm income, like many enterprising Chinese in the eighties and nineties, he diversified. He set up a truck repair business which took him away from home frequently, but also boosted household earnings. At home, it was always Joyous Li's mother who held the fort. She wore the pants at home as well as being the principal of the village school. Joyous Li remembers her mother being extremely strict with all the children, especially her own. Once as she strode past Joyous Li's classroom, she noticed her daughter gazing dreamily out of the window instead of paying attention to the lesson. Wasting no time, Principal Gao threw open the door of the classroom and pulled her daughter to her feet. She dragged Joyous Li outside and made her kneel in the snow as punishment.

Apart from her village job, Principal Gao also owned several pieces of land on the outskirts of the village where she grew vegetables. Joyous Li and her siblings were expected to help out with the farm chores after finishing their schoolwork. At harvest time, they spread the wheat stalks out on the main street to dry before threshing. If they were lucky, tractors and trucks drove over the wheat, meaning the children had less threshing to do later. Principal Gao always insisted the children keep a close watch on the crop as it dried, just in case anyone tried to pinch it.

One evening as Joyous Li stood by the road guarding the wheat, her mother called her home for dinner. The house was only 50 metres away. Within moments she had run through the gate and pushed open the wooden doors to the cottage, taking a seat at the square table surrounded by five wooden stools in the centre of the room. It was the 1990s and although life had vastly improved for many rural Chinese families, the evening meal was still basic: plain boiled rice, scrambled eggs with tomatoes, and stir-fried garlic chives flavoured with preserved pork.

The girls picked up their chopsticks hungrily. Their father was away on business, but there was still one empty seat. Joyous Li's mother scowled and made the girls put down their bowls.

'Where is he?' Principal Gao said. 'Where is New Sun?'

Around the table there was silence. No-one knew.

'Mother insisted she would beat him when he turned up,' Joyous Li recalled. 'We were always beaten back then.'

After a few more minutes, Principal Gao impatiently pushed her stool back and went to look for him. The girls heard her open the maroon metal doors of the gatehouse, calling New Sun's name in one direction and then down the other end of path. Any moment, the girls expected to hear the thud of New Sun's shoes on the path to the cottage. Though their mother was always the disciplinarian in the family, New Sun was her favourite. For him, forgiveness – and dinner – always came quickly.

But New Sun didn't come racing through the door. By now, everyone was hungry and impatient. They ate their evening meal expecting New Sun to appear any moment. Joyous Li took his bowl of rice smothered in eggs and vegetables and put it under a plate to keep it warm. Her younger brother was almost nine and knew how to look after himself. He often forgot the time though, so she wasn't worried.

The last soft light of early evening disappeared behind the trees. It was 8 pm and soon, the moon would appear splashing peach-coloured rays across the fields and over the distant lake. The village had barely any street lighting and the sky was always spectacular with its carpet of stars. Li Village had always been safe and peaceful.

But Joyous Li began to notice something she rarely saw. She sensed fear in her mother's stern face; fear laced with anger at New Sun's prank which had gone too far. Principal Gao went out to gather a search party and told the girls to wait at a neighbour's house.

Knocking on Mrs Tao's front gate, she asked nervously, 'Have you seen New Sun? He didn't come home for dinner.'

'No,' said Mrs Tao tsking at the boy's naughtiness. 'But we've already finished our meal. I'll get my sons to find torches and they can help your Mum look for him. I suppose your Dad is away?'

Joyous Li had almost forgotten about her father.

'Yes, he's out of town. I should tell the village watchmen. Maybe someone can pass a message onto him to get him to come home quickly,' Joyous Li told her.

She waited inside Mrs Tao's home. It was warm and she could stay near the window, listening out for the sounds of the search team returning.

It was a clear night with a half moon. It was autumn, so that the leaves were starting to fall from the trees. She noticed the outline of the branches of their special tree across the road in their courtyard. According to Joyous Li's Grandma, the special tree had been there for several generations. Even Grandma had played on the tree since she was a small girl. Joyous Li and her big sister sometimes held hands around the trunk, walking around slowly to see if they could see each other. The tree was a constant presence in their lives and each child held a fondness for it, particularly for its strong branches, one for each of the children.

'Help us,' Joyous whispered quietly to the tree, because she was a good little Communist and hadn't heard of God then. 'Please bring him back.'

Principal Gao came to an old village house where large ceramic urns were lined up along the side wall. These brown earthenware pots were used to collect rainwater, but recently modern plumbing had been installed in many of the houses, so water was now piped instead of being brought from the wells and then stored in the urns. The pots were too heavy to dispose of so when they weren't needed any more, they were left beside the wall until they eventually broke and could be carried away in smaller pieces.

As soon as Principal Gao saw the urns, she smiled to herself. She was sure New Sun was hiding in one of them. By now he was probably hiding because he was too scared to return home.

'If you come out now,' Principal Gao called out, trying to sound reasonable above her concern, 'I promise not to beat you.' Under her breath she added quietly, 'Right away.'

She expected New Sun's face to appear over the top of an urn. It didn't. After searching all the places she could think of, Principal Gao returned to the farmhouse, alone.

Suddenly, there was loud knocking on the gate. It was a distant relative named Old Mr Blue. He had news. Old Mr Blue had seen New Sun and another boy together after school earlier in the afternoon. He said he saw the boys swimming in the lake used to irrigate crops. Everybody knew the lake. It was at the edge of the village, in front of a landmark known as the Treeless Hill.

Principal Gao hadn't dared to mention it, but she'd been worried the boy may have been kidnapped. Although he was a little old for this, she had read in the newspaper how babies and children were taken from the villages – especially boys – and sold to rich families or even criminal gangs in the cities. Sometimes the children who worked for the gangs had their limbs broken to make them deformed so people would feel sorry for them and give them money.

Principal Gao wondered whether New Sun had gone to his friend's home. She knew instinctively that the other child was Little Bean, her son's closest friend. Once again, the search party pounded the dusty path in the direction of Little Bean's home. The men promised to bring New Sun back to her and insisted Principal Gao wait at home.

At around 10 o'clock, Joyous Li, who was still at Neighbour Tao's home across the lane from her house, heard the search party returning. She saw the erratic torch light and ran outside to the big maroon gate and followed the men into her house.

At first she couldn't see clearly in the darkness with all the men crowded inside the small living room. There was just one light-bulb in that room. As her eyes adjusted to the light she made out three men carrying her brother's limp, wet body. She saw her mother fall onto the body, hugging the boy and weeping uncontrollably. The men were trying to lay the boy down, but Joyous Li's mother would not let go of him. She held New Sun's body, rocking him and stroking his head. 'He isn't dead, he isn't dead, he isn't dead,' she repeated.

One of the villagers tried to pump the boy's chest and water began to gush out from New Sun's mouth and nose. It made no difference. He was clearly dead. All the while, Principal Gao, who had always kept a firm control of her emotions, wept in the manner of a woman who had lost everything that ever mattered.

'He isn't dead, he isn't dead, he isn't dead.'

During this desperate scene, Joyous Li's father returned home from his business trip. He'd received the message sent by Joyous Li through the village watchman that he was to return home immediately. Driving someone else's truck, he arrived home just after midnight. By this time, the girls and their mother were in one room, inconsolable. In the second room, New Sun was lying on a tarpaulin on the bed. When Joyous Li's father saw the body, he stumbled onto the hard, dirt floor but then caught himself and stood up again, almost too quickly. Years later, he told Joyous Li he didn't want to show any weakness. That would have made everyone else's suffering worse, he reasoned. None of his family ever saw him cry over the death of his golden boy.

The villagers told Joyous Li's father that when New Sun had been pulled from the waterhole, he was already dead. His body and limbs were tangled up with the second boy, his friend, Little Bean. The tallest man in the village had been instructed to wade into the water and search the shallow water. Within minutes, his legs struck the bodies. The boys had drowned, somehow twisted together as if they had been hugging each other. Two families had been broken and were now grieving on that clear autumn night.

Joyous Li's father went out to find wooden planks to make a casket for his only son.

'Mother put blankets and toys into the coffin with New Sun and cried and hugged him again for the last time. And then my father took the coffin away and buried my little brother that very night. He never told my mother where he buried New Sun. He didn't want her to know. And that was that,' Joyous Li said matter-of-factly, although there was the sense, perhaps, that she was being stoic, just as her father had been that night.

The effects of the double drowning continued to be felt for many years. Nobody would accept that the incident was an unfortunate tragedy. Joyous Li's family never spoke to Little

Bean's family again. Each family blamed the other for dragging their boy down into his watery grave. The village was never quite the same again.

Walking through Joyous Li's childhood home in the countryside, I retraced the steps of her story. Directly over the place where the body had been placed, the ceiling of the cottage had recently collapsed into a pile of red dust. The family stayed in the house for a few more years after New Sun's death, but somehow it felt as if time had stood still since that tragic autumn night. Joyous Li made me promise I wouldn't ask her mother about losing her son. So I made mental notes of the road where the wheat was left to dry and the distance to her neighbour's house. From the gate I looked towards where her father might have buried the makeshift coffin, perhaps near the Treeless Hill.

Despite the family's quiet grief, life in the village continued.

'A few years later, after so much sadness, my Mother decided that our family couldn't carry on without a son. It made my parents feel as if they had lost their standing, their position in the village,' Joyous Li explained. 'We were a very successful family. My mum was a principal and my dad had gone from being a farmer to a businessman. In rural China, the tradition is that you have to have a son. The son is needed to lead the family in a funeral procession,' she said. 'Losing New Sun meant they lost a big part of their significance and that feeling didn't melt away.'

When Joyous Li turned fifteen, a visitor came to their village. He brought a small boy with him and left him at the house. Apparently this was a middleman with a 'try before you buy' deal. Collectively the family decided that they didn't like the small boy so the man came back to take him away. A few weeks later, the same man returned with another boy. He was two years old. Joyous Li's parents named him Great Sun and he was allowed to stay.

'My parents paid a high price for him. They paid the man 8,000 yuan ($1,600). He became my parents' son and our new brother.'

The explanation given by the middleman was that Great Sun's biological mother had become pregnant while still single. Apparently the baby's father committed a crime and went to jail. In China, it's not socially acceptable to be an unmarried mother. With an unregistered child, the woman would be unlikely to find a husband in rural China, so she chose to sell her son.

In 2016, Great Sun turned eighteen. He left school to work with his father mending trucks. At times, Joyous Li says, the boy may have sensed there was something suspicious about his past. He recently asked whether he had always part of the family. His mother quickly snapped, 'Of course!' He doesn't know that he was bought and no-one is allowed to discuss it with him.

Buying and selling children in China is illegal, but the one-child policy – and a huge wealth disparity – has created a thriving black market in a trade which exists to this very day.

Thousands of women and children in China are trafficked each year. One couple in Shanghai, China's richest city, admitted to selling three newborn babies between 2008 and 2013 for 90,000 yuan ($18,000). They used a popular instant messaging system to make the transactions. The proceeds were spent on iPhones and luxury shoes.

Chinese television interviewed a blind woman named Ms Du in 2013 who lived in poverty and sold three girls and a boy to pay for food and schooling for her eldest son and daughter. She made $1,500 selling the four children.

'Rich people give away money for their daughter's wedding,' said the blind woman. 'Middle-class people get money for a daughter's marriage and poor people sell sons and daughters.'

I asked Joyous Li what she thought about the practice of buying and selling children. I struggled with explaining the meaning of the word 'taboo' and she struggled to understand me. It was as if, in matters so deeply rooted in the heart, the idea of a social taboo doesn't merit a second thought.

'After we lost New Sun, something strange happened to our special tree. It began to lose its leaves and then it died,' Joyous Li said as if she were overriding my question.

'We didn't pull the roots up though. We left the tree in the courtyard as a reminder; a reminder that something very precious had been in our lives. Then ten years later when I was pregnant with my first daughter it began to grow branches again. The tree came back to life.'

'You see, anything or anyone can be bought in China,' Joyous Li continued, cautiously. 'Bought. Or Sold. But that's another story.'

CHAPTER 20

The Family Tree

Before we left Joyous Li's old home in Li Village, I got this eerie sense we were surrounded by ghosts. In the small room attached to the gatehouse, there was a dusty, photograph of an old woman. The wooden frame was still intact, but the glass had been broken. The room was where Joyous Li's paternal grandmother had slept and she had lived with the family for many years. I took a photo of her portrait on my iPhone, so I could remember the setting. When I checked it later, the image of the woman was blurred although everything else in the photo was in focus. Spooky. Joyous Li was keen to remind me of many happy moments she had spent here as a child. But in all its decrepitude, I could only sense the pain. Maybe it was a good time to just lock the gate and leave it for good.

Joyous Li wouldn't leave until she had shown us her special hiding places in the cottage. We made our way through the undergrowth back to the cottage. In her laughing voice, Joyous Li pointed to where the Spring Festival buns were stored on a ledge over the doorway. Grooves had been carved into the back of the vermillion door like a ladder for someone to access the secret ledge. And another favourite hiding place for the children was in the loft, just under the exposed hardwood beams, where grain and some bedding were stored.

'I loved climbing up to the loft,' Joyous Li said. 'I always discovered surprising things,' she said with a twinkle. But we didn't get to hear about the surprising things because her mother, Ms Gao, was impatient to leave. Lunchtime was approaching and the Chinese take mealtimes very seriously.

'Joyous Li,' Linda whispered, unsure whether she should mention it, in case Ms Gao would get upset, 'Where is the special tree?'

She led us out of the cottage into the overgrown courtyard and pointed to a very tall tree in the furthest corner. The tree was indeed tall, but disappointingly ordinary.

'A branch of the tree fell off when my brother died, but a few years after it began to grow a new branch.' She indicated how one of the lower branches ended in a stump and further up the trunk, the tree had grown a new thick branch, like a river dividing into two.

'It eventually grew two new branches,' Joyous Li said. 'Two branches for the two daughters who did well, that's my big sister and me.'

The conversation stopped. Awkwardly.

'There were no branches for my brother. Or my little sister: Rui Rui.' Little sister? She had mentioned a big sister but not a younger one.

After our visit to Joyous Li's home we travelled along a narrow two-lane country road for half an hour. The minivan turned into a second village. Xiao Ming dialled a number on his mobile phone and held it to his ear. Someone was giving him directions and he scrunched up his face looking for a landmark. On reaching a corner shop, holding the phone to his ear still, he turned left sharply with his free hand and pulled up alongside a huge corner house with a bright blue metal gate.

The gate was ajar. Inside was a small courtyard with some vegetable rows. The plots held the dying remnants of the last harvest with a few straggling *bok choi* plants that were ripe and ready for eating. A few steps away on the front porch, there was a scattering of farm implements and a three-wheeled electric cart. A chubby young woman with a bob haircut squatted over a basin full of clothes in soapy water. She vigorously scrubbed away on a grooved wooden washboard. She looked up when she saw us coming through the gate and her face broke into a broad smile. Rushing forward in excitement, her hands were still completely dripping. At her side was a toddler with a short, practical haircut, a serious expression and wind-burned cheeks. In fact, the child never smiled all day. Nor did she cry once. She was bundled up against the cold, wearing a quilted top and typical of Chinese toddlers, split pants, no nappy of course.

Joyous Li threw her arms around the woman with the soapy hands. They stood face to face, shouting their greetings at each other in excitement. Joyous Li's daughter Mei Lin, and the little girl called Peaches, eyed each other suspiciously. Peaches ran straight for the tricycles and offered one of them to her cousin. Although they hadn't seen each other for many months, the tricycles turned them into instant best friends.

One evening in Linda's apartment, Joyous Li sat crossed-legged and lifted her glasses to rub her eyes. Was she misting up? I couldn't tell. She had promised to tell me the story of her little sister. It was never going to be an easy conversation.

'My mother had wanted a son. She already had my big sister and me and she didn't want another girl. Our paternal Grandma (whom they called Nai Nai) lived with us at home and took care of us. But in 1985, two years after I was born, another little girl, Rui Rui came along. Mother wanted to sell her, but Mother's mother was against that. She said it wasn't right to sell your own baby.'

Joyous Li was told years later that she and her elder sister were sent to a relative's home one day while Ms Gao took her mother (named Lao Lao) and baby Rui Rui on a donkey cart to Lao Lao's home. It was a journey of about an hour each way.

'My Lao Lao cared for Rui Rui in her home and raised her by herself,' said Joyous Li.

Welfare experts call this 'informal kinship care' when someone in the family takes on the primary care of a child without the involvement of the state. It's been practised in rural China for centuries. So Rui Rui was cared for by her grandmother. But when she turned seven, her mother had a change of heart. Principal Gao decided that Rui Rui should get an education. So the little girl was brought home and started school in the village when she was eight. She attended school until Grade Four and then dropped out to care for her grandmother, Nai Nai, who was dying. Nai Nai eventually died in the spring of 1999 when Rui Rui was fourteen. The air was fluffy with pollen and the shoots of wheat were deep green and ten centimetres high.

Because Rui Rui wasn't needed as a carer anymore, her mother decided to find her a job. It isn't often Linda uses cruel words about someone but she called Joyous Li's mother, Principal Gao, a 'piece of work'. First, this woman abandoned her daughter, treated her poorly through her young life and then put her into the workforce when was she still a teenager. However, many Chinese families would have thought nothing about doing the same thing. The job Principal Gao found her was in a sprawling towelling factory. Rui Rui and the other young female workers lived like sardines, crammed into dormitories. Rui Rui worked twelve-hour shifts for six days with one day off a week. After deductions for food and board at the factory, she sent the remaining money home to support the family each month.

Dragging the secrets out of someone else's family closet was like unearthing a buried body. Joyous Li, who had shown no expression until this point, lifted her head so that I could see her face. Her eyes were swollen and she took off her glasses to wipe the tears before they rolled down her face.

'Rui Rui never had the chance of a good life,' said her big sister remorsefully, accepting a tissue. I thought of all the merit awards Joyous Li and her big sister had earned from school, displayed proudly on the walls of her old mud-brick home. All the fun of finding Spring Festival buns and playing hiding-and-seek in the loft. Rui Rui had no happy memories from school and had been treated like a servant by her mother in their home.

Despite this, Rui Rui grew up to be sweet-natured if a little shy. She had only attended primary school for four years and unlike her sisters, never shone academically. With no parental guidance, Rui Rui not surprisingly developed into a vulnerable teenager.

In the clatter of the dormitory one evening, a young woman took her under her wing. Her new friend seemed always to have money, which Rui Rui rarely did, and offered to buy her nice things. She invited Rui Rui and another young worker for lunch and some shopping at the nearby town on their day off. The three of them had lots of fun and so the following weekend they went out once again. This time, Rui Rui and the other girl were locked up and raped. Rui Rui was told she had been sold to a family who wanted a 'wife' for their son. Eventually she discovered that the 'friend' from the dormitory was an experienced trafficker. This woman had done the same thing to other teenagers; selling them to desperate families searching for 'affordable' wives. The 'friend' was paid 7,000 yuan ($1,400) for each transaction.

Sex trafficking in China has become an increasing problem and now girls and women are even kidnapped from neighbouring Vietnamese villages to feed the need for brides in China.

Sex trafficking stems from China's gender imbalance which stems from the one-child policy and the preference for sons. According to Reuters, there are currently 118 men to every 100 women.[1] In some provinces however, including Henan, the disparity is closer to 140 men to 100 women according to the *British Medical Journal*.[2] While there are laws to punish those involved in sex trafficking, in many parts of rural China it's exceedingly hard to police and penalties aren't stringent enough. Many women are tricked into leaving their homes with promises of employment, high salaries or the hope of life in a city. While most who fall victim to the trade are over twenty, it's not at all uncommon to find teenagers lured away or 'bought' as Rui Rui was.

Rui Rui was taken to a village she had never been to before. She met her new 'family' and became their servant. By day, they locked her in the farmhouse to clean and prepare meals. By night, she was forced to have sex with the eldest son. She did what she was told because she didn't know where to even begin to look for help. There is a phrase used in China: the mountains are high and the Emperor is far away. It's used to imply that rules set by the central government in Beijing often get lost in the provinces. Though selling babies and wives is illegal under Chinese law, everything depends on the quality and integrity of local officials. As such, many things that shouldn't happen manage to slip by unnoticed. Like a new wife in a poor village.

Rui Rui knew nothing about sex before she was raped. She had no idea about contraception. She didn't know how to protect or look after her body. And she didn't understand why it was changing. Her periods had stopped. Amid the fear and confusion, it was at this point she decided that she had nothing to lose. The only way to get her life back was to run away.

In the farmhouse where she was held, Rui Rui noticed that the windows always leaked when it rained. The wooden frames were papered over with newspaper to stop the wind getting through. Security came in the form of high walls and the gatehouse around the compound. Rui Rui felt confident that once she forced open the window, she could run to the small gatehouse door where she could access the roof.

She chose a night when the moon was barely visible and managed to open the window easily and clamber out. Running across the courtyard, she stumbled on farm tools that had been left beside the vegetable patches. Nobody in the house stirred, so she kept going. She opened the gatehouse door, climbed the high steps to the roof and crouched down so her silhouette wouldn't draw attention like an inexperienced thief. As soon as she caught her breath, she crawled on her growing stomach towards the wall of the gatehouse holding a coat she had brought from the house. Feeling inside the pockets of the coat, she found 100 yuan ($20) which she stuffed into her own pockets. She tied one of the arms to a metal peg used to hang drying wheat and clambered down until she was holding on to the hem of the coat. Then she dropped down to the ground. Her legs hurt, but she could take the pain. She was free. She walked and ran down the village main street and onto the county road. As dawn approached, she crouched down in a patch of spiky bushes and listened for the sound of the local bus. It took forever to come. But when she heard the distant rumble of an old diesel motor, she took her chance, clambering out of the bush and madly waving her arms.

'At that point, she thought she'd succeeded,' Joyous Li said. 'She was so relieved to have escaped that cruel family.'

The family didn't give up easily though. They had paid 7,000 yuan for Rui Rui which was more than a year's wages for a farmer. They felt they owned her. They couldn't go to the police, of course, so they decided to pursue Rui Rui by themselves and bring her back to their home.

Much to Rui Rui's dismay, the father and 'husband' managed to stop the very bus she was on.

The father asked the driver if he had noticed a young girl getting on board. 'She's run away from home,' he lied. 'We're worried about her.'

If he suspected something, the driver didn't give anything away.

So the father climbed the steps onto the bus like a citizen policeman, shouting to passengers to stand up, shoving people aside as he conducted a search for his 'daughter', the wayward teenager.

Like a scene from a suspense thriller, Rui Rui crawled on the floor to the back of the bus and pulled some luggage over her.

It was a good hiding place. Nobody turned her in.

Her captors got off the bus, defeated.

After days of riding on buses and hiding in bushes, Rui Rui found her way back to her grandmother's home where she had spent the first seven years of her life. Lao Lao saw immediately that the teenager was pregnant. She was sixteen years old. Years later, she told Joyous Li that the night she gave birth had been the most frightening night of her life. The pain had been excruciating and she thought she was dying. The labour lasted less than an hour and thankfully the baby arrived very quickly. Lao Lao severed the umbilical cord. After everything Rui Rui had been through, from her escape to giving birth, she was exhausted and traumatised. Rui Rui wrapped the baby in some of her clothing and threw it over the wall of the toilet block of her grandmother's home.

The tiny bundle was found by a relative named Aunty Bo. Aunty Bo fed the baby some rice gruel to quieten her down. A few days later, she took the child and went out and sold her for 600 yuan ($120). The child was bought by a distant cousin who had badly wanted a girl. Rui Rui saw her child just once. The little girl was very well cared for which gave Rui Rui peace of mind.

As we stood in the courtyard of Rui Rui's spacious home, Ms Gao returned with a bag of steaming hot meat buns, a local specialty.

'You have to eat these while they are hot,' she said, ushering us into the house.

We sat around a small coffee table in the living room, eating the delicious sesame-topped buns, stuffed with warm stir-fried lamb and spring onions. Rui Rui fussed around everyone, pouring out hot water from the dispenser, grabbing handfuls of serviettes for the children. She looked pleased to have so many visitors in her home. She was particularly warm and attentive towards Ms Gao, the 'piece of work', as Linda had called her, who was her mother. Now in her late twenties, Rui Rui had emerged from difficult times to become a hardworking mother, a loving sister and a loyal daughter once again. There wasn't the slightest hint of bitterness.

Rui Rui's life story, which had begun so badly had a fairy-tale ending with Chinese characteristics.

Aunty Bo had sold Rui Rui's child because she felt a teenage girl had no future as a single parent. Giving birth to a child out of marriage was and remains a taboo in China. A few years later when she was twenty-two, Rui Rui met a man named Mr Ma (which means 'horse'). He was twelve years older than her. Mr Ma came from a poor rural family who adopted him from an orphanage because they didn't have a son of their own. When the mother finally gave birth to their own son, Mr Ma took second place. The family arranged the marriage between Rui Rui and Mr Ma. At first she lived in a shack with very little money of her own. Like hundreds of millions of Chinese farmers, Mr Ma left her alone so that he could make a living in one of China's lucrative cities. He earned an excellent salary of 10,000 yuan ($2,000) a month, painting high-rise buildings.

It was a dangerous job as safety in China is often an afterthought, but the rewards can be great. Mr Ma's job took him to the far southern tourist mecca of Hainan Island in the South China Sea. He sent money home and returned to see Rui Rui twice a year. At one stage, she contemplated leaving her husband, but after she gave birth to a son, her parents-in-law would not let her leave with the baby. She would have lost her son forever.

Despite having very little education and after her experience of being sold, Rui Rui discovered that with hard work, she could earn a living and that life with her new family was becoming increasingly rewarding. She charmed Mr Ma and his family with her fortitude and humility. As a wedding gift, Mr Ma's father gave the couple a spacious house on a corner block opposite the village convenience store. Two years ago Rui Rui gave birth to the daughter she desperately wanted, serious little Peaches, who followed us everywhere during our visit.

She was not going to give away this child. She told us that she paid 5,000 yuan ($1,000) as a 'social maintenance' fine for her daughter. As she told Joyous Li, it was insignificant compared with the priceless joy the little girl had brought her.

These days, her husband comes home to visit every other month. Rui Rui manages two small plots of land (about half a hectare in total) where she grows wheat and corn. She pays someone else to harvest it and plants her own vegetables in the front courtyard of her home. Shortly after the birth of Peaches, she worked her way back into her birth family's life again. She began by visiting her mother, presenting her with armloads of fresh vegetables and a year's supply of wheat. She has never asked for an apology. And none has been given. Today, like little Peaches, she is loved and appreciated.

When I first met Joyous Li in 2013, she was pregnant with her second child. This was two years before the government relaxed the one-child policy.

'Nearly every family has two children now,' she said as she ruffled the hair of her eldest daughter, Mei Lin. Joyous Li studied my face and waited for the obvious question. After all the stories of cruelty I had heard, how was it that she could have a second child?

'It really depends on your neighbours and how nosy they are,' she said. The local family planning clinic was directly across the road from their apartment building. It was headed by an old woman with a fearsome reputation as an upholder of the family planning laws. She stood at the entrance of the clinic keeping a check of women in the neighbourhood. Spying Joyous Li several times, she warned her to get an abortion.

'They won't kill your baby these days,' Joyous Li said, referring to the practice of coerced abortion. 'They just make you pay the fine. Usually.'

But Joyous Li had reason to be nervous. The previous year, family planning officials in another province forced a twenty-three-year-old woman named Feng Jianmei to abort her seven-month-old fetus after she refused to pay a 40,000 yuan ($8,000) fine to have her second child. Her sister-in-law took photos of Ms Feng, hair strewn across her face lying in a hospital bed next to the baby's listless body with placenta and umbilical cord intact. The photos were posted on social media to an instant public outcry. Chinese citizens expressed their outrage this could happen in China in 2012. One man called the fine China's 'terror fee'. Local officials were reprimanded and officials compensated Ms Feng, but the fact that she was pursued so doggedly left people aghast. Ms Feng's husband had left her side to try to earn money to pay the fine when officials picked her up.

Joyous Li was terrified after reading about Feng Jianmei and after the woman at the family planning clinic singled her out, she didn't want to take any chances. When she reached fourteen weeks, she and Xiao Ming moved in with Linda at Gold Mountain Villas where the local cadres were much more relaxed. Shortly after their second daughter, Xia Lin, was born in December 2013, Joyous Li and her husband Xiao Ming began looking into how they might pay or get around the fine for having a second child. Probably the largest ever 'social maintenance fee' for breaching the one-child policy was handed to China's best known film director, Zhang Yimou, in 2014. He and his wife, actress Chen Ting, were fined 7.5 million yuan ($1.5 million) after admitting to having 'out of plan' children. The celebrity couple were pursued by authorities for two years. There was widespread resentment that the rich could get away with flouting the laws.

In Jiaozuo, the going rate for an 'out of plan' child was around 30,000 yuan ($6,000) according to Joyous Li, which is a lot of money for a family earning a total of 6,000 yuan ($1,200) per month. To put it in context, it was around one-third of the cost of a new apartment. Joyous Li left it up to Xiao Ming to resolve the issue. If he found the right person through a personal connection, they could escape with paying much less than 30,000 yuan. That, at least, was the goal. Without payment, they would have a 'black child', unregistered with no *hukou* or access to any benefits or social security.

Joyous Li and Xiao Ming decided to have a second child, after their first daughter Mei Lin almost died in an accident. At the entrance to their apartment building one evening, an old neighbour – who wasn't looking or didn't see the toddler – reversed her electric trike, striking the child. When Joyous Li saw what had happened, Mei Lin was lying on the ground, unconscious. She phoned Linda in Australia who told her to take Mei Lin to hospital immediately.

'I didn't know whether she was going to live or not,' Joyous Li said, her usual smile gone. 'They rushed her in for surgery and when she came out she had two pipes in her mouth and a drip in her arm. It was awful.'

Mei Lin lost her spleen, but she survived.

'Xiao Ming and I realised that if we had lost her, we would have been in a terrible state. I decided then that we had to have another child.'

Around the same time Joyous Li gave birth to Xia Lin, two baby boys turned up at the orphanage with only minor physical disabilities. Joyous Li started to think about adopting a third child although Xiao Ming wasn't initially interested. His family however thought it was a good idea and started to put pressure on him. He was the last male in the line, his father reminded him. There was no male descendant to sweep the graves, as Chinese tradition required.

One of the little orphans was the boy who was missing his left hand. Xiao Ming's family didn't approve because he wasn't physically perfect. But there was another baby boy named Xu Xu who came into the orphanage at just a few weeks old. He had a large burn mark on his leg and a 'pigeon chest' where the sternum and ribs stick out. It's a deformity that often prevents the heart and lungs from functioning optimally. Linda thought he was abandoned either because of the cost of medical treatment or maybe his biological family thought he was considered bad luck because of the scar on his leg. However, to an outsider, he looked normal so he was unlikely to face discrimination.

Xu Xu was taken into a COAT foster home specifically for babies, which was started at the urging of an Australian donor who donated her superannuation savings ($30,000).

Linda paid a 35,000 yuan ($7,000) adoption fee so that Joyous Li and Xiao Ming could adopt Xu Xu who is now Xu Lin, brother to Mei Lin and Xia Lin. Twenty years after Joyous Li's beloved little brother drowned, she brought another boy into her family to give it the gender balance she'd always wanted. The difference was that this time, it was a legal transaction, not a baby for sale.

In the meantime, Xiao Ming managed to find the right person to secure registration papers for his second daughter, Xia Lin. A friend of a friend introduced him to someone in the police department. He managed to 'legalise' his daughter's birth by agreeing to a modest social maintenance fee of 1,500 yuan ($300). He was always confident it would be sorted out, he said. It was just a matter of finding the right person. They celebrated with a studio portrait of their new family photographed against a backdrop of a gingerbread house with a white picket fence, and Linda seated in the middle, of course.

CHAPTER 21

Forgotten

The night before I left Gold Mountain Villas in March 2015 to return to Australia, Linda asked two of the older boys, Shan Shan and Pang Li, to come upstairs to her room. Shan Shan had just turned sixteen. He came to the orphanage as a round-faced baby with spina bifida and clubfeet. Now he was a studious young man with a limp. Pang Li, also sixteen, contracted Hepatitis B at birth. He was short with a long, horsey face, friendly if a little vague. If people outside the orphanage knew he had Hepatitis B, he'd be shunned like a leper.

I wanted to know what they aspired to. I wanted to know how they felt about their future. I wanted to know what it felt like to grow up in the bubble of a foster home inside a Chinese orphanage. I thought they'd probably be more relaxed speaking with Linda rather than me, so she obliged, asking the boys to come while I sat quietly in the corner of the room.

'What do you want to do when you are an adult?' asked Linda.

Shan Shan looked at each of us. His eyes blinked behind his glasses, his face completely blank.

Then it was Pang Li's turn. He became agitated and started to pull his fingers. The atmosphere was horrible. Like we were torturing him. It was as if he was about to lose the million dollar question on a TV game show. I felt annoyed at myself for putting the boys through the discomfort.

When they couldn't answer the question, Linda told them that whatever they wanted to do, she would support them. She loved them and considered them her grandsons now and always. 'Do you understand?' she asked.

'Yes Nai Nai,' they responded in English.

I felt so foolish after they left the room. What did I expect them to say? Maybe they thought they were going to be thrown out or something. God, I felt stupid. When you have spent your life in an institution, even one where you are treated with care and dignity, are you free to dream about the future?

A spirited wind swept away the smog, producing an unequivocally blue sky. As we had done on other days, Linda and I set out on the electric trike merging into the traffic. After passing the car mall, the men who fished in the irrigation channel and the wheatfields, we turned down a narrow lane across from an opulent white building with *Traffic Police* written across the top in large gold characters.

The lane became bumpier. This was definitely not the fancy part of the city. Green fields and rows of white poly-tunnels replaced apartment blocks and car showrooms. There was a whiff of an outdoor toilet backing onto the fields for easy fertiliser. Vegetable patches and cotton bushes fringed the lane as if people needed to use up every available piece of land to scratch a living. We passed a herd of dirty, fat-tailed sheep and scruffy cottages made with the nobbly bricks stolen from the construction site which became the former orphanage in 2002. We turned a corner and there in front of us, hidden from the eyes of the world, was the gatehouse to the former Jiaozuo Welfare Institute.

Today it's still a welfare compound although the orphanage is in its present high-rise premises in the east of the city. This place is where the Shums worked side by side from 2002 until Greg's death in 2006. Linda pointed out the spot where parents often abandoned their babies, a single concrete step leading to the watchman's room at the gate of the compound.

A simple sign read: Jiaozuo City Welfare House. Directly in front of us was a charity hospital where they perform cleft-palate surgery free for poor families. This was a sign of progress. Once, these children would have been abandoned. Now the government and international donors work together to deliver life-changing surgery. A large signboard showed the before and after photographs of babies who'd already had surgery. 14,363 children, according to the counter had been treated gratis as part of a 100 billion yuan investment plan delivered through hospitals around China. Apart from the charity hospital, there's a private home for the elderly and as we rounded the corner, I saw the place I'd heard so much about: the old children's orphanage.

The breeze which had cleared the smog now puffed up the fronds of willow trees that circled the grassy playground in front of the old orphanage compound. Linda, who had spent eight years working here, looked around as happy memories flashed by. She remembered times when the playground, which now resembled Frances Hodgson Burnett's *The Secret Garden*, had once been filled with the sound of children's laughter. After Greg's death, she had scattered some of his ashes on the roses that grew here. The roses died but were replaced with fig trees. If the figs were in season, Linda always picked one and thought of Greg.

Despite the warmth of the wind, this place felt creepy. The old orphanage building was right at the back of the complex, as if the intention was to keep something out of sight. The building was dark inside. Again, it seemed the lights had been turned off to save energy or money. Linda called out to the workers to open the green metal gate for us on the first floor where the children with severe impairments used to live. I wondered who was there now? I wanted to see what was on the other side, yet I was resisting. I could feel my own fear.

I heard a man's laughter which was deep and forced and heard it again and again. I sniffed that awful disinfectant, phenyl, and I knew instantly I was in an institution. Only it felt like an asylum. This is where the orphans who don't get adopted are sent to grow old. They are moved here once they reach eighteen and are considered too old to stay in the children's orphanage. When she could, Linda negotiated with Director Sun to keep the orphans out of this place. This was Jiaozuo city's adult welfare institute.

An ayi led us through a second locked gate which opened onto a large courtyard. Twelve or thirteen men stood around. They all had crew cuts. Inmates. The ground was concrete and the walls covered in white tiles. Around the perimeter of the yard, blankets and quilts were hanging on washing lines. One of the blankets had 'double happiness' characters on them, a traditional gift for newly-wed couples. None of these men would ever marry. And nothing, including the furniture, was going to walk away from this yard. Even the seating and benches were made of concrete and like the walls, covered in chipped white tiles. This way, they were easy to clean with a hose, and could not be picked-up by an inmate to use as a weapon against another inmate.

One of the men ran towards us, like a playful kid. I recognised his laughter as the sound I had heard while we had waited at the gate. Suddenly he bolted towards Linda and didn't look as if he was going stop. I was about to scream for help when he shouted a garbled 'Linda Mama!' before launching towards her with a big hug.

'Bing Bing!' Linda cried throwing her arms around this strong young man. He seemed so harmless yet despite his exuberance I sensed his strength and I feared it. I sat down on one of the tiled benches. Bing Bing came to sit next to me. He sat far too close as I smiled uneasily while Linda took a photo. A second before she pressed the shutter, he turned and firmly tugged my hair. I screamed. He threw his head back in delight like an impish child. The other men in the yard began to laugh too and some of them gathered around to see whether the show would continue. I smiled, my heart still pounding. They were just gentle giants, I told myself. Gentle, intellectually-impaired, unpredictable giants.

We left the men's yard and the ayi took us around the corner to the women's dormitory and a smaller white-tiled courtyard. A locked door connected the men's yard with the women's. One woman was crouching, rocking, in a cubicle, like an open-air cell. The others roamed around aimlessly. Like the men, they had crew cuts and most of them were barefoot. Two of them squatted, contorted hands playing with contorted feet. Linda called me from the far side of the yard. She was holding hands with a girl named Chun Hua. Chun Hua wasn't quite a dwarf, but not much taller. Unlike the other inmates she looked clean and tidy. She wore a pair of hot pink velcro trainers, jeans that were a perfect fit despite her short legs, and a striped red and black pullover.

Chun Hua's face looked familiar. In fact, I knew I had seen Chun Hua and Bing Bing somewhere before but I couldn't think where. And then it struck me as I was watched Chun Hua taking Linda to see the neatly folded clothes in her cupboard. She was one of the children featured in the Shums' video newsletters from 1998. This was the little woman Linda had once tried to bath in the courtyard of the first orphanage, only to be told by the staff that she wasn't a child but a mature woman. Bing Bing, the man who had just pulled my hair, was the boy from the video who didn't like to wear pants and played around the courtyard dressed in a long shirt.

I had seen enough of the courtyard and felt shaken by the unfairness of it all. The adult orphans spent the morning doing very little. There were no activities and apart from the ayi who let us in, staff were barely visible. After the yard we went upstairs, where there was a common room with a TV. A group of men and women crowded onto the sofas to watch a soap opera.

'This is the ward for deranged men and women,' Linda said matter-of-factly. 'Some of them were little kids when I first came to China in 1998.' There again was her old-fashioned choice of words. I knew she was using the language she was brought up to use. Insane, mad, disturbed, unbalanced, demented, neglected. It was unlikely any of these people had ever been diagnosed yet they were all intellectually challenged.

Around the orphanage and in her foster homes, she always spoke of the children as if she were a proud grandmother. The orphanage still had many practices she didn't like, including children being tied to beds and potty-chairs for 'safety' but overall conditions were a world away from when she first came to China in 1998. In this adult welfare institute however, it was hard to feel pride.

The men and women around us were yesterday's unwanted children grown-up. Some would have been among the earliest children abandoned after the implementation of the one-child policy. Others would have been brought here as adults once it became too difficult or unaffordable to care for them at home or perhaps because a parent had died. In the past, if no-one adopted a child by the time they reached the age of fourteen, they were supposed to come here. It was usually children with multiple impairments who weren't adopted; who were never matched with loving parents to complete their 'forever families'. It was a lottery with the worst, most unfair odds in the world.

In the 1990s, as *The Dying Rooms* revealed, many of China's abandoned children were left to die in overcrowded, underfunded orphanages. Ever since that time, the Chinese government has worked to lift its game, aided by an army of academics and hundreds of NGOs including COAT. Abandoned special needs children are now surviving beyond expectation and frequently go on to live productive lives. But despite the vast improvements, for orphans, there are too few alternatives to damaging institutions. Days are filled with pacing the courtyards, rocking themselves for stimulation, or if nothing else, there's always the cheapest care alternative in the world: TV. For most of the inmates at least, this place was out of harm's way. They are fed. But beyond that, what more can you expect?

Up the stairs from the courtyards, an old sign reads, 'The Chinese Orphans Assistance Team Welfare Centre'. This was the site of Linda's first school, founded in 2004. She called out a cheery, '*Ni Hao*, Hello!' to the ayis to let them know we were there. They responded, greeting her warmly: 'Linda Nai Nai, how are you?!' 'You've come back again!'

Linda led the way down a dark corridor with green paint flaking off the lower part of the walls and white paint peeling off the top half. As we reached the door of each room, the inmates came out to greet us. Though many of them were intellectually impaired, the ones who lived in this part of the centre were not classified as such, so they could wander freely around the dormitories. There were old men, young men, strange-looking men, toothless laughing men, men who just stared ahead and shuffling men. I lost count of them. But they all seemed genuinely happy to see us and didn't frighten me like the men with crew-cuts in the courtyard.

We turned into a room with two single beds off a small built-in balcony. The light came from a single neon strip. The Diamond brand wall fan and a power point were held in place with yellowing Sellotape, empty water bottles and cockroach spray lay about. The clock had a lucky '*Fu*' sign on it.

In the second bed was a balding young man. He was propped up with pillows and had a bedspread pulled up around him. His forehead was furrowed as if he had just heard bad news. Something was wriggling under the bedspread.

The bedridden man smiled when he saw us and called out weakly, 'Linda Mama!'

I watched as his bed covers rippled. His awkward, claw-like hands pulled the cover back a little so that we could see his new friend. It was a scrawny white kitten with terrible mange. I looked at the young man as his brow melted with affection for the sickly little creature. They had each other. Two outcasts, inmates, with nowhere to go.

Linda introduced him as Wang Chen.

'I haven't had an email from you in a while,' Linda said.

'It's given up at the moment,' he said pointing to a dusty keyboard and a monitor by his bedside. 'It's been fixed many, many times. It's no use anymore.'

The Internet was Wang Chen's only link with the world. He couldn't walk, so when his computer broke a month earlier, life went very quiet.

'We'll see if we can fix it,' Linda said. 'If not, maybe we can get you a new one.'

I asked Wang Chen if he could show me his kitten. He rummaged under the bedspread and drew the timid creature out by the scruff of its neck. The poor cat's eyes were red and swollen. It had dark brown marks on its face. It didn't look like it had too long to live.

'I have another cat here too. Did you see the white one?' Someone gave them to me a few months ago,' he said pointing to the balcony where a large, clean cat wrapped itself around a small satellite dish. 'The little one is sick,' he said explaining the obvious, 'just like me.'

He clearly loved the creature with all he could muster and wasn't going to let it out of his sight.

Wang Chen was forty-one-years old and had never expected to end up in a welfare institution. He didn't even know what it was before he came here.

He grew up in a poor household with his parents and older brother. His father, a railway worker, died when Wang Chen was only five. By the early 1980s, the reform era under paramount leader Deng Xiaoping was rolling out across the country. China loosened the shackles of Communism and put a greater emphasis on private enterprise. But Wang Chen and his family never experienced the fruits of China's transformation. Caring for two children, his mother couldn't get ahead and never remarried. The family fell between the cracks. By the time Wang Chen was a young adult, Socialism was just a word, it was no longer China's reality. Even things like hospitals now required hard cash. One day when he was seven, Wang Chen fell ill. All he remembered was that he had a high temperature.

'The fever affected my brain,' he said, stroking the kitten's head, a little too vigorously. 'Then after it subsided, I had trouble moving my arms and legs. My brain recovered, but I couldn't feel anything in my legs and from then on I had to stay in bed all the time,' he said without any self-pity.

Wang Chen never went to school. His mother took care of him at home and then her health began to fail. There was never enough to eat. Sometimes there was just one meal a day, perhaps a sweet potato baked in the coals, simple rice gruel flavoured with a bit of dried fish or leftover meat that a neighbour had given them. Their stomachs were always empty, Wang remembers, but he always felt valued and loved. Talking made the deep furrow return to his brow.

'She had such a hard life,' he said pausing to think of his dead mother. 'Her generation had lived through The Great Famine and The Cultural Revolution. Socialism had been a broken promise to the common people of China. They never had money for the hospital or fixing their health.'

Then in 1993, as the pace of reform quickened and many Chinese managed to turn their lives around by starting small enterprises, Wang Chen's beloved mother died. His brother tried to care for him, but having an invalid in his home caused friction with his brother's wife and eventually Wang Chen was brought here to the Jiaozuo Welfare Institute. He was eighteen years old.

In April 2016 China's parliament passed a law by a vote of 174–1 (curiously with one abstention), which could affect the operation of 7,000 foreign NGOs in China including COAT.[1] The law, which came into force in January 2017, limits the type of work overseas NGOs can engage in and gives oversight to the Public

Security Ministry which runs the national police force. Numerous governments, including Australia's, voiced concerns because of 'the potential to affect the activities of Australian business, educational, cultural and civil society organisations in China'.[2]

Linda is extremely concerned, even though COAT has official Chinese registration which many of the NGOs do not. Don White works on behalf of Love Without Boundaries. He's the father of twins Sydney and Reagan adopted from the Jiaozuo orphanage in 2004. Don fears the current Chinese government wants to remove most foreign organisations from China regardless of how much good they do for the Chinese citizenry. According to *The Wall Street Journal*, 'The thrust of the new law is very clear: it is consistent with a vigorous neo-Maoist campaign launched by President Xi Jinping against foreign ideologies and other influences on Chinese social and political development, and is intended to strengthen control by the Chinese Communist Party over Chinese society.'[3]

'Would China be crazy enough to get rid of organisations that are doing things that otherwise wouldn't be done?' asked Linda.

She knows it's not the first time China has changed the rules. Since becoming a registered Chinese entity in 2013, Linda hopes COAT will be capable of weathering the latest storm. She believes that once again, change is a matter of maintaining face. China wants the rest of the world to believe it doesn't need help from foreign countries.

'I can understand that President Xi doesn't want foreign religions to influence Chinese society,' she said. 'But the truth is the Christian church in China is now a Chinese religion as all missionaries were expelled when the Communists took over in 1949. If only the government would realise that it has nothing to fear from citizens believing in God because the Bible teaches Christians to obey the laws of the land and to have integrity.'

In August 2016, a cardboard box arrived at the COAT office in China. Linda unwrapped a perspex trophy which now sits as a paperweight on her desk in Jiaozuo. It was a Henan Province Good Person's Award, presented to her by the government in 2012, but for whatever reason only posted out four years later.

Since her first trip to China in 1998, and with the input of her passionate committee and local team, Linda has moved small mountains. She certainly wouldn't claim credit for all of the initiatives COAT has funded. But she certainly saw each of them through with determination and vigour. From an inexperienced volunteer wiping dirty faces and changing the nappies of neglected babies, she laid the groundwork for transforming the way the Jiaozuo orphanage viewed its charges. She grew the sponsorship base for the orphans, raised money to found a small school and then began to train dozens of Chinese workers in child-care and special needs education. Most of these staff were not experts in their new fields, but she taught them to harness the resources at hand, which gave them (after many years of conflict) a sense of power and control. She backed her committee members who led the charge to set up COAT's first foster home after her husband's death in late 2006, an initiative which then grew to become eight small foster homes.

The COAT school (again after many battles and setbacks) is now a registered special school with nearly 100 pupils including forty from the orphanage and fifteen from the community. This number continues to rise as more residents hear about the success of the school. It employs nineteen teachers and receives funding from donors, the Chinese welfare lottery, the Chinese government itself and the Australian embassy in Beijing.

Between 2011 and mid–2016, fifty-six children were adopted from the Jiaozuo orphanage and though there are no precise figures before that, it's likely there were at least as many since 2003. That was the year the first adoption, of a little girl named Patricia, took place.

Each of the fifty-six adoptions since 2011 were orphans who were transferred to Linda's foster homes where they were taught well, treated well and loved well, providing the foundation for future development and happiness with their new American families. Those adoptions also brought an incredible windfall – more than $200,000 to the orphanage.

Linda and her team have quietly found and encouraged scores of adoptive parents through her social media advocacy. She has rescued around 300 children from dismal institutional life and provided an education for at least 200 others who were once deemed incapable of learning. Over the years, she gave gifts of money, medicine, formula, clothes and equipment to countless others who weren't orphans, but who touched her life and who helped and supported her in many ways, or simply taught her about the intricacies of Chinese life and culture.

The most frustrating thing about Linda Shum is that she is poor at keeping records. I wanted the numbers and proof of her success and have had to settle for her estimates. The school is a source of pride to local officials and appears to run well, but to whose benchmarks?

Before the death of her father, Charles, in 2015, Linda visited China two or three times a year. Now she is able to travel up to five times a year, returning to Australia for her monthly eye injections for macular degeneration and checks on her health. One former volunteer made a valid observation about whether the fly-in fly-out nature of COAT was in the organisation's best interests. Then, of course, there is the issue of its ongoing use of 'voluntourism', which as a movement is out of step with the current standards and ethics of international aid.

The biggest setback was COAT's funding shortfall, which nearly saw the operation fold in 2015 before Linda regretfully sacked ten long-term workers on her sixty-seventh birthday and reduced the number of children in the foster homes, though this was largely due to natural attrition as once adopted they weren't replaced. She attributes the shortfall to circumstances beyond her control; mainly rapidly rising costs and a loss of interest by donors and sponsors who no longer viewed China as a poor and needy country.

Admitting to a lack of business sense, Linda said: 'I am hopeless at managing many things including the funding. However, it's up to me to dream up new ways to raise funds. I am not good at much, so I have to forgive myself for what I'm no good at and get on with what I am.'

'I'm a hopeless housekeeper. My home and classroom were always messy. But my home was full of love and children learned very well in my classroom. That for me is the bottom line.'

Through all of this, Linda stuck it out, at times close to despair, but knowing she will never turn her back on the children. It is her full-time purpose, her life and her calling.

CHAPTER 22

Forever Families

The Long March of family planning,[1] China's one-child
policy, formally ended on 31 December 2015 more than
thirty-five years after its implementation. In the words of *Time*
magazine, it worked too well.

'Just at the point where China would naturally be profiting
from a youth bulge to fuel its economy, the nation is facing a
decline in its labor force. By 2030, China's population will
begin to shrink.'[2] The policy also ended up changing China's
demographics, with too many males and too many elderly people.

While the media focused on how China's urban population
wasn't interested in having more than one child, Linda
wondered whether the end of the policy would change attitudes
to infant abandonment. This is also about welfare policy which
is moving quickly to ensure rural families have health insurance
and enough to live on. For me, this is the big moral issue at the
heart of this story. What is the Chinese government doing to
stop people abandoning children with disabilities?

Since the 1990s, more than 140,000 Chinese orphans have
found homes overseas,[3] the majority of them going to 'forever

families' in the United States. Australian families have adopted fewer than 700 Chinese orphans since 2004.[4] Adoption has long been the subject of intense ethical debate concerning the commodification of children exchanged across families, institutions and nations according to academic Leslie Wang.[5] The Hague Convention[6] implemented by China in 2005 says foreign adoption should be treated as a last resort. As a result, after more than a century of steady increase, according to Professor Wang, international adoptions to the United States (and many other countries including Australia) have plummeted. In China's case, the reduced availability of healthy girls, has contributed to a substantial decrease in adoptions since the mid-2000s.

According to Amy Eldridge who heads the US NGO Love Without Boundaries:

> A critical statistic to understand is that 90–98 per cent of children now being abandoned in China are children with medical needs, depending on which orphanage director you speak with. For gender, it is now an equal number of boys and girls entering institutions. Chinese institutions today are filled with children with heart defects, cleft lip and palate, cerebral palsy, and every other sort of medical need possible. The 'healthy' baby girls are few and far between.[7]

For the past five years, an average of one child a month has left the Jiaozuo orphanage for an American home under the Waiting Child Program. More than 9,000 orphans have been matched with US families since the program began in 2000. Embraced by America's evangelical adoption movement, the program offers older children and special needs orphans for adoption. It takes between twelve and eighteen months to process. As for Australia, we certainly don't make it easy to adopt from overseas. According to the government's intercountry adoption website, the waiting time for adopting from China is more than seven years.

Linda is part of an unofficial network of international adoption advocates. Predominantly Christian, they are usually (though not always) connected with an international NGO. There are dozens of orphan advocates who, via blogs and social media, share photos, videos and stories of Chinese babies and children in need of a home and/or life-saving medical attention. When advocates happen to meet children through orphanage visits or summer camps, they often post personal stories of their connection with them, encouraging prospective parents to adopt. And apart from these advocates, dozens of families who have already adopted or are in the process of adopting special needs children from China, share their experiences online.

Once the paperwork is approved for a Jiaozuo orphan, usually a child who has already been transferred to a COAT foster home, excitement ripples through the organisation. Members of the management team including Joyous Li, school principal Xing, the teachers and the carers, have mixed feelings: happiness for the child and, naturally, sadness to see them leave the Jiaozuo family. Sometimes it's a highly emotional departure for the child. And the children who stay behind feel a mixture of emotions. Perhaps it will be their turn next? And there are those children who suffer quietly; the older children who are no longer cute or adoptable. According to Chinese law, once a child reaches fourteen, the adoption door slams shut.

Walking through the hallway of the COAT school in 2015, I peered into the senior classroom where a maths class was in progress. Through the window, there was Wen Xuan, the boy in the wheelchair I met at the airport during my first visit in October 2013. In March 2015 aged eleven, it seemed as if he was going to be a Jiaozuo lifer. He wasn't featured on any international adoption list. A few years away from the adoption cut-off age of fourteen, time was running out.

Xing is the principal of the COAT school and daycare centre. She's in her early thirties, black wavy hair pulled from her face which has two default settings: calm or smiling/laughing. She wears the maroon tracksuit top which is the COAT uniform. Like everyone who works here, she has risen to the challenge of her job, never imagining she would find employment at a special needs school in a city orphanage.

Xing studied business English at university and always hoped to find work in one of China's big cities. Her mother, Ms Gu,

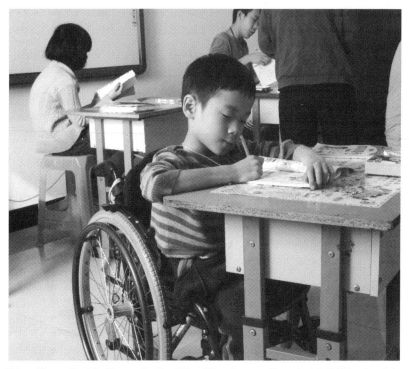

Wen Xuan Smith (formerly Fu Wen Xuan) attending the COAT school in October 2013. He was diagnosed with spina bifida as a baby, although after his adoption, American doctors described his condition as caudal regression syndrome, a congenital disorder where there's abnormal development of the lower spine. (Author photo)

the assistant manager of the foster homes, didn't want her only daughter to leave Jiaozuo. Xing decided to leave anyway. She knew she had to experience life beyond a provincial city (basically a big town) where she'd spent all her life. After graduating, she headed south to brash Guangzhou, intent on finding a job there. With its flashing neon advertisements, spaghetti freeways and endless construction, China's southern mega-city was no match for a girl from small-town Jiaozuo. It was everything she was not: big, loud and unfriendly. People in Guangzhou spoke Cantonese instead of Mandarin. She didn't like the pace of life there. And so without waiting to see if she would ever get used to the south, she retreated homeward to Jiaozuo.

'When I first came to work at COAT,' she said, 'I didn't like it. Like most Chinese people, I had never experienced working with disabled children before.' In front of us was a printout with the names and photographs of the fostered children, all of whom attended the school or daycare centre. She had brought it along to help me identify the children she was talking about.

She pointed to the image of a child with a melted face that looked a like a Halloween mask. Yezi survived several years in the foreign-managed special care facility on the fourth floor before Linda quietly moved him into a foster home so that he didn't have to go back the orphanage.

'Yezi really scared me,' Xing said. 'He used to stare at me all the time and I thought he looked so cruel.'

But eventually, Yezi's face no longer disturbed her. It was just a face. He couldn't help the way he looked. It wasn't indicative of the lively little personality inside. In fact she realised that she actually got along very well with the children. Once she got to know their characters, she realised that they were all different, yet lovable. Some, like Wen Xuan, the wheelchair boy I met at the airport, were extremely smart. Others, like the Down syndrome children were sweet-natured and wanted to learn.

This came as a revelation to Xing. Gradually, with support and training from Linda and education co-ordinators Michelle Baumgartner and Carolyn Wood, Xing started to shine in her job. She accepted that working here could be a satisfying and even worthwhile career.

These days Xing finds herself coaching new teachers who felt the same way she did when she first came to the school. Many of teachers started out as ayis. They were state employees who needed the job and it didn't matter that it was work they didn't love. Working with disabled or brain-damaged kids was not considered worthy in China. It was considered an indictment of someone's skills.

'These days, a lot of people just want a comfortable government job because the wages are stable,' Xing said. 'They think these kids look weird or they don't listen like normal children. But after working here for a while, they start to see that this place is really rewarding. Then, like me, after a few months most of the new staff decide to stay.'

Xing is the eldest of three children. She was twenty-nine and six months pregnant when I met her in 2015. Despite having a tertiary qualification, she confessed to knowing very little about pregnancy and childbirth. She was also nervous about the possibility of giving birth to a child with a disability.

'I was very scared,' she said, 'When I was three or four months pregnant I looked at our orphans one day and I started to get worried. I spoke to my husband, I went to see the doctor. The doctor assured me that the baby was normal.'

'I still worry a bit,' she said.

Three months later, she was to give birth to a healthy little girl.

Xing spends more time with the children than anyone else. We meet in the senior classroom during a lunch-break, seated at the children's desks. The atmosphere in the school is warm and relaxed, surrounded by children's paintings, maths posters and cheerful photographs. But in this sweet room, it was hard to forget that below us on the first floor, were children who were sometimes tied to their beds while others stared at the TV all day with no other stimulation.

And even for the lucky children in Linda's foster homes, was hope enough? What would become of the orphans whom nobody wanted to adopt? What future did a 'waiting child' have?

'I worry about what will happen to them,' Xing said gently. She tapped the photograph of Wen Xuan, the boy I met on my first trip to Jiaozuo, on the printout in front of us. 'He is very bright,' Xing said, 'but he is twelve this year and is only at grade four level.'

Looking me directly in the eye, she said, 'I don't even know how long he or all the children will attend this school for. Until they are what age? None of us knows. Not even Linda.'

I took that to mean that if Wen Xuan remained in a Chinese orphanage, he would never have had the opportunity to complete school or go to university for that matter.

Xing spoke of her own experience of education. She was schooled from age five to twenty-two through China's system of rote learning.

'For intellectually disabled kids,' she said, 'it's hard for them to understand learning by rote, so we have to think differently about how we educate them. We play a lot of games to demonstrate mathematics, we do a lot of craft, we try many different ways to teach these children. But we also have to educate the teachers.'

'Step one for the teachers is learning to change how they think. Then put it into action. Teachers often blame children for not understanding, but actually some of the older teachers need to change their mentality. This is the main problem.'

I mentioned to Xing that Linda thought Wen Xuan had a good head for figures and might end up working in a bank.

'I am not sure he could ever work in a bank,' she said. 'Physically, he couldn't get into a bank,' referring to the lack of disability access in many official buildings.

Education co-director Michelle Baumgartner agreed with Xing's assessment. 'In China, despite his intelligence, he would never get a job because of the stigma and some of the beliefs around disability. Our goal was to set him up in an online business so that people wouldn't be able to see him. If we could set him up to work behind a computer, he could earn money and live a great life,' Michelle said.

Michelle works with Linda and members of the management team to identify potential skills of the children who are getting too old for school. The aim is to start them in vocational training which includes setting up small businesses they can manage with support from the COAT team, while continuing to live in the foster homes.

'We are thinking of buying a stall in the market next door for a couple of the older girls and boys to work in. Maybe they could work in the shop and live in the apartment above it,' Michelle said. 'But let's face it, some of the kids will be with us until they die.'

Li Jia wears a permanent smile on her face. She adores pink and is always laughing. But she began her life in a state of neglect. She was brought into the orphanage as a six-year old, with a tumour the size of a cricket ball on her head. The policemen who brought her, threw her on the pavement outside the old orphanage, angry because she had vomited in their vehicle. Linda remembered doctors at the orphanage didn't want to treat her initially. Eventually they gave her injections to stop her nausea. Later surgeons operated to remove the tumour which left her with cerebral palsy in her legs and an arm, so that movement is awkward for her. When other children were starting school, Li Jia was confined to bed for a year. Linda found sponsors for her so that the ayis would give her better care. Back then, they believed a child was only worthy if he or she received a foreigner's attention and money. 'It's amazing when you feed them meat, how tall they get,' Linda joked.

Xing singled out Li Jia to explain some of the issues facing the teenagers. Li Jia, who was nearly sixteen in 2015, decided that she had to 'manage' everybody else's pocket money. Now she has finished school, she works as a teacher's aid, helping to look after the least mobile children. The government even pays her a small salary.

'Li Jia has a lot of emotional intelligence and asks a lot of questions about life on the outside,' said Xing. 'I tell all the older kids that it's normal to have these feelings and ideas about life beyond the orphanage.' Then she paused. 'Yesterday I asked Li Jia, what is your biggest dream? She didn't miss a beat. She said "I want more freedom. If I want make-up I should be allowed to have it. If I want to wear a skirt I should be able to do that. I don't like the teachers or ayis controlling me".'

Xing laughed. 'And then she said, "I want to look for a boy who is very handsome and rich".'

Could a girl like Li Jia find a partner in China?

If she lived in Australia or America, finding friends, a spouse or partner wouldn't be difficult. But in Jiaozuo where people just stare at someone because they happen to be in a wheelchair or on crutches, how easy would it be for her to meet her match?

'I told her if you study hard, then you can look for a job. The problem is, here at the orphanage or the school at the moment, they don't have these opportunities. I tell her "when you go into society you can look for a boy who is handsome or rich",' said Xing.

'Li Jia should be in senior school. She is very clever but didn't start school until far too late because children like this were never expected to go to school in the past, many of the older children here missed such a lot of education.'

'All I know is that in a normal society, you go to school, you learn and then when you grow up you have the chance to get a good job. I truly hope these kids can learn things. To be honest, I don't know what kinds of jobs they will get in future. All I can do is to give them as much knowledge as I can.'

Her eyes looked into mine questioningly; searching, wishing for a different outcome.

'Unfortunately, I don't have what it takes for our children to become part of real society and get a job.'

I asked Xing if she knew why parents abandoned their children to orphanages like this one. 'People abandon their kids because they don't want to have an imperfect one. In addition to that, there's the so-called 4-2-1 problem; the expectation that one child these days has to look after two parents and four grandparents in their old age. How do you care for your parents and grandparents if you have a disability?'

'These days, a small disability is ok,' she said. 'A serious one … well, that's hard.' She finds many people think that a physical disability deems a disabled person stupid.

But there are signs of change.

She pointed to the photograph of a boy named Little Chang. During the week, he lived in the foster home in Linda's apartment at Gold Mountain Villas where I was staying. Little Chang was boisterous and confrontational. He would stand firmly in front of me shouting 'Ni Hao,' over and over again, even after I had stopped responding. Sometimes he would grab my elbow and try to drag me to the dining table. He didn't know his own strength. Little Chang was intellectually impaired. His parents had spent a lot of money taking him to different hospitals to have him assessed. One doctor finally told his parents the truth, that Little Chang had something wrong with his brain and that he would never get better.

'He can't be healed completely, but now he is not too bad. He needs to go to school. A public school wouldn't accept him because of his behaviour, so his parents heard about us and brought him to the COAT school a few months ago.'

Xing said that unlike what she had seen in the past, Little Chang's parents persisted in getting a diagnosis and the best possible treatment for their precious only son.

'I think it is great that his parents wanted to keep him. They didn't want to abandon him. They have spent a lot of money trying to make him well. Maybe for two or three years, they won't be well-off because of the boy's condition, but at least they didn't give him up.'

'I truly believe that every parent wants to keep their child, no matter how sick or disabled. The difference is, Little Chang's family is rich. The father told me that he has two or three homes. He sold one to keep the boy in the hospital and to pay for different therapies. Little Chang has been to lots of different hospitals all over the country.'

'Another major change in the past decade,' she said, 'is that there are not as many girls in the orphanage. Now, boy or girl, they are equally desired. At least in the cities. Even my parents think that way.'

The village of Pinehurst in Moore County, North Carolina was the venue for the 2014 US Open and US Women's Open golf championships. Apart from a golfing mecca, Pinehurst is quaint and picturesque; the kind of place you might visit for a weekend in the country. Anna and Wesley Smith grew up in Moore County. It's a place that feels like it's far from the rat race but where you still find interesting people and experiences. A local magazine described returnees like them as 'boomerang kids'. They moved away to pursue studies and find jobs, but returned to start a family in the same place where they had such memorable childhoods. Anna and Wesley invest in and renovate real estate for a living. They are committed church-goers.

The Smith's first son, Rand, was born in 2011. Conceiving him hadn't been easy. They had always spoken of adopting domestically, but after getting started, they hit some roadblocks. They didn't want to just have their names added to a baby waiting list.

'Our faith led us to believe we had a child that was already born, somewhere out there,' Anna said.

When she and Wes discovered the Waiting Child program in China, at the suggestion of their adoption agency, they knew it was right for them. Apart from their belief in God, both of them had lost their fathers and knew how it felt to lose a parent.

In March 2015, the Smiths arrived at the COAT foster homes in Jiaozuo to take home Philip, an energetic toddler whose bilateral clubfoot had been repaired. Rand, the Smith's three-year-old son, also travelled along and was excited to have a new little brother. Now they were a family of four. During the wait for Philip's paperwork to be finalised, Anna frequently scoured the internet for photos and videos trying to catch glimpses of Philip. It was then she spotted another face from Jiaozuo that caught her attention. He appeared to have a sweet temperament and a sharp intellect. When she showed her husband Wes a video, he responded, 'That kid looks like he could be a Smith kid!'

The only trouble was, this boy wasn't listed as being available on any of the adoption websites and the Smith's learned that he didn't yet have any adoption paperwork done, most likely because his physical impairments were too severe and he was already eleven years old, close to the cut-off age for adoption. Anna smiles, recalling a conversation with Wesley about their ability as a family to handle this child's medical needs. It was a short conversation about a major decision. Wesley said to Anna: 'If not us, then who else?'

'That was the day we knew we had an older son in China. We just hoped he would want us too.'

Anna said the adoption agency offered her several orphans already on the Waiting Child (special needs) list. She refused. By now she had learned the name of the boy she was searching for. She told the agency it was that boy or none other. Rand and Philip began to pray before meals and at bedtime for their 'older brother in China'. Rand remembered his trip to the orphanage when he was three. He was upset by what he'd seen and would often start to cry thinking about his older brother and all the other kids waiting for mums and dads.

As they were finalising Philip's American passport in the southern city of Guangzhou, Anna received an email from the agency. She was told the other child she and Wesley wanted to adopt was now officially available for adoption. The orphan was due to turn twelve on 28 November 2015. It became the Smiths' priority to get him adopted before his birthday and home to Pinehurst in time for Christmas.

Child number three, was Wen Xuan, the wheelchair boy. My Chinese Oliver Twist.

Long Yuan Hu Park is a sprawling concrete expanse built around a lake near a landmark called the Jiaozuo TV tower. In summer, with boats on the man-made lake, it's attractive. But on a polluted autumn day it feels very Communist: the people's park. What it lacks in charm, it makes up for in trees which surround the plaza and its pathways, creating a verdant green belt in spring and summer. In a corner of the park, there's a place I named the Selfie Field. It's a field the size of a basketball court bursting with yellow rapeseed flowers. It's packed with couples, taking selfies amid the colour. It's a simple idea but the completely natural backdrop was like a scene from Provence. New Chinese cities are not the most attractive places, so the Selfie Field was a surprising oasis in an otherwise concrete Legoland.

China is a communal society. People like to be out with their friends and families. On weekends and in the evenings, the park fills up with people wanting to exercise, to dance or indulge in one of China's favourite pastimes: flying kites. Kites in a grey city are precious. Incredible creations – giant orange squids with fluttering tentacles, rainbow dragons, neon manta-rays – fill the sky above the plaza. There is something magical about a kite and the skill of its handler when life on the ground can be so congested and challenging. After kites, the next most popular pastime at the park is roller-blading. Battalions of children line up in neat rows, hands clasped obediently behind their backs listening to the instructor.

At the entrance to the plaza is a plinth of brown marble holding up a statue of a muscular, semi-naked man. He has long flowing hair, and an enormous hand reaching upwards towards the sun. The character is Kua Fu from a legend which dates back thousands of years. He was a proud, ambitious giant who decided to chase and catch the sun. Kua Fu could cover hundreds of kilometres in a few strides. He uprooted a tree to help him in his goal. But in tracking the sun from east to west, the challenge proved more difficult than he expected. He ran on and on in spite of his fatigue, quenching his thirst by draining the rivers and lakes he came across. Eventually he got near enough to touch the sun, but when he stretched out his hand to grasp it, he realised he didn't have any energy left. So he failed in his quest and ultimately died of exhaustion. It's said that the tree he uprooted became a peach grove and his body became a mountain.

The meaning of Kua Fu's quest is this: the person who strives beyond his or her imagination may achieve more than he or she ever thought possible.

In the months before his parents came to collect him, Wen Xuan had several conversations with the adults at COAT about what it meant to be adopted. At almost twelve, he was old enough to understand the transition about to happen in his life. Linda recalled Wen Xuan's episodes of grief when some of his closest friends had left, leaving him behind.

'In my opinion,' Linda said, 'Chinese orphans should be adopted by Chinese families and grow up with their own culture, language, education system, even food.' But in Wen Xuan's case, and for the vast majority of Jiaozuo's special needs orphans, local families are not keen to adopt children with disabilities although they are happy to adopt healthy children.

One of the final stages in the adoption process is that the orphanage places an advertisement in the provincial newspaper, the *Henan Daily*. Called a finding advertisement, the notices are very obvious because the page is covered in snapshots of little babies. They are usually the earliest photo in the orphanage's possession, sometimes from the day the child arrived. The advertisement describes the child's age, the location where he or she was abandoned and a few details that might jog a few memories. Birth parents have two months to claim the child before an overseas adoption can be finalised.

Here's what Wen Xuan's 'finding advertisement' from 7 August 2014 said:

Fu Wen Xuan, male, born on Nov 28, 2003. He was abandoned in front of the Jiaozuo City Helping Centre on Feb 24, 2004. On the same day, he was sent to the Jiaozuo Welfare House by police. His face is the shape of a sunflower seed, small eyes, white skin. He was born with spina bifida.

In the past few years, Linda had grown concerned about Wen Xuan's health. A visiting pediatrician told her that his scoliosis (curvature of the spine) could exert pressure on the heart and lungs as he grew bigger. She told Wen Xuan that she could not afford to give him the medical attention he needed and that, as well as loving parents, he would get the best medical care in America. When Wen Xuan was told that an American family wanted to adopt him and that he was to be the eldest child in the family and that his parents already adopted Philip from Jiaozuo, the little face in the shape of a sunflower seed, burst with elation.

Two weeks before his parents came to collect him, Wen Xuan packed all his belongings. When Anna and Wes arrived, Wen Xuan took them to buy presents for all of his close friends at the foster home. He took his parents to see where he slept, ate and played. He was especially proud of his favourite place, the library, funded by the Australian embassy in Beijing. By now, Anna was pregnant with another son, Bo, who would grow the number of Smith children from one to four in the space of twelve months. On the final part of the tour, Wen Xuan took Anna and Wesley to the see the cubby house, which was under the weight of a November snowfall, as well as the slide, monkey bars and swings in front of the welfare building where he had spent many happy hours.

Before leaving Jiaozuo, Wen Xuan asked if he could make one last stop at the market next to the orphanage. It's a bustling place with rows of shops selling everything from cutlery to pyjamas. Wen Xuan expertly navigated his parents through the freezing market to the exact store he wanted to visit. It was a hole-in-the-wall toy shop he'd been to many times. The only two things he wanted were a Lego set he'd been eyeing for himself and a set of action hero collectable cards for his friend, Jay, an orphan like himself adopted from Jiaozuo by American parents sixteen months earlier.

During the journey to the provincial capital Zhengzhou, Wen Xuan sat quietly in the van with his dad, Wesley, hoping there wasn't a repeat of the motion sickness which hounded him every time he got into a vehicle. Anna was ready with some medicine just in case. Though the blizzard had stopped by now,

The four Smith boys in August 2016. From left to right: Philip (who also came from the Jiaozuo orphanage), Wen Xuan, Bo and Rand. (Wesley and Anna Smith)

snow still lay on the road, on the branches of the trees, even on the head of the statue of brave, foolish Kua Fu at the entrance to Long Yuan Hu Park. It was a slow ride given the slushy conditions and the driver proceeded cautiously. Eventually, puddles of water began to replace clumps of snow as the van approached the bridge across the Yellow River.

Wearily, Wen Xuan looked out of the window, as he had on the infamous journey to the airport, where I met him two years earlier. Outside the air was thick with smog, turning a soft tangerine colour as the light faded.

The boy thought of his life in China up to that point. In the past, whenever he used to dream of what he would do when he grew up, of what he might become, all he'd hoped for one simple thing: to drive a car.

Now he knew the sky was the limit. He didn't look back.

ENDNOTES

Chapter 2

1 Stack, P.F., 'Who are evangelicals? Are they fundamentalists? Pentecostals?', www.theaquilareport.com, originally published *Salt Lake Tribune*, 9 March 2012.

2 Author interview.

Chapter 3

1 Hutcheon, S., 'Beijing rejects claims of abuse in orphanages', *Sydney Morning Herald*, 9 January 1996.

2 'U.S. Rights Group Asserts China Lets Thousands of Orphans Die', *New York Times*, 6 January 1996, p. 1., 4

3 Poole, T., 'China starves babies by the thousand', *The Independent*, 6 January 1996.

4 Gillan, A., 'Lost babies, found babies', *The Guardian*, 12 October 2002.

Chapter 4

1 Greenhalgh, S., *Just One Child*, University of California Press, p. 54.

2 www.alphahistory.com/chineserevolution/quotations-great-leap-forward

3 Author interview, *One Plus One*, 8 May 2015.

4 Author interview, *One Plus One*, 7 May 2015.

5 *Control Science and Technology for Development*, Proceedings of the IFAC/IFORS Symposium, Beijing, August 1985.

6 Ibid.

7 Johnson K. A., *Wanting a Daughter, Needing a Son*, Yeong & Yeong, p. xxi.

8 Wang, L. K., *Outsourced Children*, Stanford University Press, p. 49.

9 Johnson, p. 6.
10 'China says its gender imbalance "most serious" in the world', Reuters world news, 21 January 2015.
11 'How China's one-child policy led to forced abortions, 30 million bachelors', npr.org, 1 February 2016.
12 Ibid.
13 I am indebted to Shang & Fisher's research

Chapter 5
1 These days it's called orphanage tourism or voluntourism: short-term visits by unskilled volunteers. And it's widely discouraged, because it's seen as detrimental to the welfare of institutionalised children. Does the organisation vet or carry out police checks on its team-members? And what about the Chinese government's child safety policy? Why does it permit orphanage tourism?

Chapter 6
1 Some reasons for why children with disabilities are abandoned in China can be found in Chapter 3.

Chapter 7
1 Sacks, O. *Hallucinations*, Knopf (e-book).
2 Ibid.
3 'The Reality of World Religion: God Wins', *National Review*, 10 December 2015.
4 'Half of Americans believe in angels', *Washington Times*, 19 September 2008.
5 All dollar figures are Australian dollars at the approximate exchange rate at the time of publication (5 yuan = AUD$1).
6 'Reform of state-owned enterprises in China', China Labour Bulletin (clb.org.hk), 19 December 2007.

Chapter 8
1 Shang, X. & Fisher, K., *Caring for Orphaned Children in China*, Lexington Books, p. 86.
2 Hutchings, G., *Modern China, A companion to a Rising Power*, Penguin, 2000, p. 117.
3 www.china.org.cn/english/education/184879.htm

Chapter 10
1 Powell, A., 'Breathtakingly awful', *Harvard Gazette*, 5 October 2010.
2 Gillan, A., 'Lost babies, found babies', *The Guardian*, 12 October 2002.

Chapter 11

1   Gawande, A., *Being Mortal: Medicine and What Matters in the End*,
    Metropolitan Books, p. 183.

Chapter 13

1   Wang, H., *The Chinese Dream*, Bestseller Press, p. 2.
2   Economy, E. & Segal, A., 'China's Olympic Nightmare', *Foreign
    Affairs*, July/August 2008.
3   Shang, X. & Fisher, K., *Caring for Orphaned Children in China*,
    Lexington Books, p. 42.
4   'Lives Like Garbage: Children with Birth Defects Abandoned', www.
    chinasmack.com, 5 September 2011.
5   'Orphanage Blaze Stirs China', www.womenofchina.cn.
6   It was this incident that prompted Linda to make contact with me. See
    Chapter 1.

Chapter 14

1   Burkitt, L., 'China's Remedy for Stressed Workers: "They Need the
    Hoohah"', *Wall Street Journal*, 14 September 2011.
2   Yu, R., 'China Soon to Have Almost as Many Drivers as U.S. Has
    People', *Wall Street Journal*, 28 November 2014.

Chapter 15

1 See Chapters 7 and 8.

Chapter 17

1   The term 'cadre' refers to a public official holding a responsible or
    managerial position, usually full time, in the party and government.
    A cadre may or may not be a member of the CCP, although a person
    in a sensitive position would almost certainly be a party member.
    Worden, R. L., Matles Savada, A., & Dolan, R. E., eds., *China:
    A Country Study*, Library of Congress, 1987. (countrystudies.us/
    china/113.htm).
2   Lubman, S., 'After the One-Child Policy: What Happens to China's
    Family-Planning Bureaucracy?', *The Wall Street Journal*, 12 November
    2015.

Chapter 18

1   Campbell, C., 'China's Leader Xi Jinping Reminds Party Members to
    be "Unyielding Marxist Atheists"', *Time*, 25 April 2016.

2 Stark, R., *A Star in the East: The Rise of Charitinity in China,* Templeton Press, p. 115. This is an excellent book for understanding the contemporary spread of Christianity in China.

Chapter 20
1 'China says its gender imbalance "most serious" in the world', Reuters world news, January 21 2015.
2 'China's excess males, sex selective abortion, and one child policy: analysis of data from 2005 national intercensus survey', *British Medical Journal*, 2009: p. 338

Chapter 21
1 Wong, E., 'Clampdown in China Restricts 7,000 Foreign Organizations', *New York Times*, 28 April 2016.
2 'China's Foreign NGO Management Law', Australian Department of Foreign Affairs and Trade media release, 4 May 2016.
3 Lubman, S., 'China's New Law on International NGOs – And Questions about Legal Reform', *Wall Street Journal*, 25 May 2016.

Chapter 22
1 LaFraniere, S., 'As China Ages, Birthrate Policy May Prove Difficult to Reverse', *The New York Times*, 6 April 2011.
2 Beech, H., 'The End of China's One-Child Policy Has Put Huge Pressure on the Nation's Sperm Banks', *Time*, 21 September 2016.
3 Wang, L. K., *Outsourced Children*, Stanford University Press, p. 49.
4 www.ag.gov.au/FamiliesAndMarriage/IntercountryAdoption/ Documents/Table10Aintercountryadoptionsbycountryoforigin.pdf Adoptions Australia 2014–2015, www.aihw.gov.au/WorkArea/ DownloadAsset.aspx?id=60129553828
5 Wang, p. 48.
6 Hague Convention of 29 May 1993 on Protection of Children and Co-operation in Respect of Intercountry Adoption.
7 www.lovewithoutboundaries.com/adoption/changing-face

ACKNOWLEDGEMENTS

In December 2016, ten children from the first floor of the orphanage – most of whom had been tied to their beds over the years, were allowed to be brought upstairs to the COAT school on the ninth floor of the welfare building.

There, they were given a good bath and clean clothes. Then, for the first time in their lives, they attended half a day of daycare sessions where they were encouraged to move, to play, listen to stories being read to them in the library and to interact. Within months, two of the children graduated to full-time classes.

Everyone is excited by the development as COAT's brand of care and education is finally reaching the neediest children in the Jiaozuo welfare building.

But it has taken nearly two decades.

Four years ago when I approached Linda Shum to ask whether I could write a book about her, I had no idea how long it would take and how much of her time it might involve. I held my breath for only one second before her reply. Without hesitation, she said 'yes'.

I conducted several lengthy interviews with her, visited her home, her friends and her church in Gympie, met her in Sydney, travelled twice to Jiaozuo to see her at work and then when that still wasn't quite enough, we began a dialogue over email, phone, Skype and Facebook which continues to this day. She's an avid user of gadgets and technology. My only problem was working out which email address she happened to be using that particular week.

Her generosity and patience was incredible. She did not try to hide or sugar-coat anything. I can't thank her enough for her devotion to the children and her generosity to me.

No child or animal was harmed during the writing of this book, although my daughter wasn't happy that her bedtime routine was disrupted for far too long. My husband, Michael is the house chef, so we continued to eat well while I used the evenings to write. Thank you Michael and Isla for your love (good food) and support. Baking and holding tightly to the wise words of other writers' kept me focused and calm enough (Zen is a popular word in our house) until the job was complete.

We are incredibly lucky in Australia to have Professors Karen Fisher and Xiaoyuan Shang from the Social Policy Research Centre at the University of New South Wales. They are international leaders in the field of China's orphans and welfare policy and they were extremely generous with their research, statistics and observations. Their reports have transformed Chinese policy. Karen and Xiaoyuan have already written widely on this field and I hope this book shines a light on their work.

At one stage I was hoping to include chapters that told the story of the one-child generation here in Australia. Despite lengthy interviews with some wonderful individuals who shared their hopes and dreams with me, this seemed like another story altogether and the resulting work didn't make it into the book. However I would like to thank the artist Wu Di, Trevor Watson and Professor Hans Hendrischke of the University of Sydney Business School, Cherry, Sibella, Eunice and Wendy, and Sean in Beijing for their time and helping me to understand the circumstances of their lives and the impact of the one-child policy.

Cecily Huang, who was in Sydney working on her MA in Journalism, assisted me with research on the one-child policy and with translations as my written Chinese wouldn't get me further than a restaurant. Actually, I once sat down in a dog meat restaurant in China because I was a little unclear of the character that came before 'meat'.

Helen Littleton was my warm, encouraging publisher at ABC Books. We met at colleague Zoe Daniel's book launch in 2014. That event opened the door to my *China Baby Love* pitch. Helen and Brigitta Doyle gave me sound advice, plenty of encouragement and a deadline extension for which I was mightily grateful. I worked closely with Senior Editor Lachlan McLaine who has eagle eyes, excellent grammar and a forthright yet kind manner. Thank you Lachlan. I was delighted with the cover design by Hazel Lam. Hazel used a traditional Chinese paper cut, which I adored. Publicist Matt Howard also deserves a big 'thank you' for his hard work and being helpful beyond what was required.

Apart from the good people at HarperCollins/ABC Books, I also consulted editors Nikki Lusk and Virginia Lloyd for advice on the manuscript's structure, focus and voice.

In my day job, I am the host of the television interview show *One Plus One*, where I get to interview, among talented others, authors from Australia and overseas. Many authors gave me off-camera advice as well as on-camera inspiration. Lily Brett was particularly kind. I had the pleasure of meeting Xinran Xue at the Sydney Writers' Festival in 2015 and many others probably didn't realise they were helping me.

Thanks to author Hugh Mackay for his support and advice.

Deepest thanks to my parents Robin and Bea who remind me every day that life is about love, kindness and doing those things that bring you satisfaction. Thank you to my family in London, Sydney, the Gold Coast and the Blue Mountains for just being you.

And finally, to everyone connected to Linda and COAT who told me their stories, provided photos, clarifications and helped me in great and small ways, thank you. Special thanks to Anna and Wesley Smith, Dinah, Louis and Fu Yang DeLuca, Michelle Baumgartner, Margaret Mason, Donna Laurie and Rob. I have the utmost respect for what you do.

'Every day, every child, happiness' is COAT's motto. It's still a work in progress I know, but next year – 2018 – marks twenty years since Linda's arrival in Jiaozuo. She will also turn seventy. I for one am so glad she decided to walk in other people's shoes. And I'm grateful too, that you have this book in your hands.

Jane Hutcheon, Sydney, February 2017

Here's how to contact Linda:

www.eagleswingschina.org
Facebook: Eagles Wings China or Linda McCarthy Shum

You can reach me here:

www.janehutcheon.com
Twitter: @JHutcheon
Facebook: @JaneHutcheon.au

Jane Hutcheon began her career in radio and television in Hong Kong, where she was born. She has witnessed ground-breaking news unfolding over thirty years as a broadcast journalist. Jane has served as the ABC-TV Correspondent in China, the Middle-East and Europe. She's interviewed world leaders, CEOs, mavericks, freedom-fighters and justice-seekers, reported on 9/11, the Iraq War, London Bombings and Hurricane Katrina. Jane published her first book From *Rice to Riches* in 2003, documenting her family connections and correspondent days in China. She wrote and directed the 2013 ABC News documentary *From Mao to Now*. Jane's people-centred approach to journalism is at the core of her weekly ABC-TV show *One Plus One* where she conducts face-to-face conversations with celebrities and people from all walks of life.